WEBSTER'S NEW WORLD

LEGAL
WORD FINDER
Second Edition

Compiled by
Linnea Leedham Ochs

Prentice Hall Press
New York

Published by New World Dictionaries/Prentice Hall Press
A Division of Simon & Schuster, Inc.
Gulf + Western Building
One Gulf + Western Plaza
New York, NY 10023

PRENTICE HALL PRESS, TREE OF KNOWLEDGE, WEBSTER'S
NEW WORLD and colophons are trademarks of Simon & Schuster, Inc.

Manufactured in the United States of America

1 2 3 4 5 6 7 8 9 10

Library of Congress Cataloging-in-Publication Data

Ochs, Linnea Leedham.
  Webster's new world legal word finder.

  Rev. ed. of: Legal word finder. 1983.
  1. Legal secretaries—United States—Handbooks,
manuals, etc. 2. Law—United States—Terms and
phrases. 3. English language—Syllabication.
4. English language—Orthography and spelling.
I. Ochs, Linnea Leedham. Legal word finder.
II. Title.
KF319.027 1987   340′.03′21   87-2361
ISBN 0-13-947300-9

Preface

Here's a unique reference tool for everyone who uses legal words and expressions. Arranged like a conventional dictionary, this instant reference solves the difficult word problems you face every working day. With the Legal Word Finder at your fingertips, you will be able to:

Spell Any Legal Word Correctly You don't want to take chances with legal words, many of which are derived from Latin, a language unfamiliar to most. You will be able to spell correctly nearly 20,000 legal words quickly with the aid of this volume.

Divide Any Legal Word Correctly Many legal words contain several syllables and some phrases contain several hyphens. With this master guide, you'll be able to break and correctly hyphenate the seemingly simple words that trip up people regularly, and the long and complex words that always require extra attention.

Pronounce Any Legal Word Correctly Every word in this comprehensive volume is clearly marked for perfect pronunciation. The system of markings leave no room for error.

Find the Special Help You Need in the Reference Section In addition to the spelling, hyphenation and pronunciation you'll find in this volume, we have included a special section that enables you to locate immediately the information that most legal professionals need and use daily. Until now, this information could only be found by searching through many different volumes. This special section includes forms of address, abbreviations, Latin words and phrases, Courts of Record and Judicial Circuits, authentication of instruments, official reports and how they are cited, and other practical reference data.

914360

Because this is a dictionary without definitions, you can find the words you want in seconds—not the minutes it often takes to find words in conventional legal dictionaries. And when you find the word you are looking for, it's easy to read. On the average, there are about half the number of words on each page as you might find in a conventional dictionary. And each word is printed in a large typeface that was specially selected for its high legibility.

How to Use the *Legal Word Finder*

The markings are easy to understand. A slash indicates word division, and a word may be separated only where a slash appears. For example, Ju'/ris/pru'/dence can be broken at three different points. However, a word should be broken at the most logical place whenever possible. Here, juris/prudence would be the most easily understood break.

If a dot or a stress mark is not followed by a slash, do not break the word at this point. These marks are aids to pronunciation only. Also, a single letter should never be separated from either the beginning or the end of a word. For example, e'qual and su'o are spelled solidly, although pronunciation indicates two syllables in each case.

Hyphenated words may be divided only after the hyphen. For example, daughter-/in-/law could be broken as follows:

daughter-   or   daughter-in-
in-law   law.

Because proper names should not be divided, they are not included in this book. Heavy stress marks are used in this book to indicate syllables receiving primary stress. The lighter marks indicate secondary stress.

The Legal Word Finder is a complete, up-to-date, and easy-to-use reference for legal secretaries, lawyers, law students, paralegals and everyone who must write or speak on the subject of the law.

CONTENTS

CONTENTS

Section One

ALPHABETICAL WORD LIST

A

ab/ac′/tion
ab/a′li·en/ate′
    ab/a′li·en/at′/ed
    ab/a′li·en/at′/ing
a·ban′/don
    a·ban′/doned
    a·ban′/don/ing
a·ban′/don/ee′
a·ban′/don/ment′
aban′/te
a·bat′/able nui′/sance
a·bate′
    a·bat′/ed
    a·bat′/ing
a·bate′/ment
a·ba′/tor
ab/broach′/ment
ab′/di/cate′
    ab′/di/cat′/ed
    ab′/di/cat′/ing
ab′/di/ca′/tion
ab/duc′/tion
a·bet′
    a·bet′/ted
    a·bet′/ting
a·bet′/ment
a·bet′/tor
a·bey′/ance
a·bide′
    a·bode′
    a·bid′/ing
a·bil′/i/ty

ab in′/con/ve/nien′/ti
ab i·ni′/tio
ab in/vi′/to
ab′/ju/ra′/tion
ab/jure′
    ab/jured′
    ab/jur′/ing
a′ble-/bod′ied
a·bode′
a·bol′/ish
ab′/o/li′/tion
ab/o·rig′/i/nal ti′/tle
a·bort′
    a·bort′/ed
    a·bort′/ing
a·bor′/ti/fa′/cient
a·bor′/tion
a·bor′/tion/ist
a·bor′/tus
a·bout′
a·bove′
a·bridge′
    a·bridged′
    a·bridg′/ing
a·bridg′/ment
ab′/ro/gate′
    ab′/ro/gat′/ed
    ab′/ro/gat′/ing
ab′/ro/ga′/tion
ab/scond′
    ab/scond′/ed
    ab/scond′/ing
ab′/sence
ab′/sent
ab′/sen/tee′

ab′/so/lute′
ab′/so/lute′/ly
ab′/so/lu′/tion
ab′/so/lut′/ism′
ab/solve′
    ab/solved′
    ab/solv′/ing
ab/sorb′
    ab/sorbed′
    ab/sorb′/ing
ab/sorp′/tion
abs′/que
ab/sten′/tion
ab′/sti/nence
ab/stract′ *v*
    ab/stract′/ed
    ab/stract′/ing
ab′/stract′ *n, adj*
ab/surd′
ab/sur′/di/ty
a·buse′
    a·bused′
    a·bus′/ing
a·buse′ *n*
    —— of dis/cre′/tion
    —— of pro′/cess′
a·bu′/sive
a·but′
    a·but′/ted
    a·but′/ting
a·but′/ment
a·but′/tal
a·but′/ter
ac′/a/deme′
ac′/a/de′/mi·a

ac′/a/dem′/ic
a·cad′/e/my
ac/cel′/er/ate′
    ac/cel′/er/at′/ed
    ac/cel′/er/at′/ing
ac/cel′/er/a′/tion
ac/cept′
    ac/cept′/ed
    ac/cept′/ing
ac/cep′/tance
ac′/cess′
ac/ces′/sion
ac/ces′/so/ry
ac′/ci/dent
ac′/ci/den′/tal
ac/com′/mo/date′
    ac/com′/mo/dat′/ed
    ac/com′/mo/dat′/ing
ac/com′/mo/da′/tion
ac/com′/pa/ny
    ac/com′/pa/nied
    ac/com′/pa/ny/ing
ac/com′/plice
ac/cord′ *v*
    ac/cord′/ed
    ac/cord′/ing
ac/cord′ *n*
ac/cor′/dance
ac/cor′/dant
ac/couche/ment′
ac/count′
    —— an/nexed′
    —— debt′/or
    —— ren′/dered
    —— stat′/ed

ac/count'/a·bil'/i/ty
ac/count'/a·ble
ac/coun'/tant
ac/count'/ing
ac/counts'
    _____ pay'/a·ble
    _____ re/ceiv'/a·ble
ac/cou·ple'
ac/cred'/it
    ac/cred'/it/ed
    ac/cred'/it/ing
ac/cre'/tion
ac/cru'/al ba'/sis
ac/crue'
    ac/crued'
    ac/cru'/ing
ac/cu'/mu/late'
    ac/cu'/mu/lat'/ed
    ac/cu'/mu/lat'/ing
ac/cu'/mu/la'/tion
ac/cu'/mu/la/tive
ac'/cu/sa'/tion
ac/cu'/sa/to'/ry
    _____ in'/stru/ment
    _____ plead'/ing
    _____ pro/ce'/dure
ac/cuse'
    ac/cused'
    ac/cus'/ing
ac/cus'/er
ac/cus'/tomed
ac/knowl'/edge
    ac/knowl'/edged
    ac/knowl'/edg/ing
ac/knowl'/edg/ment

ac/quaint'
    ac/quaint'/ed
    ac/quaint'/ing
ac/quain'/tance
ac/quest'
ac'/qui/esce'
    ac'/qui/esced'
    ac'/qui/esc'/ing
ac'/qui/es'/cence
ac'/qui/es'/cent
ac/quire'
    ac/quired'
    ac/quir'/ing
ac'/qui/si'/tion
ac/quit'
    ac/quit'/ted
    ac/quit'/ting
ac/quit'/ment
ac/quit'/tal
ac/quit'/tance
a'/cre
a·cross'
ac'/ti·o
ac'/tion
    _____ in per/so'/nam
    _____ in rem
ac'/tion/a·ble
    _____ mis/rep/re/
    sen/ta'/tion
    _____ neg'/li/gence
    _____ nui'/sance
ac'/tion/a·ry
ac'/tive
    _____ con/ceal'/ment
    _____ neg'/li/gence

act of God
ac'/tor
ac'/tu/al
—— au/thor'/i/ty
—— con'/tro/ver/sy
ac/tu/ar'/i/al
ac'/tu/ar·y
ac'/tum
ac'/tus
ad ar/bi'/tri/um
ad coe'/lum doc'/trine
ad cul'/pam
ad cu'/ri/am
ad dam'/num
ad/den'/dum
   ad/den'/da
ad/dict' *v*
   ad/dict'/ed
   ad/dict'/ing
ad'/dict *n*
ad di'/em
ad/di'/tion
ad/di'/tion/al
ad'/di/tur
ad/dress' *v*
   ad/dressed'
   ad/dress'/ing
ad/dress'*or* ad'/dress *n*
ad/duce'
   ad/duced'
   ad/duc'/ing
a·deem'
   a·deemed'
   a·deem'/ing
a·demp'/tion
ad'/e/quate

ad ex'/i/tum
ad/here'
   ad/hered'
   ad/her'/ing
ad/her'/ence
ad/he'/sion
ad hoc
ad ho'/mi/nem
ad i'dem
ad in'/fi/ni'/tum
ad in'/ter/im
ad/ja'/cent
ad'/jec/tive law
ad/join'
   ad/joined'
   ad/join'/ing
ad/journ'
   ad/journed'
   ad/journ'/ing
ad/journ'/ment
ad/judge'
   ad/judged'
   ad/judg'/ing
ad/ju'/di/cate'
   ad/ju'/di/cat'/ed
   ad/ju'/di/cat'/ing
ad/ju'/di/ca'/tion
ad/ju'/di/ca'/tive
ad'/junct'
ad/junc'/tion
ad'/ju/ra'/tion
ad/jure'
   ad/jured'
   ad/jur'/ing
ad/just'
   ad/just'/ed

ad/just′ (contd.)
    ad/just′′/ing
ad/just′′/er
ad/just′′/ment
ad′/ju/tan/cy
ad′/ju/tant gen′′/er/al
ad/le/gi/a′′/re
ad li′/tem
ad/mea′′/sure/ment
ad/mi/nic′/u/lar
ad/min′′/is/ter
    ad/min′′/is/tered
    ad/min′′/is/ter/ing
ad/min′/is/tra′′/tion
ad/min′/is/tra′′/tive
ad/min′′/is/tra/tor
    ____ de bo′′/nis non
    ____ pen/den′′/te li′/te
ad/min′/is/tra′′/trix
ad′′/mi/ral/ty court
ad/mis′′/si/ble
ad/mis′′/sion
ad/mit′
    ad/mit′′/ted
    ad/mit′′/ting
ad/mit′′/tance
ad/mon′′/ish
    ad/mon′′/ished
    ad/mon′′/ish/ing
ad′/mo/ni′′/tion
ad/mon′′/i/tor′′/y
a·dopt′
    a·dopt′′/ed
    a·dopt′′/ing
a·dopt′/ee′
a·dop′′/tion

a·dop′′/tive
ad pro′/se/quen′′/da
ad rec′/tum
ad re′/spon/den′′/dum
ad sec′/tam
a·dult′
a·dul′′/ter/ate′
    a·dul′′/ter/at′′/ed
    a·dul′′/ter/at′′/ing
a·dul′′/ter/a′′/tion
a·dul′′/ter/er
a·dul′′/ter/ess
a·dul′′/ter/ine
a·dul′′/ter·y
ad va/lo′′/rem
ad/vance′
    ad/vanced′
    ad/vanc′′/ing
ad/vance′/ment
ad/van′′/tage
ad′/van′/ta′′/geous
ad′/ven/ti′′/tious
ad/ven′′/ture
ad/ven′′/tur/er
ad′′/ver/sar·y
    ____ pro/ceed′′/ing
    ____ sys′′/tem
ad/verse′
    ____ en/joy′′/ment
    ____ in′′/ter/est
    ____ pos/ses′′/sion
    ____ wit′′/ness
ad′′/ver/tise′
    ad′′/ver/tised′
    ad′′/ver/tis′/ing
ad′′/ver/tise′′/ment

ad/vice′
ad/vise′
    ad/vised′
    ad/vis′/ing
ad/vis′/ed/ly
ad/vise′/ment
ad/vi′/so/ry
ad′/vo/ca/cy
ad′/vo/cate′ *v*
    ad′/vo/cat′/ed
    ad′/vo/cat′/ing
ad′/vo/cate *n*
ad/vow′/son
ae′/quus
aes/thet′/ic
af/fair′
af/fect′
    af/fect′/ed
    af/fect′/ing
af/fec′/tion
af/fec′/tus
af/feer′
    af/feered′
    af/feer′/ing
af/fi′/ance
    af/fi′/anced
    af/fi′/anc/ing
af/fi′/ant
af′/fi/da′/vit
    —— of de/fense′
    —— of mer′/its
    —— of ser′/vice
af/fil′/i/ate′ *v*
    af/fil′/i/at′/ed
    af/fil′/i/at′/ing
af/fil′/i/ate *n*

af/fil′/i/a′/tion
af/fin′/i/ty
af/firm′
    af/firmed′
    af/firm′/ing
af/fir′/mance
af/fir′/mant
af′/fir/ma′/tion
af/fir′/ma/tive
af/fix′
    af/fixed′
    af/fix′/ing
af/flic′/tion
af/force′
    af/forced′
    af/forc′/ing
af/fray′
af/freight′/ment
af/front′
a·fore′/said′
a·fore′/thought′
a for′/ti/o′/ri
af′/ter
af′ter-/ac·quired′
    —— prop′/er/ty
    —— ti′/tle
af′ter-/born′ heir
af′ter-/dis·cov′ered ev′/
i/dence
af′ter-/mar′ket
af′/ter/noon′
af′/ter/thought′
af′ter/ward
a·gainst′
age
    aged

age (contd.)

    ag'/ing

a'gen/cy

a·gen'/da

a·gen'/dum

a'gent

a'ger

ag'/gra/vate'

    ag'/gra/vat'/ed

    ag'/gra/vat'/ing

ag'/gra/vat'/ed

    ____ as/sault'

    ____ bat'/ter·y

ag'/gra/va'/tion

ag'/gre/gate *n*

ag'/gre/ga'/tion

ag/gres'/sion

ag/gres'/sive

ag/gres'/sor

ag/grieved' par'/ty

a'gio

ag'/i/tate'

    ag'/i/tat'/ed

    ag'/i/tat'/ing

ag'/i/ta'/tor

ag/no'/men

ag/nom'/i/na'/tion

ag/nos'/tic

ag'/o/ny

a·grar'/i/an

a·gree'

    a·greed'

    a·gree'/ing

a·greed'

    ____ judg'/ment

    ____ or'/der

a·greed' (contd.)

    ____ state'/ment on

   ap/peal'

a·gree'/ment

ag'/ri/cul'/ture

ag'/ri/cul'/tur/al

    ____ com/mod'/i/ty

    ____ em/ploy'/ment

    ____ pro'/duce

aid

    ____ and a·bet'

    ____ and com'/fort

aid'/er and a·bet'/tor

aid'/er by ver'/dict

ail'/ment

air pi'/ra/cy

a la'/te/re

al'/bum bre'/ve

al'/co/hol

al'/co/hol'/ic

al'/co/hol'/ism'

al'/der/man

a'le/a/to'/ry con'/tract

a'lias

    ____ dic'/tus

    ____ ex'/e/cu'/tion

    ____ pro'/cess

    ____ sum'/mons

al'/i/bi'

a'li·en

    ____ a·my'

    ____ and se/di'/tion

  laws

    ____ im'/mi/grant

a'li·en/a·bil'/i/ty

a'li·en/age

a'li·en/ate'
   a'lien/at'/ed
   a'lien/at'/ing
a'li·en/a'/tion
   ——— in mort'/main'
   ——— of af/fec'/tions
a'li·en/ee'
a'li·en/ism'
a'li·en/ist
a'li·en/or'
a·lign'/ment
a·like'
al'/i/men'/ta
al'/i/mo'/ny
al'/i/quot'
al'/i/ter
al'/i/un'/de
a·live'
al'/le/ga'/tion
al/lege'
   al/leged'
   al/leg'/ing
al/le'/giance
al/le'/gi/a'/re
al/li'/ance
al/lied'
al'/lo/ca/ble
al'/lo/cate'
   al'/lo/cat'/ed
   al'/lo/cat'/ing
al'/lo/ca'/tion
al'/lo/cu'/tion
al'/lo/graph'
al/longe'
al/lot'
   al/lot'/ted

al/lot' (contd.)
   al/lot'/ting
al/lot'/ment
   ——— cer/tif'/i/cate
   ——— sys'/tem
al/low'
   al/lowed'
   al/low'/ing
al/low'/ance
al/lu'/sion
al/lu'/vi/on
al'/ly', *pl* al'/lies
alms'/house'
a·lone'
a·long'
al'/so
al'/ter
   al'/tered
   al'/ter/ing
al'/ter/a'tion
al'/ter/ca'/tion
al'/ter e'go
al'/ter/nate *n, adj*
al'/ter/nate' *v*
   al'/ter/nat'/ed
   al'/ter/nat'/ing
al/ter'/na/tive
   ——— con'/tract'
   ——— ob'/li/ga'/tion
   ——— plead'/ing
   ——— re/main'/ders
al'/to et bas'/so
a·mal'/gam/a'tion
a·man'/u/en'/sis
am/bas'/sa/dor
am'/bi/dex'/ter

am′/bi/gu′/i/tas
am′/bi/gu′/i·ty
am/big′′/u/ous
am′′/bit
am′′/bi/tus
am′′/bu/lance chas′′/er
am′′/bu/la/to′′/ry
am′′/bush′
a·me′′/lio/rate′
    a·me′′/lio/rat′/ed
    a·me′′/lio/rat′/ing
a·me/lio/ra′′/tion
a·me′′/na/ble
a·mend′
    a·mend′′/ed
    a·mend′′/ing
a·mend′′/ment
a·men′′/i/ty
a men′′/sa et tho′′/ro
a·merce′
    a·merced′
    a·merc′/ing
a·merce′′/ment
a·mi′
am′′/i/ca/ble
    _____ ac′′/tion
    _____ com/pound′′/er
am·i′′/cus cu′′/ri/ae′
am/ne′′/sia
am′′/nes/ty
a·mong′
am′′/or/ti/za′′/tion
am′′/or/tize′
    am′′/or/tized′
    am′′/or/tiz′′/ing
a·mo′′/tion

a·mount′
    _____ in con′′/tro/ver′′/
sy
    _____ re′′/al/ized′
a·muse′′/ment
a·nal′′/o/gous
a·nal′′/o/gy
an′/aph′′/ro/di′′/sia
an′′/ar/chist
an′′/ar/chy
a·nat′′/o/cism
an′′/ces′′/tor
an/ces′′/tral
an′′/cient writ′′/ings
an′′/cil/lar′y
    _____ ad/min′′/is/tra′′/
tion
    _____ at/tach′′/ment
    _____ ju′′/ris/dic′′/tion
    _____ leg′/is/la′′/tion
    _____ pro/ceed′′/ing
a·new′
an′′/ga/ry
an′′/ger
an′′/guish
an′i/mal
an′i/mo
an′i/mus
    _____ can′/cel/lan′′/di
    _____ do/nan′′/di
    _____ fu/ran′′/di
    _____ ma/nen′′/di
    _____ tes/tan′′/di
an′′/nals
an′′/nex′ *n*

an/nex′ *v*
 an/nexed′
 an/nex′/ing
an′/nex′/a′tion
an′/ni/ver′/sa/ry
an′/no Dom′/i/ni
an′/no/tate′
 an′/no/tat′/ed
 an′/no/tat′/ing
an′/no/ta′/tion
an/nounce′
 an/nounced′
 an/nounc′/ing
an/noy′/ance
an′/nu/al
 ____ as/say′
 ____ de/pre′/ci/a′/
 tion
 ____ ex/clu′/sion
an′/nu/al/ly
an/nu′/i·ty
an/nul′
 an/nulled′
 an/nul′/ling
an/nul′/ment
an′/nus
a·nom′/a/lous
a·non′/y/mous
an/oth′/er
an′/swer
 an′/swered
 an′/swer/ing
an′/te
an′/te/ced′/ent
an′/te/date′
 an′/te/dat′/ed

an′/te/date′ (contd.)
 an′/te/dat′/ing
an/ten′/na
an′/te/nup′/tial
 ____ a·gree′/ment
 ____ con′/tract′
an/tic′/i/pa′/tion
an/tic′/i/pa/to′/ry
 ____ breach of con′/
 tract′
 ____ nui′/sance
 ____ of/fense′
an/tig′/ra/phy
a·part′/ment
a′pex′
a·pha′/sia
a·pho′/nia
ap′/o/plex′y
a pos/te′/ri/o′/ri
ap′/pa/ra′/tus
ap/par′/el
ap/par′/ent
 ____ au/thor′/i/ty
 ____ ne/ces′/si/ty
ap/peal′
 ap/pealed′
 ap/peal′/ing
ap/peal′/a·ble
ap/pear′
ap/pear′/ance
ap/pel′/lant
ap/pel′/ate
 ____ ju′/ris/dic′/tion
ap′/pel/lee′
ap/pend′
 ap/pend′/ed

ap/pend′ (contd.)
    ap/pend′/ing
ap/pend′/age
ap/pen′/dant
ap/pen′/dix
ap′/per/tain′
    ap/per/tained′
    ap/per/tain′/ing
ap′/pli/ca/ble
ap′/pli/ca′/tion
ap/ply′
    ap/plied′
    ap/ply′/ing
ap/point′
    ap/point′/ed
    ap/point′/ing
ap/poin′/tee′
ap/point′/ive
ap/point′/ment
ap/point′/or
ap/por′/tion
ap/por′/tion/ment
ap/pose′
    ap/posed′
    ap/pos′/ing
ap′/po/site
ap′/po/si′/tion
ap/prais′/al
ap/praise′
    ap/praised′
    ap/prais′/ing
ap/praise′/ment
ap/prais′/er
ap/pre′/cia/ble
ap/pre′/ci/ate′
    ap/pre′/ci/at′/ed

ap/pre′/ci/ate′ (contd.)
    ap/pre′/ci/at′/ing
ap/pre′/ci/a′/tion
ap′/pre/hend′
    ap′/pre/hend′/ed
    ap′/pre/hend′/ing
ap′/pre/hen′/sion
ap/pren′/tice
ap/proach′
ap/pro′/pri/ate *adj*
ap/pro′/pri/ate′ *v*
    ap/pro′/pri/at′/ed
    ap/pro′/pri/at′/ing
ap/pro′/pri/a′/tion
ap/pro′/pri/a′/tor
ap/prov′/al
ap/prove′
    ap/proved′
    ap/prov′/ing
ap/prove′/ment
ap/prov′/er
ap/prox′/i/mate *adj*
ap/prox′/i/ma′/tion
ap/pur′/te/nance
ap/pur′/te/nant
a pri/o′/ri
ap′/ti/tude′
a quo
ar′/a/ble
ar′/bi/ter
ar′/bi/trage′
ar/bit′/ra/ment
ar′/bi/trar′i/ly
ar′/bi/trar′y
ar′/bi/tra′/tion
ar′/bi/tra′/tor

ar/bit′/ri/um
ar′/bor civ′/i/lis
ar′/che/type′
ar′/chi/tect′
ar′/chi/tec′/tur/al
ar′/chives
ar′/chi/vist
ar′/e·a
ar′/gue
   ar′/gued
   ar′/gu/ing
ar′/gu/en′′/do
ar′/gu/ment
a·rise′
ar′/is/toc′/ra/cy
armed neu/tral′/i/ty
ar′/mi/stice
ar′/mor·y
ar′/my
a·round′
ar/raign′
   ar/raigned′
   ar/raign′′/ing
ar/raign′′/ment
ar/range′′/ment
ar/ray′
ar/rear′′/age
ar/rears′
ar/rest′
   ar/rest′/ed
   ar/rest′/ing
ar/riv′/al
ar/rive′
   ar/rived′
   ar/riv′′/ing
ar′/ro/ga′/tion

ar′′/se/nal
ar′′/son
ar/te′′/sian
ar′/ti/cle
ar′/ti/cles
   ——— of a·gree′′/ment
   ——— of ap/pren′′/
tice/ship
   ——— of as/so′/ci/a′/
tion
   ——— of con/sol′/i/da′/
tion
   ——— of dis/so/lu′′/tion
   ——— of in/cor′/po/ra′/
tion
ar′/ti/fice
ar/ti′′/fi/cer
ar′/ti/fi′′/cial
   ——— per′/son
   ——— pre/sump′′/tion
   ——— suc/ces′′/sion
ar′/ti/fi′′/cial/ly
ar′′/ti/san
as/cend′
as/cen′/dant
as/cent′
as′′/cer/tain′
   as/cer/tained′
   as/cer/tain′′/ing
a·side′
as′/pect′
as/per′/sion
as/phyx′/ia
as/phyx′/i/a′′/tion
as′′/por/ta′′/tion
as/sas′′/sin

as/sas′/si/nate′
    as/sas′/si/nat′/ed
    as/sas′/si/nat′/ing
as/sas′/si/na′/tion
as/sault′
    _____ and bat′/ter·y
    _____ with in/tent′ to
com/mit′ man′/
slaugh′/ter
    _____ with in/tent′ to
com/mit′ mur′/der
as/say′
    as/sayed′
    as/say′/ing
as/say′/er
as/sem′/blage
as/sem′/ble
    as/sem′/bled
    as/sem′/bling
as/sem′/bly
as/sent′
    as/sent′/ed
    as/sent′/ing
as/sess′
    as/sessed′
    as/sess′/ing
as/sess′/ment
    _____ com′/pa/ny
    _____ dis′/trict
    _____ in/sur′/ance
    _____ pe′/ri/od
    _____ ra′/tio
as/ses′/sor
as′/set
as/sev′/er/ate′
    as/sev′/er/at′/ed

as/sev′/er/ate′ (contd.)
    as/sev′/er/at′/ing
as/sev′/er/a′/tion
as/sign′
    as/signed′
    as/sign′/ing
as/sign′/a·bil′/i/ty
as/sign′/a·ble
as/sign/ee′
as/sign′/er *or* as′/sign/or′
as/sign′/ment
as/sist′
    as/sist′/ed
    as/sist′/ing
as/sis′/tance
as/sis′/tant
as/size′
as/so′/ci/ate *n, adj*
as/so′/ci/ate′ *v*
    as/so′/ci/at′/ed
    as/so′/ci/at′/ing
as/so′/ci/a′/tion
as/soil′
as/sume′
    as/sumed′
    as/sum′/ing
as/sump′/sit
as/sump′/tion
    _____ of in/debt′/
ed/ness
    _____ of mort′/gage
as/sur′/ance
as/sure′
    as/sured′
    as/sur′/ing
as/tip′/u/la′/tion

a·sy**/**lum
a te**/**/ne/ris an**/**/nis
a**/**the/ist
at**/**/om/ize**/**
    at**/**/om/ized**/**
    at**/**/om/iz**/**/ing
a·tro**/**/cious
a·troc**/**/i/ty
at/tach**/**
    at/tached**/**
    at/tach**/**/ing
at**/**/ta/ché**/**
at/tach**/**/ment
at/tain**/**
    at/tained**/**
    at/tain**/**/ing
at/tain**/**/der
at/tempt**/**
    at/tempt**/**/ed
    at/tempt**/**/ing
at/ten**/**/dant
at/ten**/**/tion
at/test**/**
    at/test**/**/ed
    at/test**/**/ing
at**/**/tes/ta**/**/tion
at/tes**/**/ter
at/torn**/**
    at/torned**/**
    at/torn**/**/ing
at**/**/tor/nar**/**/re
at/tor**/**/ney
at/tor**/**/ney/ship**/**
at/trac**/**/tive nui**/**/sance
doc**/**/trine
auc**/**/tion

auc**/**/tion/eer**/**
au**/**/di/ence
au**/**/dit
    au**/**/dit/ed
    au**/**/dit/ing
au**/**/di/tor
aug**/**/men/ta**/**/tion
au/then**/**/tic
au/then**/**/ti/ca**/**/tion
au**/**/thor
au/thor**/**/i/ty
au**/**/tho/rize**/**
    au**/**/tho/rized**/**
    au**/**/tho/riz**/**/ing
au/toc**/**/ra/cy
au**/**/to/graph**/**
au**/**/to/mat**/**/ic
au**/**/to/ma**/**/tion
au/tom**/**/a/tism**/**
au**/**/to/mo/bile**/**
au/ton**/**/o/my
au**/**/top**/**/sy
au/top**/**/tic prof/fer**/**/ence
au**/**/tre droit
aux/il**/**/ia/ry
a·vail**/**/a·ble
av**/**/e/nue
a·ver**/**
    a·verred**/**
    a·ver**/**/ring
av**/**/er/age
a**/**vi/a**/**/tion
a vin**/**/cu/lo ma**/**/tri/mo**/**/
nii
a·vo/cat**/**
av**/**/o/ca**/**/tion

a·void**'**
 a·void**'**/ed
 a·void**'**/ing
a·void**'**/a·ble con**'**/se/
quenc/es
a·void**'**/ance
av**'**/oir/du/pois**'**
a·vow**'**
 a·vowed**'**
 a·vow**'**/ing
a·vow**'**/al
a·vow**'**/ry
a·vul**'**/sion
a·wait**'**
 a·wait**'**/ed
 a·wait**'**/ing
a·ward**'**
 a·ward**'**/ed
 a·ward**'**/ing

B

bab**'**/ble
bach**'**/e/lor
back**'** bond
back**'**/date
 back**'**/dat/ed
 back**'**/dat/ing
back**'**/ing
back**'**/ward
back**'**/ward/a**'**tion *or*
 back**'**/a/da**'**/tion
back**'**/wa**'**/ter

bad
 _____ char**'**/ac/ter
 _____ mo**'**/tive
 _____ ti**'**/tle
badge
bail
bail**'**/a·ble
 _____ ac**'**/tion
 _____ of/fense**'**
bail/ee**'**
bai**'**/liff
bai**'**/li/wick**'**
bail**'**/ment
bail/or**'** *or* bail**'**/er
bail**'**/out
bails**'**/man
bait
bal**'**/ance
 _____ of pay**'**/ments
 _____ of pow**'**/er
bal**'**/last
bal**'**/last/age**'**
bal/loon**'**
 _____ mort**'**/gage
 _____ pay**'**/ment
bal**'**/lot
ban**'**/dit
bane
ban**'**/ish/ment
bank
 _____ ac/cep**'**/tance
 _____ ac/count**'**
 _____ cred**'**/it
 _____ deb**'**/it
 _____ de/pos**'**/it
 _____ state**'**/ment

bank′/a·ble pa′/per
bank′/book
bank′/er
bank′/er's ac/cep′/tance
bank′/ing
bank′/rupt′
bank′/rupt/cy
bar *n*
    —— ad/mis′/sion
    —— as/so′/ci/a′/tion
bar *v*
  barred
  bar′/ring
bare
    —— or mere li′/cens/
  ee′
    —— pat′/ent li′/cense
    —— trust/ee′
bare′/boat char′/ter
bar′/gain
  bar′/gained
  bar′/gain/ing
bar′/gain/ee′
bar/gain/or′
bar′/on·y
bar′/ra/tor *or* bar′/ra/ter
bar′/ra/trous
bar′/ra/try
bar′/rel
bar′/ren
bar′/ren/ness
bar′/ri/er
bar′/ris/ter
bar′/ter
  bar′/tered
  bar′/ter/ing

bas′/al frac′/ture
base
    —— and me/rid′/i/an
    —— bul′/lion
    —— ten′/ure
ba/sil′/i/ca
ba′/sin
ba′/sis, *pl* ba′/ses′
bas′/tard
bas′/tard/ize′
  bas′/tard/ized′
  bas′/tard/iz′/ing
bas′/tard·y
    —— ac′/tion
    —— pro/ceed′/ings
bat′/tel
bat′/ter
  bat′/tered
  bat′/ter/ing
bat′/ter·y
bawd
bawd′y/house
bay′/gall′
bay′/ou
beach
bea′/con
bea′/con/age
bear
    —— in′/ter/est
    —— mar′/ket
bear′/er
bear′/ing date
beast
beat
  beat′/en
  beat′/ing

be/come′
    be/came′
    be/com′/ing
be/get′
    be/gat′
    be/get′/ting
    be/got′/ten
beg′/gar
be/gin′
    be/gan′
    be/gin′/ning
    be/gun′
be/half′
be/hav′/ior
be/hoof′
be/lief′
bel/lig′/er/en/cy
bel/lig′/er/ent
bel′/lum
be/long′
    be/longed′
    be/long′/ing
be/long′/ings
be/low′
bench
    ____ blot′/ter
    ____ con′/fer/ence
    ____ leg′/is/la′/tion
    ____ tri′/al
    ____ war′/rant
be′/ne
ben′/e/fice
ben′/e/fi′/cial
    ____ en/joy′/ment
    ____ es/tate′
    ____ in′/ter/est

ben′/e/fi′/cial (contd.)
    ____ own′/er
    ____ pow′/er
ben′/e/fi′/cia/ry
ben′/e/fit′
    ____ cer/tif′/i/cate
    ____ of bar′/gain rule
    ____ of cler′/gy
    ____ of dis/cus′/sion
    ____ of in′/ven/to′/ry
    ____ so/ci′/e/ties
be/nev′/o/lence
be/nev′/o/lent
    ____ as/so′/ci/a′′/tion
    ____ cor′/po/ra′/tion
    ____ so/ci′/e/ty
be/queath′
    be/queathed′
    be/queath′/ing
be/quest′
be/seech′
    be/sought′ *or* be/
    seeched′
    be/seech′/ing
be/sides′
be/sot′
best ev′/i/dence
bes′/ti/al′/i/ty
be/stow′
    be/stowed′
    be/stow′/ing
be/tray′
    be/trayed′
    be/tray′/ing
be/tray′/al
be/troth′/al

be/trothed/
be/troth//ment
bet//ter/ment
bet
    bet *or* bet//ted
    bet//ting
be/tween/
bev//er/age
be/yond/
    ——— a rea//son/a·ble
    doubt
    ——— con/trol/
bi//an//nu/al/ly
bi//as
bi/cam//er/al sys//tem
bid
    bid//ding
bid//der
bi//en//ni/al ses//sion
bi//en//ni/al/ly
biens
bi//fur/cat//ed tri//al
big//a/mous
big//a/my
big//ot
bi//lat//er/al con//tract
bil//bo
bill
    ——— bro//ker
    ——— for fore/clo//sure
    ——— o·blig//a/to/ry
    ——— of ad/ven//ture
    ——— of at/tain//der
    ——— of con/for//mi/ty
    ——— of cred//it

bill (contd.)
    ——— of dis/cov//er·y
    ——— of en//try
    ——— of ev//i/dence
    ——— of ex/change/
    ——— of in/dem//ni/ty
    ——— of in/dict//ment
    ——— of in//for/ma//
tion
    ——— of in//ter/plead//
er
    ——— of lad//ing
    ——— of mor/tal//i/ty
    ——— of pains and pen//
al/ties
    ——— of par/tic//u/lars
    ——— of re/view/
    ——— of re/viv//or and
sup//ple/ment
    ——— pay//a·ble
    ——— pe//nal
    ——— re/ceiv//a·ble
    ——— ren//dered
    ——— to per/pet//u/ate/
tes//ti/mo//ny
bil//ly
bi//me/tal//lic
bind out
bind//er
bind//ing
    ——— a·gree//ment
    ——— au/thor//i/ty
    ——— in/struc//tion
    ——— re/ceipt/
bi//par//tite/

birth
bis
bish′/op
black a′cre and white a′cre
black′/jack′
black′/leg′
black′/list′
black′/mail′
blanc seign
blank
    _____ ac/cept′/ance
    _____ en/dorse′/ment
blan′/ket
    _____ in/sur′/ance
    _____ mort′/gage
    _____ pol′/i/cy
blas′/phe/my
blend′/ed price
blind
    _____ al′/ley
    _____ cor′/ner
    _____ sel′/ling
blind′/ness
block
    _____ book sys′/tem
    _____ pol′/i/cy
    _____ of sur′/veys′
    _____ to block rule
block/ade′
block′/age rule
blood
    _____ mon′/ey
    _____ re/la′/tion
    _____ rel′/a/tive
blood′/hound′

blood′/wit
blood′y
blud′/geon
    blud′/geoned
    blud′/geon/ing
blue′-/rib′bon ju′/ry
blue sky law
blum′/ba
blun′/der
blun′/der/buss′
board
    _____ mea′/sure
    _____ of ad/just′/ment
    _____ of al′/der/men
    _____ of ap/peals′
    _____ of di/rec′/tors
    _____ of ed′/u/ca′/tion
    _____ of par′/dons
    _____ of re/view′
    _____ of su′/per/vi′/
    sors
    _____ of trust/ees′
boat′/a·ble
boat′/ing
boat′/swain
bob′/tail driv′/er
bod′i/ly
bod′y
    _____ cor′/po/rate
    _____ ex′/e/cu′/tion
    _____ of a coun′/ty
    _____ of the of/fense′
    _____ pol′/i/tic
boil′/er/plate
bo/li′/to

bolt'/ing
bo'/na
_____ fi'/de'
_____ fi'/des'
_____ gra'/tia
_____ me/mo'/ria
bond
_____ and mort'/gage
_____ cred'/i/tor
_____ dis'/count
_____ div'/i/dend
_____ for ti'/tle
_____ in/den'/ture
_____ is'/sue
_____ of in/debt'/
ed/ness
_____ pre'/mi/um
_____ rat'/ing
_____ re/demp'/tion
_____ with sur'e/ty
bond'/age
bond'/ed
_____ in/debt'/ed/ness
_____ ware'/house
bonds'/man
bon'/i/fi/ca'/tion
bo'/no et ma'/lo
bo'/nus
boo'/dle
boo'/dled
boo'/dling
book
_____ ac/count'
_____ en'/try

book (contd.)
_____ val'/ue
booked
book'/ing
book'/keep'/er
book'/mak'/er
book'/mak'/ing
boom'/age
boot'/leg'/ger
boot'/leg'/ging
boo'/ty
born a·live'
bor'/ough
bor'/row
bor'/rowed
bor'/row/ing
bor'/row/er
bot'/tle
bot'/tom/ry
bot'/u/lism'
bou'/le/vard'
bou'/le/ver/sé/ment
bounc'/er
bound'/ar·y
bound'/ed
bound'/ers
bounds
boun'/ty
bour/geois'
bourse
bo'/vine
boy'/cott'
branch
_____ pi'/lot

branch (contd.)

    ____ rail'/road

brass knuck'/les

bras'/sage

brawl

breach

    ____ of con'/tract'

    ____ of cov'/e/nant

    ____ of du'/ty

    ____ of pris'/on

    ____ of prom'/ise

    ____ of priv'/i/lege

    ____ of war'/ran/ty

break'/ing and en'/ter/ing

breath'/a/ly'/zer test

breath'/ing

breed

breth'/ren

bre'/ve

bre'/vet

bre'/vi·a

bre'/vi/ate *n*

brew'/er

brib'/er·y

bridge se/cu'/ri/ties

brief

broad in/ter'/pre/ta'/tion

broad'/side ob/jec'/tion

bro'/kage

bro'/ken

bro'/ker/age

    ____ con'/tract'

    ____ list'/ing

broth'/el

broth'/er

broth'er-/in-/law

bru'/tum ful'/men

buck'/et/ing

bud'/get

buff'/er

buf'/fet

bug'/ger·y

bug'/ging

build'/er

build'/ing

    ____ and loan as/so'/ci/a'/tion

    ____ per'/mit

    ____ re/stric'/tions

    ____ so/ci'/e·ty

bulk

    ____ mort'/gage

    ____ trans'/fers

bull

bul'/le/tin

bul'/lion

bum'/bail'/iff

bump'/ing

bun'/co' game

bun'/dle

bu·oy

bur'/den

    ____ of go'/ing for'/ward

    ____ of pro/ceed'/ing

    ____ of proof

bu'/reau

bu/reau'/cra/cy

burg *or* burgh
bur′/gess
bur′/glar
bur′/glar·y
bur/glar′/i/ous
bur′/glar/ize′
    bur′/glar/ized′
    bur′/glar/iz′/ing
bur′/gle
    bur′/gled
    bur′/gling
bur′/go/mas′/ter
bur′i/al
burke
    burked
    burk′/ing
burk′/ism
burn
    burned
    burn′/ing
bur′/sar
bur′/sar·y
bur′y
    bur′/ied
    bur′y/ing
bush′/el
bus′i/ness
    ——— a′gent
    ——— cor′/po/ra′/tion
    ——— en′/ter/prise′
    ——— ex/pense′
    ——— in′/vi/tee′
    ——— judg′/ment rule
    ——— loss′/es
    ——— vis′/i/tor

butt
but′/tal
butte
but′/ted and bound′/ed
butts and bounds
buy′/er
buy′/ing
    ——— dor′/mant ti′/tles
    ——— long
by′-/bid′der
by′-/bid′ding
by′/law′ *or* bye′/law′
by′/stand′/er

C

ca/bal′
ca/ban′a
cab′/a/ret′
cab′/i/net coun′/cil
ca′/ble
cab′/o/tage′
ca/dav′/er
ca/dav′/er/ous
ca′/de/re
ca/det′
ca′/dit quae′/sti·o
ca/du′/ca
ca/du′/ca′/ry
cae/sar′/e/an *or* cae/sar′/
i/an
cae′/te/ro′/rum
caf′/e/te′/ri·a

ca/hoots′
cal′/a/boose′
ca/lam′/i/ty
cal′/cu/late
    cal′/cu/lat′/ed
    cal′/cu/lat′/ing
cal′/en/dar
cal′/ends
call
    _____ op′/tion
    _____ pat′/ent
    _____ pre′/mi/um
call′/a·ble bonds
call′/er
call′/ing
    _____ an e·lec′/tion
    _____ the dock′/et
    _____ the ju′/ry
    _____ to tes′/ti/fy
    _____ up/on′ a pris′/
on/er
ca/lum′/ni·a
ca/lum′/ni/ate′
    ca/lum′/ni/at′/ed
    ca/lum′/ni/at′/ing
cal/lum′/ni/a′/tor
ca/lum′/ni/ous
cal′/um/ny
cam′/ou/flage′
cam/paign′
camp′/er
ca/nal′
can′/a/li/za′/tion
can′/cel
    can′/celed

can′/cel (contd.)
    can′/cel/ing
can′/cel/la′/tion
can′/di/date′
can′/di/da/cy
can′/on
ca/non′/i/cal
    _____ dis′/a·bil′/i/ty
can′/on/ist
can′/ons of con/struc′/tion
can′/vass
    can′/vassed
    can′/vass/ing
can′/vass/er
ca′/pa/bil′/i/ty
ca′/pa/ble
ca/pac′/i/ty
ca′/pax do′/li
ca′/per
ca′/pi/as
    _____ ad com′/pu/tan′/
dum
    _____ ad re′/spon/den′/
dum
    _____ ad sat′/is/fa′/
ci/en′/dum
    _____ ex/ten′/di fa′/
ci/as
    _____ pro fi′/ne
ca′/pi/ta
cap′/i/tal
    _____ as′/sets
    _____ con′/tri/bu′/tion
    _____ ex/pen′/di/ture
    _____ im/pair′/ment

cap′/i/tal (contd.)
    _____ in′/crease′
    _____ in/vest′′/ment
    _____ lev′y
    _____ mar′′/ket
    _____ of/fense′
    _____ out′/lay′
    _____ pun′/ish/ment
    _____ re/cov′′/er·y
    _____ re/turn′
    _____ struc′/ture
    _____ sur′/plus
cap′/i/tal/ist
cap′/i/tal/i·za′/tion meth′′/
od
cap′/i/tal/ize′
    cap′/i/tal/ized′
    cap′/i/tal/iz′/ing
cap′/i/ta′/tim
cap′/i/ta′/tion tax
ca/pit′′/u/late′
    ca/pit′′/u/lat′/ed
    ca/pit′′/u/lat′/ing
ca/pit′′/u/la′′/tion
ca/price′
ca/pri′′/cious/ness
cap′′/tain
cap′′/ta/tor
cap′′/tion
cap′′/tive
cap′′/tor
cap′′/ture
    cap′′/tured
    cap′′/tur/ing
ca′/put

car′′/at
car/ca′′/num
car/ca′′/tus
car′′/cel/age
car′′/cer
card′-/car′ry·ing
card hold′′/er
car′′/di/nal
care′/less
care′/less/ly
care′/less/ness
car′′/go
car′′/load
car′′/men
car′′/nal
    _____ a·buse′
    _____ knowl′′/edge
car′′/riage
car′′/ri/er
car′′/ry
    car′′/ried
    car′′/ry/ing
car′′/ry
    _____ a mem′′/ber
    _____ an e·lec′/tion
    _____ on bus′i/ness
car′′/ta
cart′′/age
carte blanche
car/tel′
cart′′/load
car′′/ton
car′′/tu/lar′y
case
    _____ law

case (contd.)
    ____ meth'/od
    ____ of ac'/tu/al con'/tro/ver'/sy
    ____ on ap/peal'
    ____ re/served'
case'/ment
case'/work/er
cash
    ____ ac/count'
    ____ ba'/sis ac/count'/ing
    ____ bud'/get
    ____ cy'/cle
    ____ dis'/count
    ____ div'/i/dend
    ____ e·quiv'/a/lent
    ____ mar'/ket val'/ue
    ____ re/served'
    ____ sur/ren'/der val'/ue
    ____ val'/ue op'/tion
cash/ier'
cash/iered'
cash/ier's' check
cas/sa'/re
cast a·way'
cast'/a·way' n
cas'/ti/gate'
    cas'/ti/gat'/ed
    cas'/ti/gat'/ing
cas'/ti/ga'/tion
cast'/ing vote
ca'/su/al
    ____ bet'/tor

ca'/su/al (contd.)
    ____ def'/i/cit
    ____ e·jec'/tor
    ____ em/ploy'/ment
ca'/su/al/ty
    ____ in/sur'/ance
ca'/su/ist/ry
ca'/sus
    ____ bel'/li
    ____ foe'/de/ris
    ____ for/tu'/i/tus
    ____ ma'/jor
    ____ o·mis'/sus
cat'/a/lep'/sy
cat'/a/lex'/is
cat'/a/log *or* cat'/a/logue
ca/tas'/tro/phe
cat'a/ton'/ic
catch'/ings
catch'/land
catch'/pen'/ny
catch'/pole' *or* catch'/poll'
cat'/e/gor'/i/cal ques'/tion
ca/the'/dral
cat'/tle
    ____ rus'/tling
Cau/ca'/sian
cau'/cus
cau'/da ter'/rae
cau'/sa
    ____ hos/pi/tan'/di
    ____ mor'/tis
    ____ prox'/i/ma
    ____ re/mo'/ta
    ____ si'/ne qua non

cau′/sa (contd.)
    ―――― tur′/pis
caus′/al re/la′′/tion
cau/sa′′/tion
cau′/sa/tor
cause
    ―――― cé/lè/bre′
    ―――― of ac′′/tion
    ―――― of in′′/ju/ry
cause′/way′
cau′′/tion
cau′/tion/ar′y
    ―――― in/struc′′/tion
    ―――― judg′′/ment
cau′′/tious
ca′/ve/at
    ―――― ac′′/tor
    ―――― emp′/tor
    ―――― ven′′/di/tor
    ―――― vi/a′′/tor
ca′/ve/at′/or
ca/ve′′/re
cease and de/sist′
cede
    ced′′/ed
    ced′′/ing
ce′/do
ce/la′′/tion
cel′/e/brate′
    cel′/e/brat′′/ed
    cel′/e/brat′′/ing
ce/leb′′/ri/ty
cem′/e/ter′y
cen′/sor/ship
cen′/sure

cen′′/sus
    ―――― bu′′/reau
    ―――― re/gal′′/is
cent
cen′′/ter
cen/time′
cen′′/tral
cen′/tral/i·za′′/tion
cen′′/tu/ry
ce′/pi
ce′/pit
    ―――― et ab/dux′′/it
    ―――― et as′/por/ta′′/vit
    ―――― in a′lio lo′′/co
ce′/ra
    ―――― im/pres′′/sa
cer′/e/bel′′/lum
ce/re′′/brum
cer′/e/mo′′/ni/al mar′′/riage
cer′′/tain
    ―――― con′/tract′
cer′/tain/ty
cer′/ti/fi′′/a·ble
cer/tif′′/i/cate
    ―――― cred′/it
    ―――― of ac/knowl′′/
edg/ment
    ―――― of a·mend′′/ment
    ―――― of as/size′
    ―――― of au/thor′′/i/ty
    ―――― of com′′/pe/ten/
cy
    ―――― of e·lec′′/tion
    ―――― of in/cor′′/po/ra′′/
tion

cer/tif'/i/cate (contd.)

    _____ of in/debt'/ed/ness

    _____ of in/sur'/ance

    _____ of in'/ter/est

    _____ of oc'/cu/pan/cy

    _____ of par/tic'/i/pa'/tion

    _____ of pur'/chase

    _____ of reg'/is/try

cer'/ti/fi/ca'/tion

cer'/ti/fied'

    _____ car'/ri/er

    _____ cop'y

    _____ pub'/lic ac/coun'/tant

cer'/ti/fy'

    cer'/ti/fied'

    cer'/ti/fy'/ing

cer'/ti·o/ra'/ri

ce/sar'/e/an *or* ce/sar'/i/an

ces/sa'/re

ces'/sion

cess'/ment

ces'/sor

ces/tui'

    _____ que trust

    _____ que use

    _____ que vie

chain

    _____ of cus'/to/dy

    _____ of pos/ses'/sion

    _____ of ti'/tle

chair'/man

chair'/per'/son

chair'/wom'/an

chal'/lenge

    chal'/lenged

    chal'/leng/ing

chal'/lenge

    _____ to ar/ray'

    _____ to the fa'/vor

    _____ to the poll

cham'/ber of com'/merce

cham'/bers

cham'/per/tor

cham'/per/tous

cham'/per/ty

cham'/pi/on

chance bar'/gain

chan'/cel/lor

chance'-/med'ley

chan'/cer

chan'/cer·y

change of ven'ue'

changed cir'/cum/stanc/es

chang'/er

chan'/nel

chap'/el

chap'/er/on *or* chap'/er/one

chap'/lain

chap'/man

chap'/ter

char'/ac/ter

charge

    _____ ac/count'

    _____ and dis'/charge

    _____ to the ju'/ry

char'/gé' d'af·faires'
charge'/a·ble
charg'/ing lien
char'/i/ta/ble
         ____ be/quest'
         ____ con'/tri/bu'/tion
         ____ cor/po/ṛa'/tion
         ____ de/duc'/tion
         ____ foun/da'/tion
         ____ in'/sti/tu'/tion
         ____ or'/ga/ni/za'/
tion
         ____ pur'/pose
         ____ re/main'/der
char'/i/ty
char'/la/tan
chart
char'/ta
char'/ter
         ____ a·gree'/ment
         ____ of af/freight'/
ment
         ____ par'/ty
char'/tered
char'/ter/er
char'/ter/house'
chase
     chased
     chas'/ing
chaste char'/ac/ter
chas'/ti/ty
chat'/tel
         ____ mort'/gage
         ____ pa'/per
chaud'-/med'ley
chauf'/feur

cheat
     cheat'/ed
     cheat'/ing
cheat'/er
check kit'/ing
check'/book'
check'/er/board' sys'/tem
check'/off sys'/tem
cheque
chi/cane'
     chi/caned'
     chi/can'/ing
chi/ca'/ner·y
chief
         ____ ex/ec'/u/tive
         ____ jus'/tice
         ____ mag'/is/trate'
child
         ____ a·buse'
         ____ la'/bor
         ____ wel'/fare
chil'/dren
chill'/ing a sale
chill'/ing ef/fect' doc'/trine
chi/rog'/ra/pher
chi/rog'/ra/phy
chi/rop'/o/dist
chi/rop'/o/dy
chi'/ro/prac'/tic
chi'/ro/prac'/tor
chiv'/al/ry
cho'/ate lien
chose
         ____ in ac'/tion
         ____ in pos/ses'/sion
cho'/sen free'/hold'er

Chris′/tian
chron′/ic
_____ al′/co/hol′/ism′
church
_____ prop′′/er/ty
_____ reg′/is/ter
_____ war′/den
churl
ci′/ca/trix
ci′/pher
cir′/ca
cir′/cuit
_____ court
_____ court of ap/peals′
_____ jus′/tice
cir/cu′/i/ty of ac′/tion
cir′/cu/lar let′/ter of cred′/it
cir′/cu/late′
　　cir′/cu/lat′/ed
　　cir′/cu/lat′/ing
cir′/cu/la′/tion
cir′/cum/spect′
cir′/cum/stance
cir′/cum/stan′/tial ev′/i/dence
cir′/cum/ven′/tion
cis′′/ta
ci/ta′′/tion
cite
　　cit′/ed
　　cit′/ing
cit′/i/zen
cit′/i/zen/ry
cit′/i/zen/ship′
cit′y coun′′/cil

civ′/ic
civ′/il
_____ ac′/tion
_____ au/thor′′/i/ty
_____ com/mit′′/ment
_____ con/spir′′/a/cy
_____ con/tempt′
_____ dam′′/age
_____ dis/a·bil′/i/ty
_____ dis/o·be′/di/ence
_____ dis/or′/der
_____ dock′/et
_____ in′/for/ma′/tion
_____ in′/quest
_____ li′/a/bil′′/i/ty
_____ lib′/er/ties
_____ nui′/sance
_____ ob′/li/ga′′/tion
_____ of/fense′
_____ of′′/fice
_____ of′′/fi/cer
_____ rem′/e/dy
_____ re/spon′/si/bil′′/i/ty
_____ ser′′/vant
_____ ser′′/vice
ci/vil′′/ian
ci′′/vi/lis
ci/vi′/li/ter mor′′/tu/us
civ′/i/li/za′/tion
claim
_____ ac/crued′
_____ ad/just′′/er
_____ and de/liv′′/er·y
_____ for re/lief′
_____ in eq′/ui/ty

claim (contd.)
    —— jump'/ing
    —— prop'/er/ty fund
claim'/ant
clair/voy'/ant
clam'/or
clan/des'/tine
class
    —— ac'/tion
    —— leg'/is/la'/tion
    —— rep'/re/sen/ta'/
tion
clas'/si/fi/ca'/tion
clas'/si/fy'
    clas'/si/fied'
    clas'/si/fy'/ing
clause
clau'/sum fre'/git
clear
    —— and con/vinc'/
ing proof
    —— and pres'/ent
dan'/ger
    —— an/nu'/i·ty
    —— chance
    —— ev'/i/dence
    —— ti'/tle
    —— val'/ue
clear'/ance
    —— cer/tif'/i/cate
clear'/ing
    —— ti'/tle
clear'/ing house'
clear'/ly
    —— er/ro'/ne/ous

clear'/ ly (contd.)
    —— proved
clem'/en/cy
clem'/ent
cler'/gy
cler'/gy/man
cler'/i/cal
    —— er'/ror
    —— mis/pri'/sion
cler'/i/sy
clerk
    —— of ar/raigns'
    —— of as/size'
    —— of en/roll/ments'
    —— of in/dict'/ments
    —— of rec'/ords and
writs
    —— of the mar'/ket
    —— of the peace
    —— of the priv'y seal
    —— of the sig'/nct
    —— of the ta'/ble
clerk'/ship
cli'/ent
cli'/en/tele'
clin'/i/cal
cli/ni'/cian
clipped sov'/er/eign/ty
cli'/max'
close
    —— cor/po/ra'/tion
    —— in/ter'/pre/ta'/
tion
    —— jail ex'/e/cu'/
tion

close (contd.)

_____ rel'/a/tive

closed

_____ cor/po/ra'/tion

_____ in/sur'/ance

pol'/i/cy

_____ pri'/ma'/ry

_____ shop con'/tract'

_____ trans/ac'/tion

_____ u'nion

clos'/ing

_____ ar'/gu/ment

_____ costs

_____ en'/try

_____ es/tate'

_____ state'/ment

clo'/sure

cloud on ti'/tle

club law

clus'/ter zon'/ing

clutch

co'/ad/ju'/tor

co'/ad/ju'/trix

co'/ad/min'/is/tra'/tor

co'/ad/ven'/tur/er

co'/a·gent

co'/a·lesce'

co'/a·li'/tion

co'/as'/sign/ee'

coast

coast'/ed

coast'/ing

coast wa'/ters

coast'/al

coast'/er

coast'/ing trade

coast'/wise'

cock'/pit'

code

_____ ci/vil'

_____ d'in/struc/tion'

cri/mi/nelle'

_____ of crim'/i/nal

pro/ce'/dures

_____ pe/nal'   ·

Code

_____ Na/po/le/on'

_____ of Fed'/er/al

Reg'/u/la'/tion

_____ of Jus/tin'/i/an

_____ of Mil'/i/tar'y

Jus'/tice

co'/dex

cod'/i/cil

cod'/i/fi/ca'/tion

cod'/i/fy'

cod'/i/fied'

cod'/i/fy'/ing

co'/emp'/tion

co'/e'qual

co/erce'

co/erced'

co/erc'/ing

co/er'/cion

co/er'/cive

co'/ex/ec'/u/tor

cof'/fer/er of the queen's

house'/hold'

cog'/nate'

cog/na'/tion

cog/na′/tus
cog/ni′/ti·o
cog/ni′/tion
cog′/ni/tive
cog′/ni/za/ble
cog′/ni/zance
cog/nize′
   cog/nized′
   cog/niz′/ing
cog/ni/zee′
cog′/ni/zor
cog/no′/men
cog/no′/vit
   _____ ac′/ti·o′/nem
   _____ judg′/ment
co/hab′/it
   co/hab′/it/ed
   co/hab′/it/ing
co/hab′/i/ta′/tion
co/heir′
co/heir′/ess
co/her′/ent
coif
co′/hort′
coin′/age
co′/in/sur′/ance
co′/i·tus
co/ju′/di/ces
cold blood
col/lab′/o/rate′
   col/lab′/o/rat′/ed
   col/lab′/o/rat′/ing
col/lab′/o/ra′/tion
col/laps′/i·ble
   _____ cor′/po/ra′/tion
   _____ part′/ner/ship

col/lat′/er/al
   _____ an′/ces′/tors
   _____ at/tack′
   _____ con′/san′/guin′/i/ty
   _____ cov′/e/nant
   _____ de/scent′
   _____ es/top′/pel
   _____ im/peach′/ment
   _____ in/her′/i/tance tax
   _____ is′/sue
   _____ kins′/man
   _____ lim′/i/ta′/tion
   _____ mort′/gage
   _____ neg′/li/gence
   _____ prom′/ise
   _____ se/cu′/ri/ty
   _____ un′/der/tak′/ing
col/la′/tion
col/lect′
   col/lect′/ed
   col/lect′/ing
col/lect′/i·ble
col/lec′/tive
   _____ bar′/gain/ing
col/lec′/tor
col/leg′/a/tar′y
col′/lege
col/le′/gia
col/le′/giate
col/le′/gi/um
col/lide′
   col/lid′/ed
   col/lid′/ing
col/li′/sion

col'/lo/ca'/tion
col/lo'/qui/al
col/lo'/qui/um
col/lude'
    col/lud'/ed
    col/lud'/ing
col/lu'/sion
col/lu'/sive
    _____ ac'/tion
    _____ join'/der
co/lo'/ni·al
    _____ char'/ter
    _____ sta'/tus
col'/o/nist
col'/o/ny
col'/or
    _____ of au/thor'/i/ty
    _____ of of'/fice
    _____ of ti'/tle
col'/or/a·ble
col'/ored
co'/mak'/er
com'/bat
com'/bi/na'/tion
    _____ in re/straint' of
    trade
    _____ pat'/ent
com/bus'/ti·o
com/bus'/tion
comes and de/fends'
com'/fort
    com'/fort/ed
    com'/fort/ing
co'/mi/tas
co'/mi/ty
com'/ma

com/mand'
    com/mand'/ed
    com/mand'/ing
com/mand'/er in chief
com/mand'/ment
com/mence'
    com/menced'
    com/menc'/ing
com/mence'/ment
com/mend'
    com/mend'/ed
    com/mend'/ing
com/men'/da/to'/ry
com/men/da'/ti·o
com'/ment
com'/merce
com/mer'/cia bel'/li
com/mer'/cial
    _____ a'cre
    _____ a'gen/cy
    _____ a'gent
    _____ brib'/er·y
    _____ bro'/ker
    _____ cor'/po/ra'/tion
    _____ de/liv'/er·y
    _____ do'/mi/cile'
    _____ es/tab'/lish/ment
    _____ frus/tra'/tion
    _____ im'/prac'/ti/ca/
bil'/i/ty
    _____ in/sol'/ven/cy
    _____ in/sur'/ance
    _____ in'/stru/ment
    _____ let'/ter of cred'/
it
    _____ part'/ner/ship

com/mer′/cial (contd.)
——— pa′/per
——— prop′/er/ty
——— trav′/el/er
——— u′nit
com/min′′/gle
   com/min′′/gled
   com/min′′/gling
com′/mis/sar′/i/at
com′/mis/sar·y
com/mis′′/sion
——— bro′/ker
——— gov′/ern/ment
——— mer′/chant
——— of an/tic′/i/pa′/
tion
——— of ar/ray′
——— of as/size′
com/mis′′/sioned of′/fi/cer
com/mis′′/sion/er
com/mis′′/sive waste
com/mit′
   com/mit′′/ted
   com/mit′′/ting
com/mit′′/ment
com/mit′′/tee
com/mit′′/ting mag′/
is/trate′
com/mit′′/ti/tur
com′/mo/da′′/tum
com/mod′′/i/ty
com′′/mon
——— an′′/ces/tor
——— ap/pear′/ance
——— ar′/e·a

com′′/mon (contd.)
——— bench
——— car′′/ri/er
——— coun′/cil
——— de/fense′
——— de/sign′
——— di/sas′′/ter
——— en′′/e/my
——— hu/man′′/i/ty
——— ju′/ry
——— knowl′/edge
——— nui′/sance
——— oc′/cu/pant
——— of es/to′′/vers
——— pleas
——— re/cov′′/er·y
com′′/mon/a·ble
com′′/mon/al/ty
com′′/mon/ance
com′′/mon/er
com′mon-/law
——— ac′/tion
——— as/sign′/ments
——— cheat
——— con/tempt′
——— cop′y/right′
——— ded′/i/ca′′/tion
——— ex/tor′′/tion
——— ju′/ris/dic′′/tion
——— lar′′/ce/ny
——— mar′′/riage
——— mort′/gage
——— nui′/sance
——— pro/ce′/dure
——— rem′/e/dy

com'/mon-/law (contd.)
    ____ trade'/mark
com'/mons
com'/mon/wealth'
com'/mo/ran/cy
com'/mo/rant
com'/mo/ri/en'/tes
com/mo'/tion
com'/mune' *n*
com/mu'/ni/cate'
    com/mu'/ni/cat'/ed
    com/mu'/ni/cat'/ing
com/mu'/ni/ca'/tion
com/mu'/nis
    ____ o·pin'/io
    ____ sti'/pes
com'/mu/nism
com'/mu/nist
com/mu'/ni/ty
    ____ ac/count'
    ____ of in'/ter/est
    ____ of prof'/its
    ____ prop'/er/ty
com'/mu/ta'/tion
com/mu'/ta/tive con'/
tract'
com/mute'
    com/mut'/ed
    com/mut'/ing
com/mut'/er
com'/pact' *n*
com/pact' *adj*
com/pan'/age
com/pan'/ion
com'/pa/ny

com'/pa/ra/ble
com/par'/a/tive
    ____ in/ter'/pre/ta'/
    tion
    ____ ju'/ris/pru'/
    dence
    ____ neg'/li/gence
    ____ rec'/ti/tude'
com/pare'
    com/pared'
    com/par'/ing
com'/pass
    com'/passed
    com'/pass/ing
com/pat'/i/ble
com/pat'/i/bil'/i/ty
com/pel'
    com/pelled'
    com/pel'/ling
com/pen'/di/um
com/pen'/sa/ble in'/ju/ry
com'/pen/sate'
    com'/pen/sat'/ed
    com'/pen/sat'/ing
com'/pen/sa'/tion
com/pen'/sa/to'/ry
com'/per/to'/ri/um
com/pe'/ru/it ad di'/em
com/pete'
    com/pet'/ed
    com/pet'/ing
com'/pe/ten/cy
com'/pe/tent
    ____ au/thor'/i/ty
    ____ ev'/i/dence

com′/pe/tent (contd.)
    _____ wit′/ness
com′/pe/ti′/tion
com/pet′/i/tive
    _____ bid′/ding
    _____ traf′/fic
com/pet′/i/tor
com′/pi/la′/tion
com/pile′
    com/piled′
    com/pil′/ing
com/plain′
    com/plained′
    com/plain′/ing
com/plain′/ant
com/plaint′
com/plete′
    com/plet′/ed
    com/plet′/ing
com/ple′/tion
com′/pli/cate′
    com′/pli/cat′/ed
    com′/pli/cat′/ing
com′/plice
com/plic′/i/ty
com/ply′
    com/plied′
    com/ply′/ing
com′/pos men′/tis
com′/pos su′i
com/pose′
    com/posed′
    com/pos′/ing
com/pos′/ite
com′/po/si′/tion
    _____ deed

com′/po/si′/tion (contd.)
    _____ in bank′/rupt/cy
    _____ of mat′/ter
    _____ with cred′/i/tor
com′/pound′ *n, adj*
    _____ in′/ter/est
    _____ lar′/ce/ny
com/pound′ *v*
    com/pound′/ed
    com/pound′/ing
com/pound′/er
com′/pre/hen′/sive
com′/print′
com/prise′
    com/prised′
    com/pris′/ing
com′/pro/mise′
    com′/pro/mised′
    com′/pro/mis′/ing
comp/trol′/ler
com/pul′/sa
com/pul′/sion
com/pul′/so/ry
    _____ ar′/bi/tra′/tion
    _____ at/ten′/dance
    _____ dis/clo′/sure
    _____ in/sur′/ance
    _____ non′/suit′
    _____ pay′/ment
    _____ pro′/cess
com′/pur/ga′/tor
com/pute′
    com/put′/ed
    com/put′/ing
com′/pu/ta′/tion
com′/pu/tus

con/ceal'
    con/cealed'
    con/ceal'/ing
con/ceal'/er
con/ceal'/ment
con/ceive'
    con/ceived'
    con/ceiv'/ing
con/cep'/tion
con/cern'
con/cerned'
con/cern'/ing
con'/cert *n*
con/cert'/ed ac'/tion
con/ces'/si
con/ces'/sion
con/ces'/sit sol'/ve/re
con/ces'/sum
con/ces'/sus
con/cil'/i/ate'
    con/cil'/i/at'/ed
    con/cil'/i/at'/ing
con/cil'/i/a'/tion
con/cil'/i/um
con/clude'
    con/clud'/ed
    con/clud'/ing
con/clu'/sion
con/clu'/sive
    _____ ev'/i/dence
    _____ pre/sump'/tion
con'/cord'
con/cor'/dat'
con/cor'/di·a
con/cu'/bi/nage
con'/cu/bine

con/cu'/pis/cence
con/cur'
    con/curred'
    con/cur'/ring
con/cur'/rence
con/cur'/rent
    _____ con/di'/tions
    _____ cov'/e/nant
    _____ in/sur'/ance
    _____ ju'/ris/dic'/tion
    _____ lease
    _____ neg'/li/gence
    _____ pow'/er
    _____ tort'-/feas/ors
con/cur'/so
con/cus'/sion
con/demn'
    con/demned'
    con/demn'/ing
con'/dem/na'/tion
con/dic'/ti·o
    _____ cer'/ti
    _____ ex le'/ge
    _____ in deb/i/ta'/ti
    _____ re'i fur/ti'/vae
    _____ si'/ne cau'/sa
con/di'/tion
con/di'/tion/al
    _____ as/sault'
    _____ con'/tract'
    _____ cov'/e/nant
    _____ de/vise'
    _____ en/dorse'/ment
    _____ es/tate'
    _____ in/tent'
    _____ judg'/ment

con/di′/tion/al (contd.)
    ____ lim′/i/ta′/tion
    ____ ob′/li/ga′/tion
    ____ par′/don
    ____ re/lease′
    ____ sen′/tence
con′/do/min′/i/um
con′/do/na′/tion
con/done′
    con/doned′
    con/don′/ing
con/duce′
    con/duced′
    con/duc′/ing
con/duct′ *v*
    con/duct′/ed
    con/duct′/ing
con′/duct′ *n*
con/fec′/ti·o
con/fed′/er/a/cy
con/fed′/er/ate *n, adj*
con/fed′/er/ate′ *v*
    con/fed′/er/at′/ed
    con/fed′/er/at′/ing
con/fed′/er/a′/tion
con/fer′
    con/ferred′
    con/fer′/ring
con′/fer/ence
con/fess′
    con/fessed′
    con/fess′/ing
con/fes′/si·o
con/fes′/sion
    ____ and a·void′/ance
    ____ of de/fense′

con/fes′/sion (contd.)
    ____ of judg′/ment
con/fes′/so
con/fes′/sor
con/fide′
    con/fid′/ed
    con/fid′/ing
con′/fi/dence
con′/fi/den′/tial
    ____ com/mu′/ni/
    ca′/tion
    ____ re/la′/tion
con′/fi/den′/ti/al′/i/ty
con/fine′
    con/fined′
    con/fin′/ing
con/fine′/ment
con/firm′
    con/firmed′
    con/firm′/ing
con′/fir/ma′/ti·o
    ____ char/ta′/rum
    ____ cres′/cens
    ____ di/min′/u/ens
    ____ per/fi′/ci/ens
con′/fir/ma′/tion
con/firmed′ let′/ter
con′/firm/ee′
con/firm′/or
con/fis′/ca/ble
con′/fis/ca′/re
con′/fis/cate′
    con′/fis/cat′/ed
    con′/fis/cat′/ing
con/fis′/ca/tee′
con′/fis/ca′/tion

con/fis′/ca/to′/ry
con/fi′/tens re′/us
con/flict′
    con/flict′/ed
    con/flict′/ing
con′/flict of laws
con/form′
    con/formed′
    con/form′/ing
con/for′/mi/ty
con′/frere
con′/fron/ta′/tion
con/fu′/si·o
con/fu′/sion
con/fute′
    con/fut′/ed
    con/fut′/ing
con′/ge/a·ble
con/glom′/er/ate *n, adj*
    ____ merg′/er
con′/gre/gate′
    con′/gre/gat′/ed
    con′/gre/gat′/ing
con′/gre/ga′/tion
con′/gress
con/gres′/sio/nal
con′/gress/man
con′/gress/wom′/an
con/jec′/ti·o
con/jec′/tur/al
con/joint′ rob′/ber·y
con′/ju/gal
    ____ rights
con/junc′/ta
con/junc′/tive
    ____ ob′/li/ga′/tion

con′/ju/ra′/ti·o
con′/ju/ra′/tion
con′/jur/a′/tor
con/nect′
    con/nect′/ed
    con/nect′/ing
con/nec′/tion
con/niv′/ance
con/nive′
    con/nived′
    con/niv′/ing
con′/quer
    con′/quered
    con′/quer/ing
con′/quer/or
con′/quest
con′/san/guin′/i/ty
con′/science
con′/sci/en′/tious
ob/jec′/tor
con/scrip′/tion
con′/se/crate′
    con′/se/crat′/ed
    con′/se/crat′/ing
con/sec′/u/tive
    ____ sen′/ten/ces
con/seil′
con/sen′/su/al
    ____ con′/tract′
    ____ mar′/riage
con/sen′/sus ad i′dem
con/sent′ *v*
    con/sent′/ed
    con/sent′/ing
con/sent′ *n*
    ____ de/cree′

con/sent′ (contd.)
 _____ judg′/ment
con′/se/quence
con′/se/quen′′/tial
dam′′/ag/es
con/ser′′/va/tor
con/serve′
 con/served′
 con/serv′′/ing
con/sid′′/er
 con/sid′′/ered
 con/sid′′/er/ing
con/sid′′/er/a·ble
con/si′′/de/ra′′/ti·o
cu′/ri/ae
con/sid′′/er/a′tion
con/sid′′/er/a/ture
con/sign′
 con/signed′
 con/sign′′/ing
con′/sign/ee′
con/sign′′/ment
con/sign′′/or
con/si′′/li/um
con/sist′
 con/sist′′/ed
 con/sist′′/ing
con/sis′′/tent
con/sis′′/tor
con/sole′
 con/soled′
 con/sol′′/ing
con′/so/la′′/tion
con/sol′′/i/date′
 _____ con/sol′′/i/
 dat′/ed

con/sol′′/i/date′ (contd.)
 _____ con/sol′′/i/
 dat′′/ing
con/sol′′/i/dat′′/ed
 _____ cor′′/po/ra′′/tions
 _____ mort′′/gage
 _____ se/cu′′/ri/ties
 _____ state′′/ments
con/sol′/i/da′′/tion
 _____ of ac′′/tions
 _____ of ben′′/e/fic/es
 _____ of cor′′/po/
 ra′′/tions
con/sor′′/ti·um, *pl*
con/sor′′/ti·a
con′/sort/ship′
con/spic′′/u/ous
con/spir′′/a/cy
con/spire′
 con/spired′
 con/spir′′/ing
con/spir′′/a/tor
con′/sta/ble
con′/sta/ble/wick′
con/stab′′/u/la′′/ri/us
con′/stant
con′/stant/ly
con′/stat
con′/sta′′/te
con/stit′′/u/en/cy
con/stit′′/u/ent
con′/sti/tute′
 con′/sti/tut′′/ed
 con′/sti/tut′′/ing
con′/sti/tut′′/ed au/
thor′/i/ties

con'/sti/tu'/tion
con'/sti/tu'/tion/al
    ____ al/cal'/de
    ____ con/ven'/tion
    ____ court
    ____ free'/dom
    ____ lim'/i/ta'/tion
    ____ of'/fi/cer
    ____ pro/tec'/tion
con/strain'
    con/strained'
    con/strain'/ing
con/straint'
con/struct'
    con/struct'/ed
    con/struct'/ing
con/struc'/tion
con/struc''/tive
    ____ as/sent'
    ____ au/thor'/i/ty
    ____ con'/tract'
    ____ con/di'/tion
    ____ de/ser'/tion
    ____ e·vic'/tion
    ____ in/tent'
    ____ mal'/ice
    ____ no'/tice
    ____ pos/ses'/sion
    ____ sei'/sin
    ____ tak'/ing
con/strue'
    con/strued'
    con/stru'/ing
con'/stu/prate'
    con'/stu/prat'/ed
    con'/stu/prat'/ing

con'/su/e'/tu/do
    ____ An'/gli/ca'/na
    ____ cu'/ri/ae
    ____ est al'/te/ra lex
con'/sul
con'/sul/ar courts
con/sult'
    con/sult'/ed
    con/sult'/ing
con/sul'/tar·y re/sponse'
con'/sul/ta'/tion
con/sum'/er
    ____ debt
con/sum'/mate *adj*
con'/sum/mate' *v*
    con'/sum/mat'/ed
    ____ con'/sum/
    mat'/ing
con'/sum/ma'/tion
con/sump'/tion
con'/tact'
con/tam'/i/nate'
    con/tam'/i/nat'/ed
    con/tam'/i/nat'/ing
con/tam'/i/na'/tion
con/tan'/go
con/tem'/ner
con'/tem/plate'
    con'/tem/plat'/ed
    con'/tem/plat'/ing
con'/tem/pla'/tion
    ____ of bank'/rupt/cy
    ____ of in/sol'/ven/cy
con/tem'/po/ra'/ne·a
ex'/po/si'/ti·o
con/tempt'

con/ten′/tious
con/tent′/ment
con′/tents
con/ter′/mi/nous
con′/test′ *n*
con/test′ *v*
   con/test′/ed
   con/test′/ing
con′/text′
con/tig′/u/ous
con′/ti/nent
con′/ti/nen′/tal
con/tin′/gen/cy
  _____ con′/tract′
  _____ re/serve′
con/tin′/gent
  _____ ben′/e/fi′/cia/ry
  _____ de/vise′
  _____ es/tate′
  _____ in′/ter/est
  _____ leg′/a/cy
  _____ lim′/i/ta′/tion
  _____ li′/a/bil′/i/ty
  _____ re/main′/der
con/tin′/u/al
con/tin′/u/ance
con/tin′/u/an′/do
con/tin′/ue
   con/tin′/ued
   con/tin′u/ing
con/tin′u/ing
  _____ cov′/e/nant
  _____ dam′/ag/es
  _____ ease′/ment
  _____ nui′/sance
  _____ of/fense′

con/tin′/u/ous ad/verse′
use
con/tin′/u/ous/ly
con′/tra
  _____ ac/count′
  _____ bo′/nos mo′/res
  _____ for′/mam
col/la′/ti/o′/nis
  _____ for′/mam do′/ni
  _____ for′/mam
sta/tu′/ti
  _____ jus com/mu′/ne
  _____ leg′/em ter′/rae
  _____ om′/nes gen′/tes
  _____ pa′/cem
  _____ pre′/fe/ren′/tem
  _____ ta′/bu/las
  _____ va′/di/um et
ple′/gi/um
con′tra-/bal′ance
con′/tra/band′
con′/tra/cau′/sa/tor
con′/tract′
  _____ car′/ri/er
  _____ im/plied′ in fact
  _____ im/plied′ in law
  _____ not to com/pete′
  _____ of af/freight′/
ment
  _____ of be/nef′/
i/cence
  _____ of be/nev′/
o/lence
  _____ of in/sur′/ance
  _____ of rec′/ord
  _____ sys′/tem

con/trac′/tion
con′/trac′/tor
con/trac′′/tu/al
ob′/li/ga′/tion
con/trac′′/tus
con′/tra/dict′
 con/tra/dict′′/ed
 con/tra/dict′′/ing
con′/tra/dic′′/tion
con′/tra/fac′/ti·o
con′/tra/li/ga′/ti·o
con′/tra/man/da′′/ti·o
con′/tra/man/da′′/tum
con′/tra/pla′′/ci/tim
con′/tra/pos/i′/ti·o
con′/tra/ro′′/tu/la′′/tor
con′′/trar′y
con′/tra/vene′
 con′/tra/vened′
 con′/tra/ven′′/ing
con′/tra/ven′′/ing eq′′/ui/ty
con′/tra/ven′′/tion
con′/trec/ta′′/ti·o
con/trib′′/ute
 con/trib′/ut/ed
 con/trib′/ut/ing
con′/tri/bu′′/tion
con/trib′/u/to′/ry
 _____ neg′′/li/gence
con/trol′
 con/trolled′
 con/trol′′/ling
con/trol′′/ler
con/trol′′/ment
con′/tro/ver′′/si/al
con′/tro/ver′/sy

con′/tro/vert′
 con′/tro/vert′/ed
 con′/tro/vert′/ing
con′′/tu/ma′′/ce
ca/pi/en′′/do
con′/tu/ma′′/cious
con/tu′/ma/cy
con′′/tu/max
con′′/tume′′/ly
con/tuse′
 con/tused′
 con/tus′′/ing
con/tu′′/sion
con/tu′′/tor
co′′/nu/sant
co′/nu/see′
co′′/nu/sor
con′′/va/lesce′
 con′′/va/lesced′
 con′′/va/lesc′′/ing
con′′/va/les′′/cence
con/ven′′/a·ble
con/vene′
 con/vened′
 con/ven′′/ing
con/ve′′/nience and
ne/ces′′/si/ty
con/ve′/nient
con′′/vent
con/ven′′/ti/cle
con/ven′′/ti·o
 _____ vin′/cit
 _____ le′′/gem
con/ven′′/tion
con/ven′′/tion/al
 _____ mort′′/gage

con'/ven/ti·o'/ne
con/ver'/sant
con'/ver/sa'/tion
con/verse'
   con/versed'
   con/vers'/ing
con/ver'/sion
con/vert'/i·ble
   ____ col/li'/sion
   in/sur'/ance
   ____ se/cu'/ri/ties
   ____ term in/sur'/ance
con/vey'
   con/veyed'
   con/vey'/ing
con/vey'/ance
con/vey'/anc/er
con/vey'/anc/ing
con/vey'/or
con'/vict' *n*
con/vict' *v*
   con/vict'/ed
   con/vict'/ing
con/vic'/tion
con/vinc'/ing proof
con'/vo/ca'/tion
con'/voy'
co'-/ob'ligor
cool'ing-/off' pe'/ri/od
co/op'/er/ate'
   co/op'/er/at'/ed
   co/op'/er/at'/ing
co/op'/er/a'/tion
co/op'/er/a/tive
   ____ a·part'/ment
   ____ as/so'/ci/a'/tion

co/op'/er/a/tive (contd.)
   ____ cor'/po/ra'/tion
   ____ fed'/er/al/ism
   ____ in/sur'/ance
   ____ neg'/li/gence
co/op'/er/tum
co/op'/er/tus
co'-/op'ta'tion
co/or'/di/nate *n, adj*
   ____ ju'/ris/dic'/tion
   ____ sys'/tem
co/or'/di/nate' *v*
   co/or'/di/nat'/ed
   co/or'/di/nat'/ing
co/par'/ce/nar'y
co/par'/ce/ner
co'/part'/ner
co'/part'/ner/ship'
cope'/man *or* copes'/man
copes'/mate'
cop'/u/la
cop'/u/la'/tive term
cop'y
cop'/ied
cop'y/ing
cop'y/hold'
cop'y/right'
co'/ram
   ____ dom'/i/no re'/ge
   ____ ip'/so re'/ge
   ____ no'/bis
   ____ non ju'/di/ce
   ____ pa/ri'/bus
   ____ sec'/ta/tor'/i/bus
   ____ vo'/bis
co'/re/spon'/dent

cor′/ner
    cor′/nered
    cor′/ner/ing
cor/net′
cor′/o/dy
cor′/ol/lar′y
co/ro′/na
cor′/o/na′/tion
cor′/o/ner
cor′/o/ner′s
    ____ in′/quest′
    ____ ju′/ry
corp′/ner/ship
cor′/po/ral
    ____ her′/e/dit′/
    a/ments
    ____ im′/be/cil′/i/ty
    ____ pun′/ish/ment
cor′/po/rate
    ____ a′gent
    ____ al′/ter e′go
    ____ au/thor′/i/ty
    ____ bod′y
    ____ cit′/i/zen/ship
    ____ do′/mi/cile′
    ____ en′/ti/ty
    ____ fran′/chise
    ____ li′/a/bil′/i/ty
    ____ of′/fi/cer
    ____ op′/por/tu′/ni/ty
    ____ pow′/er
    ____ pur′/pose
    ____ trust′/ee′
    ____ veil
cor′/po/ra′/tion
    ____ de fac′/to

cor′/po/ra′/tion (contd.)
    ____ de ju′/re
cor′/po/ra′/tor
cor/po′/re/al
    ____ her′/e/dit′/
    a/ments
    ____ prop′/er/ty
cor′/po/re et a′ni/mo
corps dip/lo/ma/tique′
corpse
cor′/pus
    ____ cor′/po/ra′/tum
    ____ cum cau′/sa
    ____ de/lic′/ti
    ____ ju′/ris
    ____ ju′/ris can/o/
    ni′/ci
    ____ ju′/ris ci/vil′/is
cor/rect′
    cor/rect′/ed
    cor/rect′/ing
cor/rect′ attest′
cor/rec′/tion
cor/rec′/tion/al
    ____ in′/sti/tu′/tion
    ____ sys′/tem
cor/rec′/tor
cor/rel′/a/tive
cor′/re/spon′/dence
    ____ au′/dit
cor′/re/spon′/dent
cor/rob′/o/rate′
    cor/rob′/o/rat′/ed
    cor/rob′/o/rat′/ing
cor/rob′/o/ra′/tion
cor/rob′/o/ra′/tive

cor/rob'/o/ra'tive (contd.)
    ev'/i/dence
cor/rob'/o/ree
cor/rupt'
    cor/rupt'/ed
    cor/rupt'/ing
cor/rup'/tion
cor/rupt'/ly
cor'/tex'
cost
    ____ ac/count'/ing
    ____ and freight
    ____ ba'/sis
    ____ con'/tract'
    ____ de/ple'/tion
    ____ of liv'/ing clause
cost'-/plus' con'/tract'
co/stip'/u/la'/tor
costs
    ____ de in/cre/men'/to
    ____ to a·bide' e·vent'
    ____ of col/lec'/tion
co/sure'/ties
co/ten'/an/cy
co/ten'/ant
co'/te/rie
co/ter'/mi/nous
cot'/tage
cot'/ti/er ten'/an/cy
cot'/ton
couch'/ant
couch'/er
coun'/cil
    ____ of con/cil'/i/
    a'/tion

coun'/cil/lor *or*
coun'/cil/or
coun'/cil/man
coun'/cil/wom'/an
coun'/sel
    coun'/seled
    coun'/sel/ing
coun'/sel/or *or*
coun'/sel/lor
count
    count'/ed
    count'/ing
coun'/te/nance
coun'/ter
coun'/ter/claim
coun'/ter/feit
coun'/ter/feit/er
coun'/ter/fe'/sance
coun'/ter/mand'
coun'/ter/part'
coun'ter-/rolls
coun'ter-/se·cu'rity
coun'/ter/sign'
coun'/ter/sig'/na/ture
coun'/ter/state'/ment
coun'/ter/vail'
    coun'/ter/vailed'
    coun'/ter/vail'/ing
coun'/ter/vail'/ing
eq'/ui/ty
coun'/tors
coun'/try
coun'/ty
    ____ af/fairs'
    ____ at/tor'/ney

coun'/ty (contd.)

_____ au'/di/tor

_____ board of e'qual/ i·za'/tion

_____ bus'i/ness

_____ com/mis'/sion/er

_____ of'/fi/cer

_____ pow'/ers

_____ pur'/pos/es

_____ su'/per/vi'/sor

_____ war'/rant

coup d'e·tat'

cou'/pled with an in'/ter/est

cou'/pon

_____ se/cu'/ri/ties

course

_____ of bus'i/ness

_____ of deal'/ing

_____ of em/ploy'/ment

_____ of ves'/sel

court

_____ a·bove'

_____ ad/min'/is/tra'/ tor

_____ be/low'

_____ en banc

_____ in bank

_____ of ap/peals'

_____ of bank'/rupt/cy

_____ of chan'/cer·y

_____ of civ'/il ap/ peals'

_____ of claims

court (contd.)

_____ of com'/mon pleas

_____ of com'/pe/tent ju'/ris/dic'/tion

_____ of con/cil'/i/a'/ tion

_____ of con'/science

_____ of cus'/toms and pat'/ent ap/peals'

_____ of do/mes'/tic re/la'/tions

_____ of eq'/ui/ty

_____ of er'/ror

_____ of first in'/stance

_____ of gen'/er/al ses'/sions

_____ of hon'/or

_____ of in'/qui'/ry

_____ of in'/ter/me'/ di/ate re/view'

_____ of law

_____ of lim'/it/ed ju'/ris/dic'/tion

_____ of o·rig'/i/nal ju'/ris/dic'/tion

_____ of ni'/si pri'/us

_____ of pro'/bate'

_____ of rec'/ord

_____ of ses'/sions

_____ of star cham'/ber

_____ of sur'/vey

_____ of the cor'/o/ner

_____ or'/der

_____ re/port'/er

court (contd.)

—— sys′/tem

court′-/bar′on

court′-/hand′

court′/house′

court′-/mar′tial

court′/yard

cous′/in

cov′/e/nant

—— a·gainst′ en/

cum′/branc/es

—— ap/pur′/te/nant

—— for fur′/ther

as/sur′/ance

—— for pos/ses′/sion

—— for qui′/et as/

sur′/ance

—— for qui′/et en/

joy′/ment

—— for ti′/tle

—— not to com/pete′

—— in gross

—— of non′/claim′

—— of right to

con/vey′

—— of sei′/sin

—— of war′/ran/ty

—— run′/ning with

the land

—— run′/ning with

ti′/tle

—— to con/vey′

—— to re/new′

—— to stand seised

cov′/e/nan′/tee′

cov′/e/nan′/tor

cov′/er

cov′/ered

cov′/er/ing

cov′/er/age

co′/vert′

cov′/er/ture′

cov′er-/up

co′/vin

co′/vi/nous

cow′/ard

cow′/ard/ice

coz′/en *or* cos′/en

craft

cran′/age

cras′/sa

—— ig′/no/ran′/ti·a

—— neg′/li/gen′/ti·a

crave

craved

crav′/ing

crazed

cra′/zy

crean′/sor

cre/ate′

cre/at′/ed

cre/at′/ing

cre/a′tion

cre/den′/tials

cred′/i/bil′/i/ty

cred′/i/ble

—— per′/son

—— wit′/ness

cred′/it

—— ad′/ver/tis′/ing

cred′/it (contd.)
 ____ bu′/reau
 ____ dis/clo′/sure
 ____ in/sur′/ance
 ____ mem′/o/ran′/
dum
 ____ mo/bi/lier′
 ____ rat′/ing
 ____ re/port′
 ____ u′nion
cred′/it
 cred′/it/ed
 cred′/it/ing
cred′/it/a·ble
cred′/i/tor
cred′/i/tors′ bill *or* suit
cred′/its
creed
cre/mains′
cre′/mate′
 cre′/mat′/ed
 cre′/mat′/ing
cre/ma′/tion
cre/pus′/cu/lum
crest
cre′/tin/ism
cre′/ti·o
crew
cri′/er
cri/ez′ la peez
crime
 ____ a·gainst′ law of
na′/tions
 ____ a·gainst′ na′/ture
 ____ a·gainst′

crime (contd.)
 prop′/er/ty
 ____ ma′/la in se
 ____ ma′/la pro/hib′/
i/ta
 ____ of o·mis′/sion
cri′/men
 ____ fal′/si
 ____ in/no′/mi/na′/
tum
 ____ lae′/sae maj′/
es/ta′/tis
 ____ rap′/tus
crim′/i/nal
 ____ ac′/tion
 ____ an′/ar/chy
 ____ at/tempt′
 ____ be/hav′/ior
 ____ ca/pac′/i/ty
 ____ con/spir′/a/cy
 ____ con/tempt′
 ____ con′/ver/sa′/tion
 ____ dam′/ag/es
 ____ for′/fei/ture′
 ____ gross neg′/
li/gence
 ____ in′/for/ma′/tion
 ____ in/san′/i/ty
 ____ in′/stru/men/
tal′/i/ty
 ____ ju′/ris/dic′/tion
 ____ jus′/tice
 ____ mal′/ver/sa′/tion
 ____ mis′/chief
 ____ mo′/tive

crim′/i/nal (contd.)
     ____ neg′/li/gence
     ____ non′/sup/port′
     ____ of/fense′
     ____ pro/ce′/dure
     ____ pro/ceed′/ing
     ____ pro′/cess
     ____ pros′/e/cu′/tion
     ____ reg′/is/tra′/tion
     ____ sanc′/tions
     ____ stat′/utes
     ____ syn′/di/cal′/ism
     ____ tres′/pass
crim′/i/nal′/i/ty
crim′/i/nate′
    crim′/i/nat′/ed
    crim′/i/nat′/ing
crim′/i/na′/tion
crim′/i/nol′/o/gy
crim′/i/nous
crimp
crip′/ple
    crip′/pled
    crip′/pling
cri′sis, *pl* cri′/ses
cri/te′/ri/on
crit′/i/cal
crit′/i/cism′
crit′/i/cize′
    crit′/i/cized′
    crit′/i/ciz′/ing
cro′/ci·a
crook
crook′/ed
crop′/per

cross
     ____ ac′/tion
     ____ ap/peal′
     ____ col/lat′/er/al
     ____ in′/ter/rog′/a/
to′/ry
     ____ re/main′/der
cross′-/claim′
cross′-/com·plaint′
cross′-/de·mand′
cross′-/er′ror
cross′-/ex·am′i·na′tion
cross′-/ex·am′ine
cross′-/file′
cross′-/in′dex′
cross′-/na′tion·al
cross′-/ques′tion
cross′-/ref′er·ence
cross′/ing
crowd
crown
     ____ cas′/es
     ____ cas′/es re/served′
     ____ court
     ____ of′/fice
     ____ of′/fice in
chan′/cer·y
     ____ pa′/per
     ____ so/lic′/i/tor
cru′/el
     ____ and in′/hu′/man
treat′/ment
     ____ and un/u′/su/al
pun′/ish/ment
cru′/el/ty

cruise
cry
    cried
    cry′/ing
cry′/er
cryp′/ta
cuck′/old
cui bo′/no
cul de sac
cul′/pa
cul′/pa/bil′/i/ty
cul′/pa/ble
cul′/prit
cul′/ti/vate′
    cul′/ti/vat′/ed
    cul′/ti/vat′/ing
cul′/ti/va′/tor
cul/tu′/ra
cul′/tus
cul′/vert
cum cop′/u/la
cum gra′/no sa′/lis
cum o′ne/re′
cum tes′/ta/men′/to
an/nex′o
cu′/mu/la/tive
    _____ div′/i/dend
    _____ ev′/i/dence
    _____ leg′/a/cies
    _____ of/fense′
    _____ re/main′/der
    _____ sen′/tence
    _____ vot′/ing
cun′/ni/lin′/gus
cu′/ra

cu/ra′′/gu/los
cu′/rate
cu/ra′′/ti·o
cur′/a/tive ad/mis′′/si/
bil′/i/ty
cu/ra′′/tor
    _____ ad hoc
    _____ ad li′/tem
cu/ra′′/tor/ship′
cu′/ra/trix
cure
    cured
    cur′/ing
cure by ver′/dict′
cur′/few
cu′/ria
    _____ ad′/vi/sa′′/ri vult
    _____ bar′/on/is *or*
    bar′/on/um
    _____ co′/mi/ta′′/tus
    _____ cur′′/sus aq′′/uae
    _____ dom′′/i/ni
    _____ mil′′/i/tum
    _____ pe′/dis pul′′/
    ver/i/za′′/ti
    _____ per/so′′/nae
    _____ re′′/gis
cur′′/ing ti′′/tle
cur′′/ren/cy
cur′′/rent
    _____ ac/count′
    _____ as/sets′
    _____ ex/pens′′/es
    _____ in′′/come
    _____ li′/a/bil′′/i/ties

cur′/rent (contd.)
  —— main′/te/nance
  —— mon′/ey
  —— ob′/li/ga′/tions
  —— rev′/e/nues
  —— val′/ue
  —— wag′/es
cur/ric′/u/lum, *pl*
cur/ric′/u/la
cur′/rit qua/tu′/or
pe′/di/bus
curse
 cursed
 curs′/ing
cur′/so/ry ex/am′/i/
na′/tion
cur/tail′
 cur/tailed′
 cur/tail′/ing
cur′/te/sy
  —— con/sum′/mate
  —— i·ni′/ti/ate
cur′/ti/lage
cur/til′/li/um
cur′/tis
cus/to′/des
  —— pa′/cis
cus′/to/dia le′/gis
cus′/to′/di/al
cus/to′/di/am lease
cus′/to/dy
cus′/tom
  —— and us′/age
  —— du′/ties
cus′/tom/ar′i/ly

cus′/tom/ar′y
  —— dis′/patch
  —— es/tates′
  —— free′/hold′
  —— in/ter′/pre/
ta′/tion
  —— ser′/vic/es
  —— ten′/ants
cus′/tom/er
cus′/tom/house′
cus′/toms
  —— bro′/ḳer
  —— ser′/vice
cus′/tos
  —— bre′/vi/um
  —— fe/ra′/rum
  —— hor′/rei re′/gi·i
  —— ma′/ris
  —— mo′/rum
  —— pla′/ci/to′/rum
co/ro′/nae
  —— ro/tu/lo′/rum
  —— ter′/rae
cus/tu′/ma
  —— an/ti′/qua si′/ve
mag′/na
  —— par′/va et no′/va
cuth′/red
cut′-/o′ver land
cut′/purse′
cut′/throat′
cy′/cle
 cy′/cled
 cy′/cling
cy′/clic

cy'/cli/cal
cy pres

D

dac'/ty/log'/ra/phy
dag'/ger
dai'/ly
_____ bal'/ance
_____ oc'/cu/pa'/tion
dale and sale
dam'/age
    dam'/aged
    dam'/ag/ing
dam'/age
    _____ fea'/sant
    _____ to per'/son
    _____ to prop'/er/ty
dam'age-/clear
dam'/ag/es
dame
damn
    damned
    damn'/ing
dam'/na
dam'/na/to'/ry
dam/na'/tus
dam'/ni/fi/ca'/tion
dam'/ni/fy'
    dam'/ni/fied'
    dam'/ni/fy/ing
dam'/num
    ab'/sque in/ju'/ri·a
    e·mer'/gens

dam'/num (contd.)
    fa/ta'/le
dan'/ger
dan'/ger/ous
    _____ crim'/i/nal'/i/ty
    _____ in'/stru/men/
    tal'/i/ty
    _____ ma/chine'
    _____ oc'/cu/pa'/tion
    _____ per se
    _____ weap'/on
dan'/ism
dap'/i/fer
da'/re
dar/raign'
    dar/raigned'
    dar/raign'/ing
dar/rein'
    _____ con/tin'/u/ance
    _____ pre/sent'/ment
    _____ sei'/sin
da'/ta
date
    _____ of cleav'/age
    _____ of in'/ju/ry
    _____ of is'/sue
    _____ of ma/tu'/ri/ty
da'/ti·o
da'/tion
da'/tive
da'/tum
daugh'/ter
daugh'ter-/in-/law
day
    _____ cer'/tain

day (contd.)
    —— in court
day'/book'
day'/light'
day'-/rule' *or* day'-/writ'
days
    —— in bank
    —— of grace
days'/man
day'/time'
dea'/con
dead
    —— as'/sets
    —— let'/ter
    —— stor'/age
dead'-/born'
dead'/lock'ed
dead'/ly weap'/on
dead man's stat'/ute
dead'-/pledge'
deaf and dumb
deaf'/ness
deal
    dealt
    deal'/ing
deal'/er
deal'/ers' talk
deal'/ings
de al'/to et bas'/so
dean
death
    —— ben'/e/fits'
    —— by wrong'/ful act
    —— cer/tif'/i/cate
    —— du'/ty

death (contd.)
    —— pen'/al/ty
    —— rec'/ord
    —— sen'/tence
    —— tax'/es
    —— war'/rant
death'/bed'
deaths'/man
de at'/tor/na'/to re/
ci'/pi/en'/do
de au'/di/en'/do et
ter'/mi/nan'/do
de ban'/co
de/bar'
    de/barred'
    de/bar'/ring
de/bar'/ment
de/base'
    de/based'
    de/bas'/ing
de/bat'/a·ble
de/bate'
    de/bat'/ed
    de/bat'/ing
de/bauch'
    de/bauched'
    de/bauch'/ing
de/bauch'/ee'
de/bauch'/er·y
de be'/ne es'/se
de/ben'/ture
    —— in/den'/ture
deb'/et
    —— et det'/i/net
    —— et sol'/et

deb′/et (contd.)

    ____ si′/ne bre′/ve

de bi/en′ et de mal

de bi/ens′ le mort

deb′/it

deb′/i/tor

deb′/i/trix

deb′/i/tum

    ____ si′/ne bre′/vi

de bo′/no et ma′/lo

de bo′/no ges′/tu

debt

    ____ ad/just′/ment

    ____ by sim′/ple
con′/tract′

    ____ by spe′/cial/ty
con′/tract′

    ____ can′/cel/la′/tion

    ____ con/sol′/i/da′/
tion

    ____ fi′/nanc′/ing

    ____ lim′/i/ta′/tions

    ____ of rec′/ord

    ____ pool′/ing

    ____ se/cu′/ri/ty

debt′/ee′

debt′/or

Dec′a/logue

de′/ca/na′/tus

de/ca′/ni·a

de/ca′/nus

de/cap′/i/tate′

    de/cap′/i/tat′/ed

    de/cap′/i/tat′/ing

de/cap′/i/ta′/tion

de/cease′

de/ceased′

de/ce′/dent

de/ceit′

de/ceit′/ful

de/ceive′

    de/ceived′

    de/ceiv′/ing

de′/cen/cy

de′/cent

de/cep′/tion

de cer′/ti/fi/can′/do

de/cer′/ti/fy′

    de/cer′/ti/fied′

    de/cer′/ti/fy′/ing

de/ces′/sus

de/cide′

    de/cid′/ed

    de/cid′/ing

dec′/i/mate′

    dec′/i/mat′/ed

    dec′/i/mat′/ing

de/ci′/sion

    ____ on mer′/its

de/claim′

    de/claimed′

    de/claim′/ing

de/clar′/ant

dec′/la/ra′/tion

    ____ a·gainst′ in′/
ter/est

    ____ of div′/i/dend

    ____ of es′/ti/mat′/ed
tax

    ____ of home′/stead′

dec′/la/ra′/tion (contd.)
    —— of in/ten′/tion
    —— of le/git′/i/
ma/cy
    —— of trust
de/clar′/a/tor of trust
de/clar′/a/to′/ry
    —— ac′/tion
    —— cov′/e/nant
    —— de/cree′
    —— judg′/ment
    —— stat′/ute
de/clare′
    de/clared′
    de/clar′/ing
de clau′/so frac′/to
dec′/li/na′/tion
de/clin′/a/to′/ry
de/cline′
    de/clined′
    de/clin′/ing
de/col/la′/tion
de′/com/pose′
    de′/com/posed′
    de′/com/pos′/ing
de con/cil′/i·o cu′/ri/ae
dec′/o/rate′
    dec′/o/rat′/ed
    dec′/o/rat′/ing
de cor′/po/re co′/mi/
ta′/tus
de′/coy′
de/creas′/ing term in/
sur′/ance
de/cree′
    —— ni′/si

de/cree′ (contd.)
    —— of dis′/tri/bu′/
tion
    —— of in/sol′/ven/cy
    —— of nul′/li/ty
    —— pro con/fes′/so
de/creet′
    —— ab/sol′/vi/tor
    —— ar′/bit/ra
    —— con′/dem/na′/tor
de/crep′/it
de/cre′/tal
    —— or′/der
de/cre′/tum
de/crim′/i/nal/i·za′/tion
de/crown′/ing
de/cry′
    de/cried′
    de/cry′/ing
de cu′/jus
de cur′/su
de deb′/i/to
de′/di
ded′/i/cate′
    ded′/i/cat′/ed
    ded′/i/cat′/ing
ded′/i/ca′/tion
de di′e in di′/em
ded′/i/mus po′/tes/ta′/tem
de/di′/tion
de do′/lo ma′/lo
de do′/mo re′/pa/ran′/da
de do′/nis
de/duct′
    de/duct′/ed
    de/duct′/ing

de/duct′/i·ble
de/duc′/tion
deed
     ____ ab′/so/lute′
     ____ for a nom′/i/nal
sum
     ____ in/dent′/ed *or*
in/den′/ture
     ____ of cov′/e/nant
     ____ of re/lease′
     ____ of sep/a/ra′/tion
     ____ of set′/tle/ment
deem
deemed trans′/fer/or
de/face′
     de/faced′
     de/fac′/ing
de fac′/to
     ____ a·dop′/tion
     ____ con′/tract′
     ____ do′/mi/cile′
     ____ gov′/ern/ment
     ____ in′/te/gra′/tion
     ____ mar′/riage
     ____ seg′/re/ga′/tion
de/fal′/cate′
     de/fal′/cat′/ed
     de/fal′/cat′/ing
de/fal′/ca′/tion
de/falk′
de/fam′/a/cast′
def′/a/ma′/tion
de/fam′/a/to′/ry
     ____ li′/bel
     ____ per quod

de/fame′
     de/famed′
     de/fam′/ing
de/fault′
     ____ judg′/ment
de/fault′/er
de/fea′/sance
de/fea′/si/ble
     ____ ti′/tle
de/fea′/sive
de/feat′
     de/feat′/ed
     de/feat′/ing
de′/fect′ *n*
     ____ of par′/ties
     ____ of sub′/stance
de/fect′ *v*
     de/fect′/ed
     de/fect′/ing
de/fec′/tion
de/fec′/tive
     ____ ti′/tle
de/fec′/tus
de/fend′
     de/fend′/ed
     de/fend′/ing
de/fend′/a·ble
de/fen′/dant
     ____ in er′/ror
de/fen′/da/re
de/fen′/de/mus
de/fend′/er
de′/fen/er/a′/tion
de/fense′
     ____ at/tor′/ney
     ____ of hab′/i/ta′/tion

de/fense' (contd.)
—— of prop'/er/ty
de/fen'/si/ble
de'/fen/si'/va
de/fen'/sive
de/fen'/so
de/fer'
    de/ferred'
    de/fer'/ring
def'/er/ence
de/fer'/ral
de/ferred'
—— an/nu'/i·ty
—— com'/pen/sa'/
tion
—— div'/i/dend
—— in'/come
—— pay'/ments
—— sen'/tence
de/fi'/ance
de/fi'/cien/cy
—— as/sess'/ment
—— de/cree'
—— div'/i/dend
—— judg'/ment
—— no'/tice
def'/i/cit
—— spend'/ing
de/file'
    de/filed'
    de/fil'/ing
de/file'/ment
de/fine'
    de/fined'
    de/fin'/ing
def'/i/nite

def/i/ni'/ti·o
def'/i/ni'/tion
de/fin'/i/tive
de/flect'
    de/flect'/ed
    de/flect'/ing
de/flo/ra'/tion
de/for'/mi/ty
de/fos'/sion
de/fraud'
    de/fraud'/ed
    de/fraud'/ing
de'/frau'/da'/tion
de/funct'
de/func'/tus si'/ne pro'/le
de fur'/to
de/gas'/ter
deg'/ra/da'/tion
de/grade'
    de/grad'/ed
    de/grad'/ing
de gra'/ti·a
de/gree'
de/grees'of neg'/li/gence
de/hy'/drate'
    de/hy'/drat'/ed
    de/hy'/drat'/ing
de in'/cre/men'/to
de in/gres'/su
de'/je/ra'/tion
de in/ju'/ri·a
de in'/te/gro
de ju'/di/ci'/is
de ju'/re
—— cor'/po/ra'/tion
—— gov'/ern/ment

de ju′/re (contd.)
    ____ seg′/re/ga′/tion
de lat′/e/re
de/la′/tor
de/lay′
    de/layed′
    de/lay′/ing
del bi/en′ es′/tre
del cre′/de/re
de/lec′/tus per/so′/nae
del′/e/gate *n*
del′/e/gate′ *v*
    del′/e/gat′/ed
    del′/e/gat′/ing
del′/e/ga′/tion
de/lete′
    de/let′/ed
    de/let′/ing
del′/e/te′/ri/ous
de/lib′/er/ate *adj*
de/lib′/er/ate′ *v*
    de/lib′/er/at′/ed
    de/lib′/er/at′/ing
de/lib′/er/a′/tion
de/lict′
de/lic′/tu/al fault
de/lic′/tum
de/lim′/it
    de/lim′/it/ed
    de/lim′/it/ing
de/lim′/i/ta′/tion
de/lin′/quen/cy
de/lin′/quent
    ____ tax′/es
de/lir′/i/ous

de/lir′/i/um
    ____ fe′/brile
    ____ tre′/mens
de/list′
    de/list′/ed
    de/list′/ing
de/liv′/er
    de/liv′/ered
    de/liv′/er/ing
de/liv′/er/ance
de/liv′/er·y
    ____ in es′/crow′
    ____ or′/der
de/lude′
    de/lud′/ed
    de/lud′/ing
de/lu′/sion
de ma′/lo
de/mand′ *n, adj*
    ____ de/pos′/it
    ____ in re/con/ven′/
    tion
de/mand′ *v*
    de/mand′/ed
    de/mand′/ing
de/man′/dant
de/man′/dress
de ma′/nu/te/nen′/do
de/mean′/or
de/means′
de/ment′/ed
de/men/te/nant′ en a·vant′
de/men′/ti·a
    ____ prae′/cox
de/mesne′

de mi′/ni/mus non cu′/rat
lex
de mi′/nis
de/mise′
   _____ and re′/de/mise′
   _____ char′/ter
   _____ of the crown
de/mised′ prem′/ise
de/mi′/si
de/mis′/sio
de/mo′/bi/li/za′/tion
de/moc′/ra/cy
dem′/o/crat′/ic
de/mol′/ish
   de/mol′/ished
   de/mol′/ish/ing
de/mon′/e/ti/za′/tion
dem′/on/strate′
   dem′/on/strat′/ed
   dem′/on/strat′/ing
dem′/on/stra′/tion
de/mon′/stra/tive
   _____ be/quest′
   _____ ev′/i/dence
   _____ leg′/a/cy
dem′/on/stra′/tor
de/mote′
   de/mot′/ed
   de/mot′/ing
de/mo′/tion
de/mur′
   de/murred′
   de/mur′/ring
de/mur′/ra/ble
de/mur′/rage
de/mur′/rant

de/mur′/rer
   _____ o′re ten′/us
   _____ to ev′/i/dence
   _____ to in′/ter/rog′/
   a/to′/ries
de/nar′/i·us de′i
de/na′/tion/al/ize′
   de/na′/tion/al/ized′
   de/na′/tion/al/iz′/ing
de/na′/tion/al/i·za′/tion
de/ni′/al
den/ier′
den′/i/za′/tion
den′/i/zen
de/nom′/i/na′/tion
de/nom′/i/na′/tion/al
de/nounce′
   de/nounced′
   de/nounc′/ing
de/nounce′/ment
de no′/vo
   _____ hear′/ing
   _____ tri′/al
den′/tist
de/nu′/me/ra′/tion
de/nun′/ci/a′/tion
de/ny′
   de/nied′
   de/ny′/ing
de of/fice′
de/part′
   de/part′/ed
   de/part′/ing
de/part′/ment
de/par′/ture

de/pend′
   de/pend′/ed
   de/pend′/ing
de/pend′/a·ble
de/pen′/dence
de/pen′/den/cy
de/pen′/dent
   _____ con/di′/tions
   _____ con′/tract′
   _____ cov′/e/nant
   _____ prom′/ise
   _____ rel′/a/tive rev′/
   o/ca′/tion
de/pe′/sas
de pla′/ci/to′
de pla′/no
de/plet′/a·ble e′co/nom′/ic
in′/ter/est
de/plete′
   de/plet′/ed
   de/plet′/ing
de/ple′/tion al/low′/ance
de/po′/nent
de/pop′/u/late′
   de/pop′/u/lat′/ed
   de/pop′/u/lat′/ing
de/pop′/u/la′/tion
de/port′
   de/port′/ed
   de/port′/ing
de/port′/a·ble
de′/por′/ta′/tion
de′/por′/tee′
de/pose′
   de/posed′
   de/pos′/ing

de/pos′/it *v*
   de/pos′/it/ed
   de/pos′/it/ing
de/pos′/it *n, adj*
   _____ ac/count′
   _____ com′/pa/ny
   _____ in/sur′/ance
   _____ of ti′/tle deeds
   _____ pre′/mi/um
de/pos′/i/tar′y
de′/po/si′/tion
   _____ de be′ne es′/se
de/pos′/i/tor
de/pos′/i/to′/ry
de/pos′/i/tum
de′/pot
de prae/sen′/ti
de/prave′
   de/praved′
   de/prav′/ing
de/prav′/i/ty
de/pre′/cia/ble
de/pre′/ci/ate′
   de/pre′/ci/at′/ed
   de/pre′/ci/at′/ing
de/pre′/ci/a′/tion
   _____ re/serve′
dep′/re/date′
   dep′/re/dat′/ed
   dep′/re/dat′/ing
dep′/re/da′/tion
de/press′
   de/pressed′
   de/press′/ing
de/pres′/sant
de/pres′/sion

de/pres′/sive
de′/pri/va′/tion
de/prive′
    de/prived′
    de/priv′/ing
dep′/u/tize′
    dep′/u/tized′
    dep′/u/tiz′/ing
dep′/u/ty
de quo
de quo′/ta li′/tis
de/raign′
    de/raigned′
    de/raign′/ing
de/rail′
    de/railed′
    de/rail′/ing
de/rail′/ment
de/range′
    de/ranged′
    de/rang′/ing
de/range′/ment
de rec′/to
der′/e/lict
der′/e/lic′/tion
der′/i/va′/tion
de/riv′/a/tive
    _____ ac′/tion
    _____ con′/tra/band′
    _____ con/vey′/ance
    _____ rule
de/rive′
    de/rived′
    de/riv′/ing
der′/o/ga′/tion

de/rog′/a/to′/ry
de sal′/vo con/duc′/tu
de/scend′
    de/scend′/ed
    de/scend′/ing
de/scen′/dant
de/scend′/er
de/scend′/i·ble
de/scent′
de/scribe′
    de/scribed′
    de/scrib′/ing
de/scrip′/tion
de/scrip′/ti·o per/so′/nae
de/scrip′/tive
des′/e/crate′
    des′/e/crat′/ed
    des′/e/crat′/ing
des′/e/cra′/tion
de/seg′/re/gate′
    de/seg′/re/gat′/ed
    de/seg′/re/gat′/ing
de/seg′/re/ga′/tion
de/sert′
    de/sert′/ed
    de/sert′/ing
de/ser′/tion
de/serve′
    de/served′
    de/serv′/ing
de/sign′
    de/signed′
    de/sign′/ing
des′/ig/nate′
    des′/ig/nat′/ed

des'/ig/nate' (contd.)
    des'/ig/nat'/ing
des'/ig/nat'/ing pe/ti'/tion
des'/ig/na'/tion
des'/ig/na'/ti·o per/so'/nae
de/sign'/ed/ly
de/sir'/a·bil'/i/ty
de/sire'
    de/sired'
    de/sir'/ing
de/sist'
    de/sist'/ed
    de/sist'/ing
    de/sis'/te/ment
de/spair'
    de/spaired'
    de/spair'/ing
de/spec'/u/la'/tion
des'/per/ate
des'/per/a'/tion
de/spite'
de/spi'/tus
de/spoil'
    de/spoiled'
    de/spoil'/ing
des'/pon/sa'/tion
des'/pot
des'/po/tism
des'/ti/na'/tion
    _____ du père de
fa/mille'
des'/ti/tute'
de/stroy'
    de/stroyed'
    de/stroy'/ing

de/struc'/tion
de/tach'/ment
de/tail'
    de/tailed'
    de/tail'/ing
de/tain'
    de/tained'
    de/tain'/ing
de/tain'/er
de/tain'/ment
de/tec'/tion
de/tec'/tive
de/tec'/tor
de/ten'/tion
de/ter'
    de/terred'
    de/ter'/ring
de/te'/ri/o/rate'
    de/te'/ri/o/rat'/ed
    de/te'/ri/o/rat'/ing
de/te'/ri/o/ra'/tion
de/ter'/min/a·ble
de/ter'/mi/nate
    _____ ob'/li/ga'/tion
    _____ sen'/tence
de/ter'/mi/na'/tion
de/ter'/mine
    de/ter'/mined
    de/ter'/min/ing
de/ter'/min/ism
de/ter'/rence
de/ter'/rent
det'/i/nue'
de/tin'/u/it
det'/o/na'/tion

de′/tour
de/tour′/ne/ment
de/tract′
    de/tract′/ed
    de/tract′/ing
de/trac′/tion
det′/ri/ment
det′/ri/men′/tal
deu′/ter/og′/a/my
de u′na par′/te
de′/val′/u/a′/tion
de′/val′/ue
    de′/val′/ued
    de′/val′/u/ing
dev′/as/ta′/tion
de′/vas/ta′/vit
de/vel′/op
    de/vel′/oped
    de/vel′/op/ing
de/vel′/op/ment
de ver′/bo in ver′/bum
de′/vi/ant
de′/vi/ate′
    de′/vi/at′/ed
    de′/vi/at′/ing
de′/vi/a′/tion
de/vice′
de vi/ci′/ne/to
de/vis′/a·ble
de/vise′
    de/vised′
    de/vis′/ing
de/vi/see′
de/vi′/sor
de′/vo/lu′/tion

de/volve′
    de/volved′
    de/volv′/ing
de/vy′
dex′/tras da′/re
di′/ag/nose′
    di′/ag/nosed′
    di′/ag/nos′/ing
di′/ag/no′/sis
di/ag′/o/nal
di′/a/lec′/tics
di/al′/lage
di′/a/logue *or* di′/a/log
di/a/nat′/ic
di/ar′/i/um
di co/lon′/na
dic′/ta
dic′/tate′
    dic′/tat′/ed
    dic′/tat′/ing
dic′/ta′/tion
dic′/ta/tor
dic/ta′/tor/ship′
dic/to′/res
dic′/tum
die
    died
    dy′/ing
die with/out′ is′/sue
di′/es
    ＿＿＿ a·mo′/ris
    ＿＿＿ ce′/dit
    ＿＿＿ com/mu′/nes in
ban′/co

di′/es (contd.)

_____ da′/tus in ban′/co

_____ da′/tus par′/ti/bus

_____ ju/ri′/di/cus

_____ non ju/ri′/di/cus

_____ u·til′/es

_____ ve′/nit

di′/et

di/e′ta

dif/fa′/ce/re

dif′/fer

    dif′/fered

    dif′/fer/ing

dif′/fer/ence

dif′/fi/cult′

dif′/for/ci/a′/re rec′/tum

dif/fuse′

    dif/fused′

    dif/fus′/ing

dig′/a/ma *or* dig′/a/my

di′/gest′

di′/ges′/ta

dig′/ni/fied′

dig′/ni/tar′y

dig′/ni/ty

di/ju′/di/ca′/tion

di/lap′/i/date′

    di/lap′/i/dat′/ed

    di/lap′/i/dat′/ing

di/lap′/i/da′/tion

dil′/a/to′/ry

_____ de/fense′

_____ ex/cep′/tions

dil′/i/gence

dil′/i/gent

di/lute′

    di/lut′/ed

    di/lut′/ing

di/lu′/tion

di/min′/ish

    di/min′/ished

    di/min′/ish/ing

di/min′/ished re/spon′/si/bil′/i/ty

dim′/i/nu′/tion

_____ in val′/ue

_____ of dam′/ag/es

di/mi′/si

di/mi′/sit

di′/nar/chy

di/oc′/e/san

di′/o/cese

di/plo′/ma

di/plo′/ma/cy

dip′/lo/mat′

dip′/lo/mat′/ic

dip′/so/ma/′ni·a

dip′/so/ma′/ni/ac′

dip′/tych

di/rect′ *v*

    di/rect′/ed

    di/rect′/ing

di/rect′ *adj*

_____ ac′/tion

_____ at/tack′

_____ con/tempt′

_____ dam′/ag/es

_____ es/top′/pel

di/rect′ (contd.)
   —— ev′/i/dence
   —— ex′/am/i/na′/tion
   —— in′/ju/ry
   —— in′/ter/est
   —— line of de/scent′
   —— pay′/ment
di/rect′/ed ver′/dict
di/rec′/tion
di/rect′/ly
di/rec′/tor
di/rec′/tor/ate
di/rec′/to/ry
   —— stat′/ute
   —— trust
dis′/a·bil′/i/ty
   —— com′/pen/sa′/
   tion
   —— in/sur′/ance
dis/a″ble
  dis/a″bled
  dis/a″bling
dis′/ad/vo″/ca/re
dis′/af/firm′
  dis′/af/firmed′
  dis′/af/firm′/ing
dis′/af/fir″/mance
dis′/af/for′/est
dis′/a·gree′/ment
dis′/al/low′
dis/alt′
dis′/ap/prov″/al
dis′/ap/prove′
  dis′/ap/proved′
  dis′/ap/prov″/ing
di/sas′/ter

di/sas″/trous
dis′/a·vow′
  dis′/a·vowed′
  dis′/a·vow″/ing
dis/band′
  dis/band′/ed
  dis/band′/ing
dis/bar′
  dis/barred′
  dis/bar″/ring
dis/bar″/ment
dis/burse″/ment
dis/charge′
  dis/charged′
  dis/charg″/ing
dis″/ci/plin/ar′y pro/ceed″/
ings
dis″/ci/pline
dis/claim″/er
dis/close′
  dis/closed′
  dis/clos″/ing
dis/clo″/sure
dis/com″/mon
dis″/con/tin″/u/ance
  —— of an es/tate′
dis″/con/tin″/u/ing ease″/
ment
dis″/con/tin″/u/ous
dis″/con/ven″/a·ble
dis′/count′
  —— bro″/ker
dis/cov″/er
  dis/cov″/ered
  dis/cov″/er/ing
dis/co″/vert

dis/cov′/er·y
dis/cred′/it
   dis/cred′/it/ed
   dis/cred′/it/ing
dis/creet′/ly
dis/crep′/an/cy
dis/crete′/ly
dis/cre′/tion
dis/cre′/tion/ar·y
   _____ dam′/ag/es
   _____ pow′/er
   _____ re/view′
dis/crim′/i/nate′
   dis/crim′/i/nat′/ed
   dis/crim′/i/nat′/ing
dis/crim′/i/na′/tion
dis/cuss′
   dis/cussed′
   dis/cuss′/ing
dis/cus′/sion
dis/ease′
dis′/en/tail′/ing stat′/ute
dis/fig′/ure
   dis/fig′/ured
   dis/fig′/ur/ing
dis/fig′/ure/ment
dis/fran′/chise′
   dis/fran′/chised′
   dis/fran′/chis′/ing
dis/fran′/chise′/ment
dis/gav′/el
dis/grace′
dis/grade′
   dis/grad′/ed
   dis/grad′/ing
dis/guise′

dis/hon′′/es/ty
dis/hon′/or
   dis/hon′′/ored
   dis/hon′′/or/ing
dis′/in/car′′/cer/ate′
   dis′/in/car′′/cer/at′′/ed
   dis′/in/car′′/cer/at′/ing
dis′/in/her′′/i/tance
dis′/in/her′′/it
   dis′/in/her′′/it/ed
   dis′/in/her′′/it/ing
dis′/in/ter′
   dis′/in/terred′
   dis′/in/ter′′/ring
dis/in′′/ter/est/ed wit′′/ness
dis/junc′′/tion
dis/junc′′/tive
   _____ al′/le/ga′′/tion
   _____ cov′/e/nant
   _____ term
dis′/lo/cate′
   dis′/lo/cat′′/ed
   dis′/lo/cat′′/ing
dis′/lo/ca′′/tion
dis/loy′/al
dis/miss′
   dis/missed′
   dis/miss′′/ing
dis/miss′′/al
   _____ a·greed′
   _____ com′/pen/sa′′/
   tion
   _____ with/out′ prej′/
   u/dice
dis/mort′′/gage
dis′/o·be′′/di/ence

dis/or′/der
dis/or′/der/ly
_____ con′/duct′
_____ house
_____ per′/son
_____ pick′/et/ing
dis/par′/age
   dis/par′/aged
   dis/par′/ag/ing
dis/par′/age/ment
dis/par′/i/ty
dis/patch′
   dis/patched′
   dis/patch′/ing
dis/pau′/per
   dis/pau′/pered
   dis/pau′/per/ing
dis/pel′
   dis/pelled′
   dis/pel′/ling
dis′/pen/sa′/tion
dis/pense′
   dis/pensed′
   dis/pens′/ing
dis/per′/so/na/re
dis/place′
   dis/placed′
   dis/plac′/ing
dis/place′/ment
dis/play′
   dis/played′
   dis/play′/ing
dis/pos′/a·ble
_____ in′/come
_____ por′/tion

dis/pose′
   dis/posed′
   dis/pos′/ing
dis′/po/si′/tion
dis/pos′/i/tive facts
dis′/pos/sess′
   dis′/pos/sessed′
   dis′/pos/ses′/sing
dis′/pos/ses′/sion
dis/prove′
   dis/proved′
   dis/prov′/ing
dis/pun′/ish/a·ble
dis/put′/a·ble pre/sump′/tion
dis/pute′
   dis/put′/ed
   dis/put′/ing
dis/qual′/i/fi/ca′/tion
dis/qual′/i/fy′
   dis/qual′/i/fied′
   dis/qual′/i/fy′/ing
dis/rate′
   dis/rat′/ed
   dis/rat′/ing
dis′/re/gard′
   dis/re/gard′/ed
   dis/re/gard′/ing
dis′/re/pair′
dis′/re/pute′
dis/rupt′
   dis/rupt′/ed
   dis/rupt′/ing
dis/sec′/tion

dis/seise′ *or* dis/seize′
   dis/seised′ *or* dis/
   seized′
   dis/seis′/ing *or* dis/
   seiz′/ing
dis′/seis/ee′ *or* dis′/seiz/ee′
dis/sei′/sin *or* dis/sei′/zin
dis/sei′/si/trix′ *or* dis/
sei′/zi/trix′
dis/sei′/
si′/tus *or* dis/sei′
/zi/tus
dis/sei′/sor *or* dis/sei′/zor
dis/sei′/sor/ess *or* dis/
sei′/zor/ess
dis/sem′/ble
   dis/sem′/bled
   dis/sem′/bling
dis/sem′/bler
dis/sent′
   dis/sent′/ed
   dis/sent′/ing
dis/sent′/er
dis/sent′/ing o·pin′/ion
dis′/si/dent
dis′/sig/na′/re
dis′/so/lute′
dis′/so/lu′/tion
dis/solve′
   dis/solved′
   dis/solv′/ing
dis/suade′
   dis/suad′/ed
   dis/suad′/ing
dis′/tance

dis/till′
   dis/tilled′
   dis/til′/ling
dis/till′/er
dis/till′/er·y
dis/tinct′
dis/tinc′/tion
dis/tinc′/tive/ly
dis/tin′/guish
   dis/tin′/guished
   dis/tin′/guish/ing
dis/tort′
   dis/tort′/ed
   dis/tort′/ing
dis/tract′/ed
dis/trac′/tion rule
dis/train′
   dis/trained′
   dis/train′/ing
dis/train′/er *or* dis/train′/
or
dis/traint′
dis/tress′
   ____ and dan′/ger
   ____ in′/fi/nite
   ____ war′/rant
dis/trib′/ute
   dis/trib′/ut/ed
   dis/trib′/ut/ing
dis/trib′/u/tee′
dis′/tri/bu′/tion
   ____ in liq′/ui/da′/
   tion
dis/trib′/u/tive
   ____ jus′/tice

dis/trib′/u/tor
dis′/trict′
—— at/tor′′/ney
—— court
—— par′/ish/es
—— reg′/is/try
dis/tric′/ti·o
di/strin′/gas
di/strin′′/ge/re
dis/turb′
   dis/turbed′
   dis/turb′/ing
dis/tur′′/bance
—— of fran′′/chise
dis/turb′/er
di/ver′′/gent
di′′/vers
di/verse′
di/ver′/si/fy′
   di/ver′/si/fied′
   di/ver′/si/fy′/ing
di/ver′/sion
di/ver′/si/ty
—— of cit′/i/zen/ship
di/vert′
   di/vert′′/ed
   di/vert′′/ing
dives
di/vest′
   di/vest′′/ed
   di/vest′′/ing
di/ves′/ti/tive fact
di/ves′/ti/ture′
di/vide′
   di/vid′′/ed

di/vide′ (contd.)
   di/vid′′/ing
di/vid′′/ed dam′′/ag/es
div′/i/dend
—— ad/di′′/tion
—— in′′/come
—— yield
div′/i/den′/da
di/vi/na′′/re
di/vine′
di/vis′/i/ble
—— con′′/tract′
—— di/vorce′
—— ob′/li/ga′′/tion
—— of/fense′
di/vi′′/sion/al
—— courts
—— se/cu′′/ri/ties
di/vorce′ *n, adj*
—— a men′′/sa et
   tho′/ro
—— a vin′′/cu/lo
   mat′/ri/mo′′/ni·i
—— by con/sent′
—— proc′′/tor
di/vorce′ *v*
   di/vorced′
   di/vorc′/ing
di/vor′/cee′
di/vulge′
   di/vulged′
   di/vulg′/ing
dock
   docked
   dock′/ing
dock′/age

dock'/et

doc'/tor

doc'/trin/al in/ter'/pre/
ta'/tion

doc'/trine

doc'/u/ment

doc'/u/men'/ta/ry

_____ ev'/i/dence

_____ in/struc'/tion

doc'/u/men/ta'/tion

dog'/ma

do'/ing bus'i/ness

dole

do'/li ca'/pax

dol'/lar

do'/lus

_____ bo'/nus

_____ ma'/lus

do/main'

dom'/bec'

do/mes'/tic

_____ an'/i/mal

_____ au/thor'/i/ty

_____ cor'/po/ra'/tion

_____ do'/mi/cile'

_____ guard'/i·an

_____ ju'/ris/dic'/tion

_____ pur'/pos/es

_____ re/la'/tions

_____ ser'/vant

do/mes'/ti/cat'/ed

do/mes'/ti/cus

do'/mi/cile

_____ of cor'/po/
ra'/tion

_____ of or'/i/gin

do'/mi/cile (contd.)

_____ of suc/ces'/sion

do'/mi/cil'/i/ate'

do'/mi/cil'/i/at'/ed

do'/mi/cil'/i/at'/ing

dom'/i/nant es/tate'

dom'/i/nate'

dom'/i/nat'/ed

dom'/i/nat'/ing

do/mi'/ni/cum

do/min'/ion

do'/mi/nus

_____ li'/tis

_____ na'/vis

do'/mus

do'/na/tar'/i/us

do'/nate'

do'/nat'/ed

do'/nat'/ing

do/na'/ti·o

_____ in'/ter vi'/vos

_____ mor'/tis cau'/sa

_____ prop'/ter nup'/
ti/as

do/na'/tion

do'/na/tive trust

do'/na'/tor

do'/na/to'/ri/us

do'/nec

do/nee'

do'/nor

dope

dor'/mant

_____ cor'/po/ra'/tion

_____ ex'/e/cu'/tion

_____ judg'/ment

dor'/mant (contd.)
 —— part'/ner
dor'/so re/cor'/di
dos'/age
dos'/sier'
dot
dot'/age
do'/tal
 —— prop'/er/ty
do/ta'/tion
do'/tis ad/min'/is/tra'/ti·o
do/tis'/sa
dou'/ble
 —— a·dul'/ter·y
 —— as/sess'/ment
 —— com/mis'/sion
 —— com/plaint'
 —— cred'/i/tor
 —— dam'/ag/es
 —— en'/try
 —— in/dem'/ni/ty
 —— in/sur'/ance
 —— jeop'/ar/dy
 —— pat'/ent/ing
 —— plead'/ing
 —— re/cov'/er·y
 —— tax/a'/tion
 —— val'/ue
 —— vouch'/er
 —— waste
dou'/bles
doubt
doubt'/ful ti'/tle
doun
dow'/a·ble

dow'/a/ger
dow'/er
 —— by com'/mon law
 —— by cus'/tom
 —— ex as/sen'/su
 pat'/ris
 —— un'/de ni'/hil
 ha'/bet
down pay'/ment
down'/ward course
dow'/ress
dow'/ry
doz'/en
dra/co'/ni/an
draff
draft
drafts'/man
drain
 drained
 drain'/ing
drain'/age dis'/trict'
dra'/ma
dra/mat'/ic
 —— com'/po/si'/tion
 —— work
draught
draw
 drew
 drawn
 draw'/ing
draw'/back
draw/ee'
draw'/er
draw'/ing ac/count'
dray'/age

dredge
    dredged
    dredg′/ing
dreit′-/dreit′
drift′-/stuff′
drink
    drank
    drunk
    drink′/ing
drink′/er
drip
drive
    drove
    driv′/en
    driv′/ing
driv′/er's li/cense
droit
    _____ com′/mon
    _____ cou/tu/mi·er′
    _____ d'ac/ces/sion′
    _____ d'ac/crois/se/
    ment′
    _____ de de/trac/tion′
    _____ in/ter/na/tion/al′
    _____ ma/ri/time′
    _____ na/tu/rel′
droit′-/droit′
droits
    _____ ci/vils′
    _____ of ad/mir′/al/ty
drop let′/ter
drov′/er's pass
drown
    drowned
    drown′/ing

drug
drunk′/ard
drunk′/en/ness
dry
    _____ dock
    _____ ex/change′
    _____ mort′/gage
    _____ re/ceiv′/er/ship′
    _____ trust
du′/al
    _____ cit′/i/zen/ship
    _____ na′/tion/al′/i/ty
    _____ pur′/pose
du′/ar/chy
du/bi′/et·y
du′/bi/ous
du′/bi/tan′/te
du′/bi/ta′/tur
du′/bi/ta′/vit
du′/ces te′/cum
due
    _____ and prop′/er care
    _____ and rea′/son/
    a·ble care
    _____ com′/pen/
    sa′/tion
    _____ con/sid′/er/
    a′/tion
    _____ course of law
    _____ date
    _____ dil′/i/gence
    _____ in′/flu/ence
    _____ no′/tice
    _____ post′/ing
    _____ pro′/cess of law

due (contd.)

    —— proof

    —— re/gard′

du′/el

    du′/eled

    du′/el/ing

du/loc′/ra/cy

du′/ly

    —— qual′/i/fied

dum

dumb′-/bid′ding

dum′/mo′/do

dum′/my

    —— cor′/po/ra′/tion

    —— di/rec′/tor

dump

    dumped

    dump′/ing

dun

    dunned

    dun′/ning

dun′/geon

dun′/nage

du′/o/de′/cem/vi/ra′/le ju/di′/ci/um

du′/o/de′/ci/ma ma′/nus

du′/plex′

    —— que/re′/la

du′/pli/cate *adj*

    —— tax/a′/tion

du′/pli/cate′ *v*

    du′/pli/cat′/ed

    du′/pli/cat′/ing

du′/pli/ca′/tion

du′/pli/ca′/tum jus

du/plic′/i/tous

du/plic′/i/ty

du′/ra/ble

    —— lease

du′/ran/te

    —— ab/sen′/ti·a

    —— mi/no′/re ae/ta′/te

    —— vi/du/i/ta′/te

    —— vir′/gin/i/ta′/te

    —— vi′/ta

du/ra′/tion

du/ress′

    —— of im/pris′/on/ment

    —— per mi′/nas

du/res′/sor

dur′/ing

    —— good be/hav′/ior

du′/ties

    —— of de/trac′/tion

    —— on im′ports′

du′/ti/ful

du′/ty

    —— of ton′/nage

    —— of wa′/ter

du/um′/vi/rate

dwell

    dwelt *or* dwelled

    dwell′/ing

dy′/ar′/chy

dy′/ing

    —— dec′/la/ra′/tion

    —— with/out′ is′/sue

dy′nas/ty

dys′/no/my

E

ea′/gle
earl
earl′/dom
ear′/mark′
earn
    earned
    earn′/ing
earned
    _____ in′/come
    _____ in′/come cred′/it
    _____ pre′/mi/um
    _____ sur′/plus
earn′/er
ear′/nest
    _____ mon′/ey
earn′/ing
    _____ ca/pac′/i/ty
    _____ pow′/er
earn′/ings
    _____ and prof′/its
    _____ re/port′
earth
ear′/wit′ness
ease
ease′/ment
    _____ by es/top′/pel
    _____ of ac′/cess′
    _____ of con/ve′/nience
    _____ of nat′/u/ral
    sup/port′
    _____ of ne/ces′/si/ty
east
east′/er/ly

east′/ern
eaves′/drop′
    eaves′/dropped′
    eaves′/drop′/ping
eb′/ba
ebb and flow
e-bri′/e/ty
ec/cen′/tric
ec′/cen/tric′/i/ty
ec/cle′/si/as′/ti/cal
    _____ au/thor′/i/ties
    _____ com/mis′/sion/
    ers
    _____ coun′/cil
    _____ courts
    _____ ju′/ris/dic′/tion
    _____ mat′/ter
ec′/di/cus
ech′o/en/ceph′/a/log′′/ra/
phy
ech′o/la′/li·a
ec·lec′/tic
    _____ prac′/tice
e-col′/o/gy
e′co/nom′/ics
e·con′/o/mize′
    e·con′/o/mized′
    e·con′/o/miz′/ing
e·con′/o/my
e con′/tra
e con/ver′/so
e′co/sys′/tem
ec′/u/men′/i/cal
e′/dict′
ed′/it
    ed′/it/ed

ed′/it (contd.)
    ed′/it/ing
e·di′/tion
ed′/i/tor
ed′/i/to′/ri/al
ed′/i/tus
ed′/u/cate′
    ed′/u/cat′/ed
    ed′/u/cat′/ing
ed′/u/ca′/tion
ed′/u/ca′/tion/al
   —— in′/sti/tu′/tion
   —— pur′/pose
ef/fect′ *v*
    ef/fect′/ed
    ef/fect′/ing
ef/fect′ *n*
   —— of pre/sump′/
    tion
ef/fec′/tive
   —— pos/ses′/sion
   —— pro/cur′/ing
    cause
ef/fects′
ef′/fi/ca′/cious
ef/fi′/cient
   —— in′/ter/ven′/ing
    cause
ef′/fi/gy
ef′/flu′/ence
ef′/flux′
ef/flux′/ion
ef′/fort
ef/frac′/tion
ef/frac′/tor
e′go

e·gre′/gious
e′gress
eigh′/teenth′
eighth
eis′/ne
ei′/ther
e·/ject′
    e·ject′/ed
    e·ject′/ing
e·jec′/ta
e·jec′/tion
e·jec′/ti/o′/ne
   —— cus/to′/di/ae′
   —— fir′/mae′
e·ject′/ment
e·jec′/tor
e·jec′/tum
e′/ju/ra′/tion
e·jus′/dem ge′/ner/is
e·lab′/o/rate′
    e·lab′/o/rat′/ed
    e·lab′/o/rat′/ing
e·lab/o/ra′/tion
el′/der
el′/dest
e·lect′
    e·lect′/ed
    e·lect′/ing
e·lec′/tion
   —— au′/di/tor
   —— dis′/trict′
   —— re/turns′
e·lec′/tion/eer′
e·lec′/tive
   —— fran′/chise′
   —— of′/fice

e·lec′/tor
e·lec′/tor/al
    _____ col′/lege
    _____ com/mis′/sion
e·lec′/tric chair
e·lec′/tro/car′/di·o/graph
e·lec′/tro/cute′
    e·lec′/tro/cut′/ed
    e·lec′/tro/cut′/ing
e·lec′/tro/cu′/tion
el′/ee/mos′/y/nar·y
e·le′/git
el′/e/ment
e·lev′/enth
el′/i/gi/bil′/i/ty
el′/i/gi/ble
e·lim′/i/nate′
    e·lim′/i/nat′ed
    e·lim′/i/nat′/ing
e·lim′/i/na′/tion
e·li′/sor
el/lip′/sis *pl* el/lip′/ses
e·loign′/ment
e′lon/ga′/ta
e′lon/ga′/tus
e·lope′
    e·loped′
    e·lop′/ing
e·lope′/ment
else′/where′
e·lu′/ci/date′
    e·lu′/ci/dat′/ed
    e·lu′/ci/dat′/ing
e·man′/ci/pa′/tion
em/bar′/go
em′/bas/sage

em′/bas/sy
em/bel′/lish
    em/bel′/lished
    em/bel′/lish/ing
em/bez′/zle
    em/bez′/zled
    em/bez′/zling
em/bez′/zle/ment
em′/blem
em′/ble/ments
em/bod′i/ment
em′/bo/lism
em′/bo/lus
em/bra′/ceor
em/brac′/er·y
e·mend′
    e·mend′/ed
    e·mend′/ing
e·men′/da
e·men/da′/tion
e·merge′
    e·merged′
    e·merg′/ing
e·mer′/gen/cy
em′/i/grant
em′/i/gra′/tion
ém′i/gré
em′i/nence
em′i/nent do/main′
em′/is/sar·y
e·mis′/sion
e·mit′
    e·mit′/ted
    e·mit′/ting
e·mol′/u/ment
e·mo′/tion

em/pan′/el
em′/per/or
em′/pire′
em/pir′/ic
em/pir′/i/cal
em/plead′
    em/plead′/ed
    em/plead′/ing
em/ploy′
    em/ployed′
    em/ploy′/ing
em/ploy′/ee′
em/ploy′/er
em/ploy′/ment
em/po′/ri/um
em/pow′/er
    em/pow′/ered
    em/pow′/er/ing
emp′/ti·o *or* em′/ti·o
emp′/tor *or* em′/tor
en/a′ble
    en/a′bled
    en/a′bling
en/a′bling
    ——— leg′/is/la′/tion
    ——— pow′/er
    ——— stat′/ute
en/act′
    en/act′/ed
    en/act′/ing
en banc
en/bre/ver′
en/ceinte′
en/close′
    en/closed′
    en/clos′/ing

en/clo′/sure
en/cour′/age
    en/cour′/aged
    en/cour′/ag/ing
en/croach′
    en/croached′
    en/croach′/ing
en/croach′/ment
en/cum′/ber
    en/cum′/bered
    en/cum′/ber/ing
en/cum′/bered as′/sets
en/cum′/brance
en/deav′/or
en de/meure′
en/den′/zie *or* en/den′/i/zen
en′/do/car/di′/tis
en/dorse′
    en/dorsed′
    en/dors′/ing
en′/dors/ee′
en/dorse′/ment
en/dors′/er
en/dow′
    en/dowed′
    en/dow′/ing
en/dow′/ment
    ——— pol′/i/cy
en/dur′/ance
en′/e/my
en fait′
en/feoff′
en/feoff′/ment
en/force′
    en/forced′

en/force′ (contd.)
   en/forc′/ing
en/force′/a·ble
en/force′/ment
en/fran′/chise′
   en/fran′/chised′
   en/fran′/chis′/ing
en/fran′/chise′/ment
en/gage′
   en/gaged′
   en/gag′/ing
en/gage′/ment
en/gen′/der
   en/gen′/dered
   en/gen′/der/ing
en′/gi/neer′
en′/gi/neer′/ing
en gros
en/gross′/ment
en/hance′
   en/hanced′
   en/hanc′/ing
e·ni′/ti·a pars
en/join′
   en/joined′
   en/join′/ing
en/joy′
   en/joyed′
   en/joy′/ing
en/joy′/ment
en/large′
   en/larged′
   en/larg′/ing
en/larg/er′ l'es/tate′
en le′/gis

en/list′
   en/list′/ed
   en/list′/ing
en/list′/ment
en masse
en mort mayne
e·nor′/mous
en ow′/el main
en/roll′
   en/rolled′
   en/roll′/ing
en/roll′/ment
   _____ of ves′/sels
en route
en/sched′/ule
   en/sched′/uled
   en/sched′/ul/ing
en/seal′
   en/sealed′
   en/seal′/ing
ens le′/gis
en/sue′
   en/sued′
   en/su′/ing
en/tail′
   en/tailed′
   en/tail′/ing
en/tail′/ment
en′/ter
   en′/tered
   en′/ter/ing
en′/ter/ceur′
en′/ter/ing
   _____ judg′/ment
en′/ter/prise′
en′/ter/tain′/ment

en/tice′
    en/ticed′
    en/tic′/ing
en/tire′
    ——— blood
    ——— con′/tract′
en/ti′re/ty
en/ti′/tle
    en/ti′/tled
    en/ti′/tling
en/ti′/tle/ment
en′/ti/ty
en′/tou/rage′
en′/trails
en′/trance
en/trap′
    en/trapped′
    en/trap′/ping
en/trap′/ment
en/treat′y
en/tre/bat′
en′/tre/pot
en′/tre/pre/neur′
en′/try
    ——— ad com/mu′/nem
    le′/gum
    ——— of judg′/ment
en′/try/man
e·nu′/mer/ate′
    e·nu′/mer/at′/ed
    e·nu′/mer/at′/ing
e·nu′/mer/a′/tor
en/vel′/op
en′/ve/lope′
en ven′/tre sa mère
en vie

en′/vi/ous
en/vi′/ron
en/vi′/ron/ment
en′/voy′
en′/vy
e′/o
    ——— di′/e
    ——— in/stan′/ti
    ——— in/tu′/i/tu′
    ——— lo′/ci
    ——— no′/mi/ne
ep′/i/dem′/ic
ep′/i/lep′/sy
e·pis′/co/pa/cy
e·pis′/co/pal
e·pis′/co/pate
ep′/i/sode′
e·pis′/to/la
e·pis′/to/lae
e·pis′/to/lar′y
e plu′/ri/bus u′num
ep′/och
e′qual
    ——— pro/tec′/tion
e·qual′/i/ty
e·qual′/i/za′/tion
e′/qual/ize′
    e′qual/ized′
    e′/qual/iz′/ing
e′qui/lib′/ri/um
e·qui/lo′/cus
e′qui/nox′
e·quip′
    e·quipped′
    e·quip′/ping
e·quip′/ment

eq′/ui/ta/ble
　　＿＿＿ ac′/tion
　　＿＿＿ ad/just′/ment
　　＿＿＿ a·dop′/tion
　　＿＿＿ as/sign′/ment
　　＿＿＿ con/ver′/sion
　　＿＿＿ de/fense′
　　＿＿＿ doc′/trine of
ap/prox′/i/ma′/tion
　　＿＿＿ ease′/ment
　　＿＿＿ e·lec′/tion
　　＿＿＿ es/top′/pel
　　＿＿＿ ex′/e/cu′/tion
　　＿＿＿ life es/tate′
　　＿＿＿ mort′/gage
　　＿＿＿ own′/er/ship′
　　＿＿＿ rate of in′/ter/est
　　＿＿＿ re/coup′/ment
　　＿＿＿ re/lief′
　　＿＿＿ sal′/vage
　　＿＿＿ ser′/vi/tude′
eq/ui′/tas se′/qui/tur
le′/gem
eq′/ui/ty
　　＿＿＿ acts in per/so′/
　　nam
　　＿＿＿ fi′/nanc′/ing
　　＿＿＿ fol′/lows the law
　　＿＿＿ ju′/ris/dic′/tion
　　＿＿＿ ju′/ris/pru′/
　　dence
　　＿＿＿ of re/demp′/tion
　　＿＿＿ to a set′/tle/ment
e·quiv′/a/lent
e·quiv′/o/cal

e·rase′
　　e·rased′
　　e·ras′/ing
e·ra′/sure
e·rect′
　　e·rect′/ed
　　e·rect′/ing
e·rec′/tion
er′/go
er′/got
e·rode′
　　e·rod′/ed
　　e·rod′/ing
e·ro′/sion
er′/rant
　　＿＿＿ wa′/ter
er/rat′/ic
er/ra′/tum *pl* er/ra′/ta
er/ro′/ne/ous
er′/ror
　　＿＿＿ ap/par′/ent of
　　rec′/ord
　　＿＿＿ co′/ram no′/bis
　　＿＿＿ co′/ram vo′/bis
　　＿＿＿ in fact
　　＿＿＿ in law
　　＿＿＿ in va′/cu·o
　　＿＿＿ no′/mi/nus
er′/rors
　　＿＿＿ and o·mis′/sions
　　＿＿＿ ex/cept′/ed
es′/ca/la′/tor clause
es/cape′
　　es/caped′
　　es/cap′/ing
es/cap′/ee′

es/cap'/ol'/o/gy
es/cheat'
es/cheat'/a·ble
es/chea'/tor
es'/cort'
es'/crow'
——— ac/count'
——— de/pos'/it
es'/ne/cy
es'/pi/o/nage'
es/pous'/al
es/pouse'
es/poused'
es/pous'/ing
es'/quire'
es'/sence
——— of the con'/tract'
es/sen'/tial
es/sen'/tial/ly
es/soin'
es/tab'/lish
es/tab'/lish/ment
es/tate'
——— at suf'/fer/ance
——— by e·le'/git
——— by en/ti'/re/ty
——— by pur'/chase
——— by stat'/ute
mer'/chant
——— by stat'/ute
sta'/ple
——— by the cur'/te/sy
——— by the en/ti'/re/ty
——— du'/ty
——— from pe'/ri/od to
pe'/ri/od

es/tate' (contd.)
——— in com'/mon
——— in co/par'/ce/
nar'y
——— in dow'/er
——— in ex/pec'/tan/cy
——— in fee sim'/ple
——— in joint ten'/
an/cy
——— in re/main'/der
——— in re/ver'/sion
——— in sev'/er/al/ty
——— in va'/di·o
——— less than free'/
hold'
——— of free'/hold'
——— of in/her'/i/tance
——— on con/di'/tion
——— on con/di'/tion/
al lim'/i/ta'/tion
——— on lim'/i/ta'/tion
——— plan'/ning
——— sub'/ject to a
con/di'/tion/al
lim'/i/ta'/tion
——— tail
——— tax
——— up/on' con/di'/
tion ex/pressed'
——— up/on con/di'/
tion im/plied'
es'/ti/mate'
es'/ti/mat'/ed
es'/ti/mat'/ing
es'/ti/ma'/tion

es/top′
  es/topped′
  es/top′/ping
es/top′/pel
  _____ by e·lec′/tion
  _____ by judg′/ment
  _____ by rec′/ord
  _____ by la′/ches
  _____ by si′/lence
  _____ by ver′/dict′
  _____ cer/tif′/i/cate
es/to′/ver
es/tray′
es/treat′
  es/treat′/ed
  es/treat′/ing
es/trepe′/ment
es′/tu/ar′y
et al′/i·a
et al′/i·us
et al′/lo/ca′/tur
et/cet′/er·a
eth′/i/cal
eth′/ic
et sic ad ju/di′/ci/um
et ux′/or
eu′/no/my
eu′/nuch
eu′/tha/na′/si·a
e·vac′/u/a′/tion
e·val′/u/ate′
  e·val′/u/at′/ed
  e·val′/u/at′/ing
e·va′/sion
e·va′/sive
e′/ven

e′/ven/ing
e·vent′
ev′/er
ev′/er·y
e·vict′
  e·vict′/ed
  e·vict′/ing
e·vic′/tion
ev′/i/dence
  _____ by in/spec′/tion
  _____ com/plet′/ed
ev′/i/dent
ev′/i/den′′/ti·a/ry
ev′/i/dent/ly
e′/vil/do′/er
e·vince′
  e·vinced′
  e·vinc′/ing
ev′/o/ca′/tion
ev′o/lu′/tion stat′/ute
e·volve′
  e·volved′
  e·volv′/ing
ex ab/un′/dan′′/ti
ex/ac′/tion
ex ad/ver′′/so
ex al′/te/re par′′/te
ex/am′′/en
ex/am′/i/na′′/tion
ex/am′/ine
  ex/am′′/ined
  ex/am′′/in/ing
ex/am′/in/er
ex/an′/nu/al roll
ex ar/bit′′/ri·o ju′′/di/cis
ex bo′′/nis

ex ca/the′/dra
ex cau′/sa
ex′/cel/len/cy
ex/cept′
ex/cept′/ing
ex/cep′/ti·o
   —— di/la/to′/ri·a
   —— do′/li ma′/li
   —— fal′/si om′/ni/um
ul′/ti/ma
   —— in fac′/tum
   —— in per/so′/nam
   —— ju′/ris/ju/ran′/di
   —— pac′/ti con/ven′/
ti
ex/cep′/tion
ex/cep′/tion/al
cir′/cum/stanc/es
ex/cess′
   —— con′/dem/na′/
tion
   —— in/sur′/ance
   —— ju′/ris/dic′/tion
   —— pol′/i/cy
ex/cess′/es
ex/ces′/sive
   —— as/sess′/ment
   —— dam′/ag/es
   —— pen′/al/ty
   —— ver′/dict′
ex/ces′/sive/ly
ex/change′
  ex/changed′
  ex/chang′/ing
ex/che′/quer

ex′/cise′
ex/clu′/sion
ex/clu′/sion/ar′y zon′/ing
ex/clu′/sive
   —— a′gen/cy
   —— con′/tract′
   —— con/trol′
   —— ju′/ris/dic′/tion
   —— li′/cense
   —— pos/ses′/sion
ex/clu′/sive/ly
ex con/sul′/to
ex con′/trac′/tu
ex′/cul/pate′
  ex′/cul/pat′/ed
  ex′/cul/pat′/ing
ex′/cul/pa′/tion
ex/cul′/pa/to′/ry
   —— ev′/i/dence
   —— state′/ment
ex cu′/ri·a
ex/cus′/a·ble
   —— as/sault′
   —— ho′/mi/cide′
   —— ne/glect′
ex/cu/sa′/tion
ex/cus′/a/tor′
ex/cuse′
  ex/cused′
  ex/cus′/ing
ex deb′/i/to jus/ti′/ti/ae
ex de/fec′/tu san′/gui/nis
ex de/lic′/to
ex/div′/i/dend
ex do′/lo ma′/lo

ex′/e/cute′
    ex′/e/cut′/ed
    ex′/e/cut′/ing
ex′/e/cut′/ed
    ____ con/sid′/er/
    a′tion
    ____ con′/tract′
    ____ cov′/e/nant
    ____ es/tate′
    ____ li′/cense
    ____ re/main′/der
ex′/e/cu′/tion
    ____ cred′/i/tor
    ____ of in′/stru/ment
    ____ of judg′/ment
    ____ sale
ex′/e/cu′/ti/o/ne ju/di′/ci·i
ex′/e/cu′/tion/er
ex/ec′/u/tive
    ____ a′gen/cy
    ____ a·gree′/ment
    ____ ca/pac′/i/ty
    ____ clem′/en/cy
    ____ or′/der
    ____ par′/don
    ____ priv′/i/lege
ex/ec′/u/tor
    ____ by sub′/sti/tu′/
    tion
    ____ lu/cra′/tus
    ____ trust′/ee′
ex/ec′/u/to′/ry
    ____ con/sid′/er/
    a′tion
    ____ con′/tract′

ex/ec′/u/to′/ry (contd.)
    ____ cov′/e/nant
    ____ de/vise′
    ____ es/tate′
    ____ in′/ter/ests
    ____ li′/cense
    ____ lim′/i/ta′/tion
    ____ pro′/cess
    ____ re/main′/der
ex/ec′/u/tress
ex/ec′/u/trix′
ex/em′/plar
ex/em′/pla/ry dam′/ag/es
ex/em′/pli/fi/ca′/tion
ex/em′/pli gra′/ti·a
ex/em′/plum
ex/empt′
ex/emp′/tion
ex/empts′
ex′/e/qua′/tur
ex′/er/cise′
    ex′/er/cised′
    ex′/er/cis′/ing
ex′/er/cised′ do/min′/ion
ex′/er/cis′/ing an op′/tion
ex fac′/to
ex gra′/ti·a
ex/haus′/tion of
ad/min′/is/tra′/tive
    rem′/e/dies
ex/hib′/e/re
ex/hib′/it
    ex/hib′/it/ed
    ex/hib′/it/ing
ex′/hi/bi′/tion

ex′/hu/ma′′/tion
ex hy/po′′/the/si
ex′/i/gence
ex′/i/gen/cy
ex′/i/gen′′/dar′y
ex′/i/gent
ex′/i/gi/ble
_____ debt
ex′/i/gi fa′′/ci/as
ex′′/ile′
ex′′/iled′
ex′′/il′/ing
ex in/dus′′/tri·a
ex in′′/te/gro
ex/ist′
ex/ist′′/ed
ex/ist′′/ing
ex/is′′/tence
ex′′/it wound
ex le′′/ge
ex le′′/gi/bus
ex lo/ca′′/to
ex ma/li′′/ti·a
ex me′′/ro mo′′/to
ex mo′′/ra
ex mo′′/re
ex mu′′/tu·o
ex of/fi′′/ci·o
ex/on′′/er/ate′
ex/on′′/er/at′/ed
ex/on′′/er/at′/ing
ex/or′′/bi/tance
ex/or′′/bi/tant
ex par′′/te
_____ di/vorce′

ex par′′/te (contd.)
_____ in/junc′′/tion
_____ ma/ter′′/na
_____ pa/ter′′/na
_____ pro/ceed′′/ing
ex/pa′′/tri/ate′
ex/pa′′/tri/at′/ed
ex/pa′′/tri/at′/ing
ex/pa′′/tri/a′′/tion
ex/pect′
ex/pect′′/ed
ex/pect′′/ing
ex/pec′′/tan/cy
_____ dam′′/ag/es
ex/pec′′/tant
_____ es/tate′
_____ heir
ex′′/pec/ta′′/tion
ex/pe′′/di/ent
ex/ped′′/i/ment
ex/pe/di′′/tion
ex/pe/di′′/tious
ex/pel′
ex/pelled′
ex/pel′′/ling
ex/pel′′/lee′
ex/pend′
ex/pend′′/ed
ex/pend′′/ing
ex/pen′′/de/re
ex/pen′′/di/tor
ex/pen′′/di/ture
ex/pen′′/sal li′′/tis
ex/pense′
ex/pe′′/ri/ence

ex/per'/i/ment
ex'/pert'
_____ ev'/i/dence
_____ wit'/ness
ex'/per/tise'
ex'/pi/ate'
    ex'/pi/at'/ed
    ex'/pi/at'/ing
ex'/pi/a'/tion
ex'/pi/la'/re
ex'/pi/ra'/tion
ex/pire'
    ex/pired'
    ex/pir'/ing
ex/plic'/it
ex/ploit'
    ex/ploit'/ed
    ex/ploit'/ing
ex'/ploi'/ta'/tion
ex'/plo/ra'/tion
ex/plo'/sion
ex/plo'/sive
ex'/port let'/ter
ex/port'
    ex/port'/ed
    ex/port'/ing
ex'/por'/ta'/tion
ex/port'/er
ex/pose'
    ex/posed'
    ex/pos'/ing
ex'/po/sé'
ex'/po/si'/tion
ex/pos'/i/to'/ry stat'/ute
ex post fac'/to

ex/pos'/tu/late'
    ex/pos'/tu/lat'/ed
    ex/pos'/tu/lat'/ing
ex/po'/sure
ex/pound'
    ex/pound'/ed
    ex/pound'/ing
ex/press'
_____ ab'/ro/ga'/tion
_____ as/sump'/sit
_____ au/thor'/i/ty
_____ con'/tract'
_____ cov'/e/nant
_____ li'/cense
_____ mal'/ice
_____ ob'/li/ga'/tion
_____ per/mis'/sion
_____ re/pub'/li/ca'/
tion
ex/press'/ly
ex/pro'/pri/ate'
    ex/pro'/pri/at'/ed
    ex/pro'/pri/at'/ing
ex/pro'/pri/a'/tion
ex pro'/pri·o
_____ mo'/tu
_____ vi/go'/re
ex/pul'/sion
ex/punge'
    ex/punged'
    ex/pung'/ing
ex'/pur/gate'
    ex'/pur/gat'/ed
    ex'/pur/gat'/ing
ex'/pur/ga'/tion

ex re/la/ti/o′/ne
ex tem′/po/re
ex/tend′
    ex/tend′/ed
    ex/tend′/ing
ex/ten′/sion
ex/ten′/sive
    ———— in/ter′/pre/ta′/
    tion
ex/tent′
ex/ten′/u/ate′
    ex/ten′/u/at′/ed
    ex/ten′/u/at′/ing
ex/ten′/u/at′/ing cir′/
cum/stanc′/es
ex/ten′/u/a′′/tion
ex/te′′/ri/or
ex/ter′/nal
ex/ter′/ri/to′/ri/al′/i/ty
ex tes′/ti/men′′/to
ex/tinct′
ex/tin′/guish
    ex/tin′/guished
    ex/tin′/guish/ing
ex/tin′/guish/ment
    ———— of com′′/mon
    ———— of cop′y/hold′
    ———— of debts
    ———— of leg′/a/cy
    ———— of lien
ex′/tir/pa′/tion
ex/tor′/sive/ly
ex/tort′
    ex/tort′/ed
    ex/tort′/ing

ex/tor′′/tion
ex′′/tra
    ———— al/low′/ance
    ———— com/mer′/ci·a
    ———— com′/pen/sa′′/
tion
    ———— fe·o′/dum
    ———— ju′/di/ci′/um
    ———— le′/gem
    ———— reg′/num
    ———— ser′′/vic/es
    ———— ter′/ri/to′′/ri/um
    ———— vi′/am
ex′/tract′ *n*
ex/tract′ *v*
    ex/tract′/ed
    ex/tract′/ting
ex′/tra/di′′/tion
ex′/tra/do′′/tal prop′′/er/ty
ex′/tra/haz′/ard/ous
ex′/tra/ju/di′′/cial
ex′/tra/lat′′/er/al right
ex′/tra/mu′′/ral
ex′/tra/na′′/tion/al
ex/tra′/ne/ous
    ———— ev′/i/dence
    ———— of/fense′
    ———— ques′′/tions
ex/tra/or′′/di/nar′y
    cir′′/cum/stanc′/es
    ———— dil′′/i/gence
    ———— div′′/i/dend
    ———— haz′′/ard
    ———— rem′′/e/dies
ex/trap′/o/la′′/tion

ex′/tra/ter′/ri/to′′/ri/
al′′/i/ty
ex/trav′/a/gant
    ____ in/ter′′/pre/
    ta′′/tion
ex/treme′
ex/tre′′/mis
ex/trem′′/i/ty
ex′′/tri/cate′
    ex′′/tri/cat′′/ed
    ex′′/tri/cat′′/ing
ex/trin′′/sic
    ____ am′′/bi/gu′′/i/ty
    ____ ev′′/i/dence
ex u′na par′′/te
ex′′/urb′
ex vol′′/un/ta′′/te
eye′′/wit′′/ness
eyre

F

fab′′/ri/ca′′/re
fab′′/ri/cate′
    fab′′/ri/cat′′/ed
    fab′′/ri/cat′′/ing
fab′′/ri/ca′′/tion
face
    ____ a·mount′
    ____ of in′′/stru/ment
    ____ of judg′′/ment
    ____ of pol′′/i/cy
fa′′/ce/re

fa′′/cial dis/fig′′/ure/ment
fa′′/ci·as
fa′′/ci/en′′/do
fa′′/cies
fac′′/ile
fa/cil′′/i/tate′
    fa/cil′′/i/tat′′/ed
    fa/cil′′/i/tat′′/ing
fa/cil′′/i/ta′′/tion
fa/cil′′/i/ty
fac/sim′′/i/le
    ____ pro′′/bate′
    ____ sig′′/na/ture
fact
fac′′/ti·o tes′′/ta/men′′/ti
fac′′/to et an′i/mo
fac′′/tor
fac′′/tor/age
fac′′/tor/ing
fac′′/tor/iz′/ing pro′′/cess
fac′′/to/ry
fac/to′′/tum
fac′′/tum
    ____ ju/rid′′/i/ci/um
    ____ pro/ban′′/dum
    ____ pro′′/bans
fac′′/ul/ta′′/tive
    ____ com′′/pen/sa′′/
    tion
    ____ re/in/sur′′/ance
fac′′/ul/ties
fac′′/ul/ty
fail
    failed
    fail′′/ing

fail′/ure
    ____ of con/sid′/er/
a′tion
    ____ of is′/sue
    ____ of rec′/ord
    ____ of ti′/tle
fail′/ures in rev′/e/nue′
faint plead′/er
fair
    ____ and eq′/ui/ta/ble
val′/ue
    ____ and fea′/si/ble
    ____ and im/par′/tial
ju′/ry
    ____ and im/par′/tial
tri′/al
    ____ and prop′/er le′/
gal as/sess′/ment
    ____ and rea′/son/a·
ble com′/pen/sa′/tion
    ____ and rea′/son/a·
ble mar′/ket val′/ue
    ____ and val′/u/a·ble
con/sid′/er/a′tion
    ____ av′/er/ag/ing
    ____ cash mar′/ket
val′/ue
    ____ com′/ment
    ____ com′/pe/ti′/tion
    ____ e·quiv′/a/lent
    ____ hear′/ing
    ____ mar′/ket val′/ue
    ____ on its face
    ____ per/sua′/sion
    ____ plead′/er

fair (contd.)
    ____ pre/pon′/
der/ance of ev′/
i/dence
    ____ price
    ____ re/turn′ on
in/vest′/ment
    ____ trade
    ____ tri′/al
    ____ us′/age
    ____ val′/u/a′/tion
    ____ val′/ue
fair′/ly
fait
    ____ ac/com/pli′
    ____ en/rol/le′
faith
faith′/ful
faith′/ful/ly
fai/tours′
fake
    faked
    fak′/ing
fak′/er
fa/kir′
fall
    fell
    fall′/en
    fall′/ing
fal/la′/cious
fal′/la/cy
Fal/lo′/pi/an tube
fal′/low
fal/sa′/re
fal/sa′/ri/us

false
_____ ac'/tion
_____ and fraud'/u/lent
_____ an'/swer
_____ ar/rest'
_____ char'/ac/ter
_____ claim
_____ dem'/on/stra'/
tion
_____ en'/try
_____ im/per'/son/
a'tion
_____ in'/stru/ment
_____ mak'/ing
_____ mis/rep'/re/sen'/
ta'/tion
_____ per'/son/a'tion
_____ pre'/tens/es
_____ rec'/ord
_____ rep'/re/sen'/ta'/
tion
_____ re/turn'
_____ state'/ment
_____ swear'/ing
_____ to'/ken
_____ ver'/dict'
_____ weights
_____ wit'/ness
false'/hood
false'/ly
_____ im/per'/son/ate'
fal'/si/fi/ca'/tion
fal'/si/fy'
fal'/si/fied'
fal'/si/fy'/ing

fal'/si/ty
fal'/so/nar'/i/us
fal'/sus
fal'/sus in u'no, fal'/sus in
om'/ni/bus
fa'/ma
fam'/a/cide'
fa/mil'/i·a
fa/mil'/iar
fa/mil'/i·ar'/i/ty
fam'/i/ly
_____ al/low'/ance
_____ ar/range'/ment
_____ ex/pense'
_____ meet'/ing
_____ part'/ner/ship'
_____ pur'/pose
_____ ser'/vice
_____ set'/tle/ment
fa/nat'/ic
fa/nat'/i/cal
fan'/ci/ful
fan/tas'/tic
fare
farm
farmed
farm'/ing
farm'/er
farm'/ing
_____ op'/er/a'/tion
_____ prod'/uct'
_____ pur'/pose
farm'/land'
farm'-/out a·gree'/ment
far'o

far′/ther
far′/vand
fas
fas′/cism′
fas′/cist
fast bill of ex/cep′/tions
fa′/tal
    _____ er′/ror
    _____ in′/ju/ry
    _____ var′i/ance
fa′/ther
fa′ther-/in-/law′
fath′′/om
fa/tu′a mu′′/li/er
fa/tu′/i/tas
fa′/tum
fa/tu′′/um ju/di′′/ci/um
fat′/u/ous
fau/bourg′
fau′′/ces ter′/rae
fault
fau′′/tor
faux
fa′/vor
fa′′/vor/a·bly
feal
fe′/al/ty
fear
fea′/sance
fea′/sant
fea′/si/bil′′/i/ty
fea′/si/ble
fea′/so
feath′′/er/bed′/ding

fea′/ture
fec′′/er/al
    _____ cen′′/sus
    _____ cit′/i/zen/ship
    _____ com′′/mon law
    _____ dis′′/trict′
    _____ gov′/ern/ment
    _____ in′′/stru/men/
tal′′/i/ty
    _____ ju′/ris/dic′′/tion
    _____ pre/emp′′/tion
    _____ ques′′/tion
fed′/er/al/ism′
fed′/er/al/ist
fed′/er/al/i·za′′/tion
fed′′/er/ate′
    fed′/er/at′/ed
    fed′′/er/at′/ing
fed′/er/a′′/tion
fee
    _____ dam′′/ag/es
    _____ ex/pec′′/tant
    _____ farm
    _____ sim′′/ple
    _____ tail
feed
    fed
    feed′′/ing
feigned
    _____ ac/com′′/plice
    _____ ac′′/tion
    _____ dis/eas′′/es
    _____ is′′/sue
fe/lag′/us

fel/la′/ti•o
fel′/low
_____ heir
_____ ser′/vant
fel′o-/de-/se
fel′/on
fe/lo′/ni•a
fe/lo′/ni/ce
fe/lo′/ni/ous
_____ as/sault′
_____ ho′/mi/cide′
_____ in/tent′
_____ tak′/ing
fe/lo′/ni/ous/ly
fel′/o/ny
fel′ony-/mur′der rule
fe′/male
feme *or* femme
_____ co′/vert
_____ sole
fem′/i/cide′
fem′/i/nine
femme
_____ cou/leur′ lib′/re
fence
_____ coun′/ty
fenc′/ing pat′/ent
fend′/er
fen′/er/a′/tion
fe•od
fe•o′/dal
_____ ac′/tions
fe•o′/dum
fe•off′/ment

fe•of′/for
fe′/rae
_____ bes′/ti/ae
_____ na/tu′/rae
fer′/i•a
ferme
fer/ment′
fer/ment′/ed
fer/ment′/ing
fer/men/ta′/tion
fer/ra′/tor
fer′/ri
fer′/ri/age
fer′/rum
fer′/ry
fer′/ried
fer′/ry/ing
fer′/ry/man
fer/til′/i/ty
fes′/ti/num re/me′/di/um
fes′/ti/val
fe′/tal
fe′/ti/cide′
fet′/ter
fet′/tered
fet′/ter/ing
fe′/tus
feud
feu′/dal
_____ courts
_____ sys′/tem
feu′/dal/ism′
feu/dal′/i/ty

feu′/dal/ize′
    feu′/dal/ized′
    feu′/dal/iz′/ing
feu′/dar·y
feud′/bote′
feud′/ist
feu′/dum
    —— an′/ti′/qu/um
    —— fran′′/cum
    —— hau/be′/ti/cum
    —— im′/pro′′/pri/um
    —— in′′/di/vi′/du/um
    —— lai′′/cum
    —— li′′/gi/um
    —— ma/ter′/num
    —— mil′/i/ta′′/re
    —— no′/bi/le
    —— no′′/vum
    —— no′′/vum ut an′′/
ti′′/qu/um
    —— pa/ter′′/num
    —— pro′′/pri/um
    —— tal′/li/a′′/tum
few
fi′/at
    —— ju′′/sti′′/ti·a
    —— mon′′/ey
    —— ut pe′′/ti/tur
fi′/aunt
fic′′/ti·o
fic′′/tion
fic/ti′′/tious
    —— ac′′/tion
    —— pay/ee′

fic/ti′′/tious (contd.)
    —— per′′/son
    —— plain′′/tiff
    —— prom′′/ise
fi′/dei/com′′/mis/sar′y
fi′′/de/jus′′/si·o
fi/del′′/i/tas
fi/del′′/i/ty
fi′′/des
fi/du′/cial
fi/du′′/ci·a/ry
    —— ca/pac′′/i/ty
    —— con′′/tract′
    —— re/la′′/tion
field
    —— au′′/dit
    —— book
    —— vi′′/sion
fi′/e·ri fa′′/ci·as
fif/teenth′
fifth
fight
    fought
    fight′′/ing
fig′/ur/a/tive
fig′/ure
    fig′/ured
    fig′/ur/ing
filch
    filched
    filch′′/ing
file
    filed
    fil′′/ing

file
_____ wrap'per es/top''/
pel
fil'/i·al
fil'/i/a''/tion
_____ pro/ceed'/ing
fi'/li/us
_____ nul''/li/us
_____ po''/pu/li
fill
filled
fill'/ing
fil'/thy
fi'/lum
_____ a'quae
_____ for/est''/ae
_____ vi'/ae
fi'/nal
_____ ap/peal''/a·ble
or''/der
_____ a·ward'
_____ de/ci''/sion
_____ dis'/po/si''/tion
_____ hear'/ing
_____ in/junc'/tion
_____ or''/der
_____ pas''/sage
_____ set''/tle/ment
_____ sub/mis''/sion
fi'/nance' charge
fi'/nance'
fi'/nanced'
fi'/nanc'/ing

fi/nan''/cial
_____ in'/sti/tu''/tion
fi'/nan/cier'
find
found
find''/ing
find''/er's fee
find''/ing of fact
fine
fined
fin''/ing
fi'/nem fa''/ce/re
fin''/ger/print'
fi'/nis
fin''/ish
fin''/ished
fin''/ish/ing
fi/ni'/ti·o
fire
_____ dis''/trict'
_____ es/cape'
_____ ex'/it
_____ in/sur''/ance
_____ mar''/shal
_____ or/deal'
fire'/arm'
fire'/bare
fire'/bug'
fire'/fight''/er
fire'/man
fire'/proof'
fire'/works'
firm
_____ of''/fer

fir′/ma
fir/ma′/ri/us
firm′/ly
first
    ____ blush
    ____ class
    ____ de′/vi/see′
    ____ im/pres′/sion
    ____ mort′/gage
    ____ of ex/change′
    ____ of/fend′/er
    ____ pur′/chas/er
first-/class ti′/tle
first-/de·gree mur′/der
first′/hand′
fisc
fis′/cal
    ____ a′gent
    ____ pe′/ri/od
fish′/er·y
fish′/garth
fit
    fit′/ted *or* fit
    fit′/ting
fix
    fixed
    fix′/ing
fixed
    ____ as′/set
    ____ cap′/i/tal
    ____ in′/come
    ____ in/debt′/ed/ness
    ____ li′/a/bil′/i/ties
    ____ o·pin′/ion
    ____ sal′/a/ry

fix/a′/tion
fix′/ture
fla′/co
flag
fla′/grans′
    ____ bel′/lum
fla′/grant
    ____ ne/ces′/si/ty
fla/gran′/te
    ____ bel′/lo
    ____ de/lic′/to
flash check
flat mon′/ey
flat′/ter·y
fleet
flesh and blood
flex′/i/bil′′/i/ty
flex′/i/ble
flight
flim′/flam′
    flim′/flammed′
    flim′/flam′/ming
float
    float′/ed
    float′/ing
float′/a·ble
float′/ing
    ____ cap′/i/tal
    ____ ease′/ment
    ____ in′/ter/est rate
    ____ lien
    ____ pol′/i/cy
flog
    flogged
    flog′/ging

flood
floor
    ____ plan fi′/nanc′/ing
floored
flo′/tage
flo/ta′/tion
flo/ter′/i·al
flo/til′/la
flot′/sam
flour′/ish
    flour′/ished
    flour′/ish/ing
flow′/age
flow
    flowed
    flow′/ing
fluc′/tu/ant
fluc′/tu/ate′
    fluc′/tu/at′/ed
    fluc′/tu/at′/ing
fluc′/tu/a′/tion
fluc′/tus
flume
flu′/vi/us
flux′/us
fo′/cus
fod′/der
foe′/ner/a′/tion
foe′/tus
fog
fol′/ge/re
fol′/gers
fo′/li·o
fol′/low
    fol′/lowed

fol′/low (contd.)
    fol′/low/ing
foot
    ____ a′cre
    ____ front′/age
foot′/print′
for ac/count′ of
for/bar/rer′
for/bear′/ance
force
    forced
    forc′/ing
force
    ____ ma/jes/ture′
    ____ ma/jeure′
forced sale
forc′/es
forc′/i·ble
    ____ de/tain′/er
    ____ en′/try
    ____ tres′/pass
for col/lec′/tion
fore′/bear′
fore/close′
    fore/closed′
    fore/clos′/ing
fore/clo′/sure
fore′/fa′/ther
fore′/gift′
fore′/gone′ con/clu′/sion
for′/eign
    ____ af/fairs′
    ____ a′gent
    ____ ap/pos′/er
    ____ com′/merce

for/'/eign (contd.)
    _____ con/'/su/late
    _____ cor/'/po/ra/'/tion
    _____ di/vorce/'
    _____ doc/'/u/ment
    _____ ex/change/'
    _____ im/mu/'/ni/ty
    _____ judg/'/ment
    _____ ju/'/ris/dic/'/tion
    _____ rep/'/re/sen/'/ta/
tive
    _____ pro/ceed/'/ing
    _____ re/ceiv/'/er
    _____ ser/'/vice
    _____ sub/'/stance
for/'/eign/er
fore/judge/'
    fore/judged/'
    fore/judg/'/ing
fore/'/man
fo/ren/'/sic
    _____ med/'/i/cine
fore/'/or/dain/'
    fore/'/or/dained/'
    fore/'/or/dain/'/ing
fore/see/'/a·ble
fore/'/shore/'
fore/'/sight/'
for/'/est
fore/stall/'
    fore/stalled/'
    fore/stall/'/ing
for/'/est/er
fore/'/thought
for/ev/'/er

for/ev/'/er/more/'
for/'/feit
    for/'/feit/ed
    for/'/feit/ing
for/'/feit/a·ble
for/'/fei/ture/'
forge
    forged
    forg/'/ing
forg/'/er
forg/'/er·y
for/get/'
    for/got/'
    for/got/'/ten
    for/get/'/ting
for/get/'/ful
for/give/'
    for/gave/'
    for/giv/'/en
    for/giv/'/ing
for/give/'/ness
for/go/'
fo/'/ris
fo/'/ris/fac/'/tu/ra
fo/'/ris/fa/'/mi/li/a/'/re
fo/'/ris/ju/'/di/ca/'/ti·o
fo/'/ris/ju/'/di/ca/'/tus
fo/'/ris/ju/ra/'/re
form
    formed
    form/'/ing
for/'/ma
    _____ pau/'/per/is
for/'/mal
    _____ con/'/tract/'

for′/mal (contd.)
    _____ par′/ty
for/mal′/i/ty
for′/mal/ize′
    for′/mal/ized′
    for′/mal/iz′/ing
for/ma′/ta bre′′/vi·a
formed
    _____ ac′/tion
    _____ de/sign′
for′/me/don
for′/mer
    _____ ac/quit′/tal
    _____ jeop′/ar/dy
    _____ re/cov′/er·y
    _____ tes′/ti/mo′/ny
forms of ac′/tion
for′/mu/la
for′/mu/lae
for′/mu/lar′y
for′/ni/cate′
    for′/ni/cat′/ed
    for′/ni/cat′/ing
for′/ni/ca′′/tion
for′/schel
for/sake
    for/sook′
    for/sak′′/en
    for/sak′′/ing
for/swear′
    for/swore′
    for/sworn′
    for/swear′′/ing
for/taxed′
forth′/com′′/ing

for′/ti/o′′/ri
fort′′/night′
for/tu′′/i·tous
for/tu′′/i·ty
for′′/tu/nate
for′′/tune
fo′′/rum
    _____ ac′/tus
    _____ con′/sci/en′/ti/ae
    _____ con/ten′/ti/o′′/
sum
    _____ con/trac′′/tus
    _____ con/ve′/ni/ens
    _____ do/mes′′/ti/cum
    _____ do′′/mi/ci′′/li·i
    _____ ec′/cle′/si/as′′/
ti/cum
    _____ li′′/ge/an′′/ti/ae
re′i
    _____ non con/ve′′/
ni/ens
    _____ o·rig′′/i/nis
    _____ re′i
    _____ re′i gest′′/ae
    _____ re′i sit′′/ae
    _____ sec′/u/la′′/re
for val′′/ue re/ceived′
for′′/ward
for′′/ward/er
fos/sa′′/tum
fosse way
fos′′/ter
    _____ child
    _____ par′′/ent
fos′′/ter/age

found
foun/da′′/tion
found′′/ed
found′′/er
found′′/ers' shares
found′′/ling
four cor′′/ners
four′/teenth′
fourth
foy
frac′/ti·o
frac′/tion
frac′/tion/al
frag/men′′/ta
frame′-/up′
frame
    framed
    fram′′/ing
fran′′/chise
    fran′′/chised
    fran′′/chis/ing
fran′/chis′′/ee′
fran′/chis′′/er
fran′/chis′′/or′
fran′′/cus
    _____ ban′′/cus
    _____ ten′′/ens
frank
frank′′/ing priv′′/i/lege
fra/ter′′/nal
    _____ ben′′/e/fit as/so′′/
    ci/a′′/tion
    _____ in/sur′′/ance
fra/ter′′/ni/ty
frat′′/er/nize′
    frat′′/er/nized′

frat′′/er/nize′ (contd.)
    frat′′/er/niz′′/ing
frat′′/ri/cide′
fraud
    _____ in the in/duce′′/
    ment
    _____ in trea′/ty
    _____ or′/der
fraud′/u/lence
fraud′/u/lent
    _____ a′/li·en/a′/tion
    _____ a′/li·en/ee′
    _____ con/ceal′′/ment
    _____ con/ver′′/sion
    _____ con/vey′′/ance
    _____ in/tent′
    _____ mis/rep′′/re/sen′′/
    ta′′/tion
    _____ pref′′/er/ence
    _____ rep′/re/sen′′/ta′′/
    tion
fray
frec′/tum
fre′/dum
free
    _____ a·long′′/side′
    _____ and clear
    _____ and e′qual
    _____ bench
    _____ e·lec′′/tion
    _____ en′′/ter/prise′
    _____ en′′/try, e′gress,
    and re′′/gress
    _____ in/ter′′/pre/ta′′/
    tion
    _____ share′/hold′/er

free (contd.)

    ____ so′/cage

    ____ ten″/ure

free′/dom

    ____ of ex/pres″/sion

    ____ of re/li″/gion

free′/hold′

    ____ es/tate′

free′/hold′/er

free′/man

freight

    ____ book′/ing

    ____ for′/ward/er

freight″/er

fre/net′/i/cus

fre·o″/ling

fre′/quen/cy

fre′/quent *adj*

fre/quent′ *v*

    fre/quent″/ed

    fre/quent″/ing

fre′/quen′/ta″/tion

fre/quent″/er

fres′/ca

fresh

    ____ com/plaint′

    ____ pur/suit′

fresh″/et

fre′/tum

fri′/ar

friend

    ____ of the court

friend″/less

friend″/ly

    ____ so/ci″/e·ty

    ____ suit

fri/gid′/i/ty

frisk

    frisked

    frisk″/ing

friv′/o/lous

    ____ ap/peal′

    ____ de/fense′

front″/age

front′-/foot′ rule

fron′/tier′

front″/ing and a·but″/ting

fro′/zen

    ____ ac/count′

    ____ as″/sets

fruc′/tus

    ____ fun″/di

    ____ in/dus″/tri/a″/les

    ____ le″/gis

    ____ pen/den″/tes

frus′/tra

frus″/trate′

    frus″/trat′/ed

    frus″/trat′/ing

frus/tra″/tion

fu″/gam fe″/cit

fu/ga″/tor

fu′/gi/ta″/tion

fu′/gi/tive

    ____ from jus″/tice

    ____ of/fend′/er

full

    ____ an′/swer

    ____ cop′y

    ____ cous′/in

    ____ cov′/e/nant

    ____ cov′/er/age

full (contd.)
   ____ de/fense′
   ____ dis/clo′/sure
   ____ hear′/ing
   ____ ju′/ris/dic′/tion
   ____ proof
   ____ set′/tle/ment
   ____ war′/ran/ty
ful′/ly ad/min′/is/tered
func′/tion
func′/tion/al de/pre′/ci/a′/tion
func′/tion/ar′y
func′/tus of/fic′/i·o
fund
   fund′/ed
   fund′/ing
fun′/da/men′/tal
   ____ er′/ror
   ____ law
fun/da′/mus
fun′/da/tor
fund′/ed pen′/sion plan
fun′/di pub′/li/ci
fun′/dus
fu′/ner/al
fun′/gi/ble
fu/ran′/di an′/i/mus
fu′/ri/o′/sus
fu′/ri/ous
fur′/long′
fur′/lough
fur′/nish
   fur′/nished
   fur′/nish/ing

fur′/ni/ture
fu′/ror′ bre′/vis
fur′/ther
   ____ ad/vance′
   ____ con/sid′/er/a′tion
   ____ in/struc′/tions
fur′/ther/ance
fur′/tive
fur′/tum
   ____ man′/i/fes′/tum
   ____ ob/la′/tum
fus′/tis
fu′/ture
   ____ ac/quired′ prop′/er/ty
   ____ dam′/ag/es
   ____ earn′/ings
   ____ in′/ter/ests
   ____ per/for′/mance
fu′/tures con′/tract′
fu/tu′/ri

G

gab′/el
gab′/la/to′/res
gab′/lum
gaf′/ol
gain
   gained
   gain′/ing
gain′/age

gain′/er
gain′/er·y
gain′/ful
    _____ em/ploy′/ment
    _____ oc/cu/pa′/tion
gale
gal′/lon
gal′/lows
ga/ma′/lis
gam′/ble
   gam′/bled
   gam′/bling
gam′/bler
game
   _____ of chance
game′/keep′er
gam′/ing
gang′/ster
gaol
gaol′/er
ga/rage′
gar′/ble
   gar′/bled
   gar′/bling
gar′/dein
gar′/den
gar′/di·a
gar′/di/a′/nus
ga/rene′
gar′/nish
   gar′/nished
   gar′/nish/ing
gar′/nish/ee′
gar′/nish/ment
gar′/nish/or

gar′/ri/son
gar/rote′ *or* gar/rotte′
   gar/rot′/ed *or*
   gar/rot′/ted
   gar/rot′/ing *or*
   gar/rot′/ting
gar′/ter
gas′/o/line′
gas/tal′/dus
gas/tine′
gauge
   gauged
   gaug′/ing
gav′/el
gav′/el/kind′
ga/zette′
geld
geld′/a·ble
geld′/ing
ge′/ne/a/log′/i/cal
ge/ne/al′/o/gy
gene′/arch′
gen′/er/al
   _____ a′gen/cy
   _____ ap/pear′/ance
   _____ as/sem′/bly
   _____ bus′i/ness
   _____ as/sign′/ment
   for ben′/e/fit of
   cred′/i/tors
   _____ as/sump′/sit
   _____ av′/er/age
   con′/tri/bu′/tion
   _____ be/quest′
   _____ cir′/cu/la′/tion

gen**′**/er/al (contd.)

    ____ con**′**/trac**′**/tor

    ____ cov**′**/e/nant

    ____ cred**′**/i/tor

    ____ dam**′**/ag/es

    ____ de/ni**′**/al

    ____ e·lec**′**/tion

    ____ es/tate**′**

    ____ ex/cep**′**/tion

    ____ ex**′**/e/cu**′**/tion

    ____ ex/ec**′**/u/tor

    ____ fee con/di**′**/tion/
al

    ____ fund

    ____ guard**′**/i·an

    ____ ju**′**/ris/dic**′**/tion

    ____ in/tan**′**/gi/ble

    ____ in**′**/ter/est

    ____ leg**′**/a/cy

    ____ man**′**/ag/er

    ____ mort**′**/gage

    ____ oc**′**/cu/pant

    ____ own**′**/er

    ____ par**′**/don

    ____ part**′**/ner/ship**′**

    ____ pow**′**/er of ap/
point**′**/ment

    ____ re/pri**′**/sals

    ____ rep**′**/u/ta**′**/tion

    ____ ver**′**/dict**′**

    ____ war**′**/ran/ty deed

gen**′**/er/al/i·za**′**/tion

gen**′**/er/al/ly

gen**′**/er/ate**′**

    gen**′**/er/at**′**/ed

    gen**′**/er/at**′**/ing

gen**′**/er/a**′**/tion

gen**′**/er/a/tive

ge/ner**′**/ic

gen**′**/er/os**′**/i/ty

gens

gen**′**/tes

gen/til**′**/es

gen**′**/tle/man

gen**′**/tle/wom**′**/an

gen**′**/u/ine

ge**′**/nus

ge**′**o/graph**′**/ic mar**′**/ket

ge**′**/rens

ger**′**/man

ger/mane**′**

ger/ma**′**/nus

ger**′**/ry/man**′**/der

    ger**′**/ry/man**′**/dered

    ger**′**/ry/man**′**/der/ing

ges/ta**′**/tion

ges**′**/ti·o

ges**′**/tum

ges**′**/ture

gib**′**/bet

gift

    ____ cau**′**/sa mor**′**/tis

    ____ deed

    ____ en**′**/ter/prise**′**

    ____ in**′**/ter vi**′**/vos

    ____ o**′**/ver

    ____ split**′**/ting

gild

gi/ran**′**/te

gise**′**/ment

gis**′**/er

gise**′**/tak**′**/er

gist
gist tak′/er
give
 gave
 giv′/en
 giv′/ing
give
 ____ and be/queath′
 ____ col′/or
 ____ no′/tice
giv′/er
glean′/ing
glide
 glid′/ed
 glid′/ing
gloss
glos′/sa
glos′/sa/ry
go
 went
 gone
 go′/ing
go′/ing
 ____ and com′/ing
 rule
 ____ con/cern′/val′/ue
 ____ pri′/vate
 ____ pub′/lic
 ____ wit′/ness
gold stan′/dard
gold′/smiths' notes
gon′/or/rhe′a
good
 ____ and val′/id
 ____ be/hav′/ior
 ____ char′/ac/ter

good (contd.)
 ____ con/sid′/er/
 a′tion
 ____ faith pur′/chas/er
 ____ rec′/ord ti′/tle
 ____ re/pute′
 ____ Sa/mar′/i/tan
 doc′/trine
 ____ ti′/tle
goods
 ____ and chat′/tels
 ____ sold and de/liv′/
 ered
goods, wares, and
mer′/chan/dise′
good-/time al/low′/ance
gov′/ern
 gov′/erned
 gov′/ern/ing
gov′/ern/ment
 ____ de fac′/to
 ____ de ju′/re
 ____ in′/stru/men/
 tal′/i/ty
gov′/ern/men′/tal
 ____ ac/tiv′/i/ty
 ____ du′/ties
 ____ en′/ter/prise′
 ____ func′/tion
 ____ im/mu′/ni/ty
 ____ pur′/pose
 ____ sub′/di/vi′/sion
 ____ tort
gov′/er/nor
grace pe′/ri/od

grade
    grad′/ed
    grad′/ing
grad′/ed of/fense′
grad′/u/ate *n*
grad′/u/ate′ *v*
    grad′/u/at′/ed
    grad′/u/at′/ing
gra′/dus
graft
grain′/age
gram
gram′/mar school
gramme
grand
    _____ ju′/ry
    _____ lar′/ce/ny
    _____ re/mon′/strance
    _____ theft
grand′/child′
grand′/daugh′/ter
grand′/fa′/ther clause
grand′/moth′/er
grand′/par′/ent
grand′/son′
grand′/stand′
grange
    _____ cas′/es
gran′/ge/ar′/i/us
grant
    _____ and to freight let
    _____ pat′/ent
    _____ of per′/son/al
    prop′/er/ty
grant, bar′/gain, and sell
grant/ee′

grant/or′
graph′/ic
grat′/i/fi/ca′/tion
grat′/i/fy′
    grat′/i/fied′
    grat′/i/fy′/ing
gra′/tis
    _____ dic′/tum
grat′/i/tude′
gra/tu′/i·tous
    _____ al/low′/ance
    _____ bail/ee′
    _____ con′/tract′
    _____ li′/cens/ee′
    _____ pas′/sen/ger
gra/va′/men
grave
grav′/en dock
grave′/yard′ in/sur′/ance
gra′/vis
great
    _____ bod′i/ly
    in′/ju/ry
    _____ dil′/i/gence
great′-/grand′chil′dren
green′/back
    gref′/fi/er
    gref′/fi/um
gre′/mi/um
greve
griev′/ance
    _____ com/mit′/tee
    _____ pro/ce′/dure
griev′/ant
grieve
    grieved

grieve (contd.)
    griev'/ing
griev'/ous
gro'/cer
gross
    ____ al'/i/mo'/ny
    ____ earn'/ings
    ____ in/ad'/e/qua/cy
    ____ in'/come
    ____ mar'/gin
    ____ mis'/de/mean'/or
    ____ neg'/li/gence
    ____ pre'/mi/um
    ____ prof'/it
    ____ re/ceipts'
ground
    ____ of ac'/tion
    ____ wa'/ter
group
    ____ an/nu'/i·ty
    ____ boy'/cott
    ____ in/sur'/ance
grow
    grew
    grown
    grow'/ing
guar'/an/tee'
    guar'/an/teed'
    guar'/an/tee'/ing
guar'/an/teed' pay'/ment
guar'/an/tor'
guar'/an/ty
guard'/age
guard'/i·an
    ____ ad li'/tem
    ____ by na'/ture

guard'/i·an (contd.)
    ____ by es/top'/pel
    ____ by stat'/ute
    ____ for nur'/ture
    ____ in so'/cage
guard'/i·an/ship'
gu'/ber/na/to'/ri/al
guer'/don
guer/pi' *or* guer/py'
guest stat'/ute
guild
guild'/hall'
guil'/lo/tine'
guilt
guilt'y
    ____ ver'/dict'
gun
gyn'/arch·y
gyn'/e/coc'/ra/cy
gyn'/e/col'/o/gist
gyn'/e/col'/o/gy

H

ha'/be/as cor'/pus
    ____ ad de/li'/be/ren'/
    dum et re/ci'/pi/en'/
    dum
    ____ ad fa'/ci/en'/
    dum et re/ci'/pi/en'/
    dum
    ____ ad pro'/se/quen'/
    dum
    ____ ad re'/spon/den'/
    dum

ha′/be/as cor′/pus (contd.)
    ____ ad sa′/tis/fa′/ci/
en′/dum
    ____ ad sub/ji′/ci/en′/
dum
    ____ ad tes′/ti/fi/can′/
dum
    ____ cum cau′/sa
ha/ben′/dum clause
ha/be′/re
hab′/il/is
hab′/it
hab′/it/a·bil′/i/ty
hab′/it/a·ble
hab′/i/tan/cy
ha′/bi/tant
hab′/i/ta′/tion
ha/bit′/u/al
    ____ crim′/i/nal
    ____ in/tox′/i/ca′/tion
ha/bit′/u/al/ly
ha′/ci/en′/da
haec est fi/na′/lis
con/cor′/di·a
hae/re′/des
    ____ prox′/i/mi
hae′/res
    ____ de fac′/to
    ____ ex as′/se
    ____ ex/tra′/ne/us
    ____ in′/sti/tu′/tus
    ____ le/git′/i/mus
    ____ na′/tus
    ____ rec′/tus
half
    ____ broth′/er

half (contd.)
    ____ dol′/lar
    ____ ea′/gle
    ____ sec′/tion
    ____ sis′/ter
    ____ tongue
half′-/tim′er
half′/way′
hall′/mark′
hal/lu′/ci/nate′
    hal/lu′/ci/nat′/ed
    hal/lu′/ci/nat′/ing
hal/lu′/ci/na′/tion
hal/lu′/ci/na/to′/ry
hal/lu′/ci/no/gen
halved note
halves
ham′/let
ham′/mer
hand mon′/ey
hand′/bill′
hand′/cuffs′
han′/dle
    han′/dled
    han′/dling
hand′/sale′
hand′/sel
hand′/writ′/ing
hand′y/man
hang
    hung *or* hanged
    hang′/ing
hanged, drawn, and
quar′/tered
hang′/man
hanse

hap′/pi/ness
hap′/py
ha/rangue′
    ha/ranged′
    ha/rangu′/ing
ha/rass′
    ha/rassed′
    ha/rass′/ing
ha/rass′/ment
har′/bor
    har′/bored
    har′/bor/ing
hard
    _____ cas′/es
    _____ of hear′/ing
hard′/ship
harm′/ful er′/ror
harm′/less er′/ror
har/mon′/ic plane
har′/mo/nize′
    har′/mo/nized′
    har′/mo/niz′/ing
har′/mo/ny
har′/ness
    har′/nessed
    har′/ness/ing
har′/ry
    har′/ried
    har′/ry/ing
harsh
har′/vest
    har′/vest/ed
    har′/vest/ing
hash′/ish′
hatch
hatch′/way

haul
    hauled
    haul′/ing
haul′/age
have and hold
ha′/ven
hawk′/er
haz′/ard
haz′/ard/ous
    _____ con′/tract′
    _____ em/ploy′/ment
    _____ neg′/li/gence
head
    _____ mon′/ey
    _____ of a fam′/i/ly
    _____ of wa′/ter
head′/land′
head′/mas′/ter
head′/mis′/tress
head′/note′
head′/right′
head′/stream′
head′/wa′/ter
heal′/er
health of′/fi/cer
health′y
hear′/ing
    _____ de no′/vo
    _____ ex/am′/in/er
    _____ of′/fi/cer
hear′/say′
heart balm act
hearth
heat
    _____ of pas′/sion
    _____ pros/tra′/tion

heave to
hec′/tare
hedge
 hedged
 hedg′/ing
heed′/less
he/ge′/mo/ny
heif′/er
height
heir
 _____ ap/par′/ent
 _____ ben′/e/fi′/cia/ry
 _____ by a·dop′/tion
 _____ by cus′/tom
 _____ by de/vise′
 _____ col/lat′/er/al
 _____ con/ven′/tion/al
 _____ ex/pec′/tant
 _____ of the bod′y
 _____ pre/sump′/tive
 _____ spe′/cial
 _____ tes′/ta/men′/
 ta/ry
 _____ un′/con/di′/
 tion/al
heir′/dom
heir′/ess
heir′/looms′
heirs and as/signs′
heir′/ship′
hem′i/ple′/gi·a
hence′/forth′
hench′/man
hep′/tarch′y
her′/ald
her′/ald/ry

herb′/age
herd′/er
here/af′/ter
her′/e/dit′/a/ment
he/red′/i/tar′y
 _____ dis/ease′
 _____ suc/ces′/sion
here′/in′/a·bove′
here′/in/af′/ter
here′/in′/be/fore′
here′/in′/be/low′
here/of′
here/on′
her′/e/sy
her′/e/tic′
here/to′
here′/to/fore′
here/un′/der
here/un′/to
here′/u·pon′
here/with′
her′/i/ot
her′/is/cin′/di/um
her′/i/ta/ble
 _____ ju′/ris/dic′/tion
 _____ ob′/li/ga′/tion
her′/i/tage
her′/i/tor
her/maph′/ro/dite′
her′/me/neu′/tics
her′/ni·a
her′/o/in
he′/rus
het′/er·o/sex′/u/al
hid′/den
 _____ as′/set

hid**/**/den (contd.)
_____ de**/**/fect
hide
hid**/**/den *or* hid
hid**/**/ing
hi**/**/er/ar**/**/chi/cal
hi**/**/er/arch**/**y
high
_____ crimes and
mis**/**/de/mean**/**/ors
_____ de/gree**/** of care
and dil**/**/i/gence
_____ de/gree**/** of
neg**/**/li/gence
high**/**/bind**/**/er
high**/**/er and low**/**/er scale
high**/**/est
_____ de/gree**/** of care
_____ proved val**/**/ue
high**/**/ness
high**/**-/wa**/**ter mark
high**/**/way
_____ cross**/**/ing
_____ rob**/**/ber·y
high**/**/way**/**/man
hig**/**/ler
hi**/**/jack**/**
hi**/**/jacked**/**
hi**/**/jack**/**/ing
hi**/**/jack**/**/er
hin**/**/der
hin**/**/dered
hin**/**/der/ing
hire
hired
hir**/**/ing

his ex**/**/cel/len/cy
his hon**/**/or
his tes**/**/ti/bus
his/tor**/**/i/cal
his**/**/to/ry
his**/**/tri/on**/**/ics
hit
hit
hit**/**/ting
hit**/**-/and-/run**/** ac**/**/ci/dent
hith**/**/er/to**/**
hoard
hoard**/**/ed
hoard**/**/ing
hob**/**/ble
hob**/**/bled
hob**/**/bling
hob**/**/by
hoc
hold
held
hold**/**/ing
hold
_____ harm**/**/less
_____ o**/**ver
hold**/**/er
_____ for val**/**/ue
_____ in due course
hold**/**/ing com**/**/pa/ny
hold**/**/up**/**
hol**/**/i/day
ho**/**/lo/graph**/**
ho**/**/lo/graph**/**/ic will
hom**/**/age
hom**/**/ag/er

ho/ma**'**/gi/um
　　—— li**'**/gi/um
　　—— pla**'**/num
　　—— red**'**/de/re
　　—— sim**'**/plex
home of**'**/fice
home**'**/own**'**/er
home**'**/stead**'**
　　—— cor**'**/po/ra**'**/tion
　　—— ex/emp**'**/tion
ho**'**/mi/cid**'**/al
ho**'**/mi/cide**'**
　　—— by mis**'**/ad/ven**'**/
ture
　　—— by ne/ces**'**/si/ty
　　—— per in**'**/for/tu**'**/
ni/um
　　—— se de**'**/fen/den**'**/
do
ho**'**/mi/cid**'**/i/um
ho**'**/mi/na**'**/ti·o
homme
ho**'**/mo
ho**'**/mo/sex**'**/u/al
hon/es**'**/te vi**'**/ve/re
hon/es**'**/tus
hon**'**/es/ty
hon**'**/or
　　hon**'**/ored
　　hon**'**/or/ing
hon**'**/or/a·ble
　　—— dis**'**/charge**'**
hon**'**/o/rar**'**/i/um
hon**'**/or/ar**'**y
　　—— can**'**/on
　　—— trust**'**/ee**'**

hon**'**/or/ee**'**
hood**'**/lum
hook**'**/er
hope
　　hoped
　　hop**'**/ing
ho**'**/ra
hor**'**/i/zon**'**/tal
　　—— merg**'**/er
　　—— price**'**-/fix**'**ing
hor**'**/mone**'**
horn**'**/book**'**
horn**'**/er
horse**'**/pow**'**/er
hos**'**/pi/tal
hos**'**/pi**'**/tal/i·za**'**/tion
hos**'**/pi**'**/tal/ize**'**
　　hos**'**/pi/tal/ized**'**
　　hos**'**/pi/tal/iz**'**/ing
hos**'**/pi/ta**'**/tor
hos/pi**'**/ti·a
host
hos**'**/tage
hos**'**/tel/er
host**'**/ess
hos**'**/ti/cide**'**
hos**'**/tile
　　—— em/bar**'**/go
　　—— pos/ses**'**/sion
　　—— wit**'**/ness
hos/til**'**/i/ty
hos**'**/tler
hot**'**-/blood**'**ed
hotch**'**/pot**'**
ho/tel**'**
ho/te**'**/lier

hot′/head′/ed
hour
house
    ____ ar/rest′
    ____ burn′/ing
    ____ coun′/sel
    ____ of cor/rec′/tion
    ____ of pros′/ti/tu′/
    tion
    ____ of ref′/uge′
    ____ of wor′/ship
house′/age
house′/break′/ing
house′/hold′
house′/hold′/er
hous′/ing
house′/keep′/er
hov′/el
huck′/ster
hue and cry
hu′i
huis/si/er′
hu/man′/i/tar′/i/an
hun′/dred
    ____ sec′/ta
hun′/dred/ar′y
hun′/dred/or
hun′/dred/weight′
hun′/ger strike
hung ju′/ry
hunt
    hunt′/ed
    hunt′/ing
hurt
hus′/band
hus′/band/man

hus′/band/ry
hush mon′/ey
hus′/tings
hy′brid se/cu′/ri/ty
hy′/giene′
hyp/not′/ic
hyp′/no/tism′
hy′/po/chon′/dri·a
hy′/po/chon′/dri/ac′
hy/poc′/ri/sy
hyp′/o/crite′
hyp′/o/crit′/i/cal
hy/pos′/ta/sis
hy/poth′/e/ca
hy/poth′/e/cate′
    hy/poth′/e/cat′/ed
    hy/poth′/e/cat′/ing
hy/poth′/e/ca′/tion
    ____ bond
hy/poth′/e/sis
hy′/po/thet′/i/cal
    ____ ques′/tion
hys/ter/ec′/to/my
hys/te′/ri·a
hys′/ter/ot′/o/my

I

i′bi/dem′
i·de′a
i′dem
    ____ per i′dem
    ____ so′/nans
i·den′/ti/cal

i·den'/ti/fi/ca'/tion
    —— ev'/i/dence
i·den'/ti/ty
id'e/ol'/o/gy
ides
id est
id'/i/o/cy
id'/i/om
id'/i·o/syn'/cra/sy
id'/i/ot
ig/nite'
    ig/nit'/ed
    ig/nit'/ing
ig/ni'/tion
ig'/no/min'/i/ous
ig'/no/mi'/ny
ig'/no/ra'/mus
ig'/no/rance
ig'/no/rant
ig'/no/ran'/ti·a
    —— fac'/ti ex/cu'/sat
    —— le'/gis nem'/i/
    nem ex/cu'/sat
ig'/no/ra'/re le'/gis est
la'/ta cul'/pa
ig'/no/ra'/ti·o e·len'/chi
ig/nore'
    ig/nored'
    ig/nor'/ing
il/le'/gal
il'/le/gal'/i/ty
il/le'/gal/ly ob/tained'
ev'/i/dence
il/le/git'/i/ma/cy
il'/le/git'/i/mate

il/lic'/it
    —— co'/hab'/i/ta'/
tion
    —— con/nec'/tion
    —— dis/till'/er·y
    —— re/la'/tions
il/lit'/er/a/cy
il/lit'/er/ate
ill'/ness
il/loc'/a·ble
il'/lud
il/lu'/sion
il/lu'/so/ry
    —— ap/point'/ment
    —— prom'/ise
il/lus'/tri/ous
im·ag'/i/nar'y
im·ag'/i/na'/tion
im·ag'/ine
    im·ag'/ined
    im·ag'/in/ing
im'/be/cil'/i/ty
im'/i/tate'
    im'/i/tat'/ed
    im'/i/tat'/ing
im'/i/ta'/tion
im'/ma/te'/ri/al
    —— a·ver'/ment
    —— ev'/i/dence
    —— var'/i/ance
im/me'/di/a/cy
im/me'/di/ate
    —— con/trol'
    —— dan'/ger
    —— de/scent'

im/me′/di/ate (contd.)
    ____ is′/sue
    ____ no′/tice
im/me′/di/ate/ly
im′/me/mo′/ri/al
    ____ pos/ses′/sion
    ____ us′/age
im′/mi/grant
im′/mi/gra′/tion
im′/mi/nent
    ____ dan′/ger
im/mis′/ce/re
im/mo′/bile
im/mod′/er/ate
im′/mo/la′/tion
im/mor′/al
im′/mo/ral′/i/ty
im/mov′/a·ble
im/mu′/ni/ty
im′/mu/ni/za′/tion
im/pair′
    im/paired′
    im/pair′/ing
im/pair′/ing the ob′/li/
ga′/tion of con′/tracts′
im/pan′/el
    im/pan′/eled
    im/pan′/el/ing
im/parl′
    im/parled′
    im/parl′/ing
im/par′/lance
im/par′/tial
    ____ ex′/pert
    ____ ju′/ry

im/par′/ti/ble
im/peach′
    im/peached′
    im/peach′/ing
im/peach′/ment
    ____ of an/nu′/i·ty
    ____ of ver′/dict′
    ____ of waste
    ____ of wit′/ness
im/pede′
    im/ped′/ed
    im/ped′/ing
im/pe′/di/ent
im/ped′/i/ment
im/per′/a/tive
im/per′/fect
im/per′/son/ate′
    im/per′/son/at′/ed
    im/per′/son/at′/ing
im/per′/son/a′tion
im/per′/ti/nence
im/per′/ti/nent
im/pig′/no/ra′/tion
im′/pi/ous
im/pla′/ci/ta′/re
im/plead′
    im/plead′/ed
    im/plead′/ing
im′/ple/ment
im′/pli/cate′
    im′/pli/cat′/ed
    im′/pli/cat′/ing
im′/pli/ca′/tion
im/plic′/it

im/plied'
 ____ a'gen/cy
 ____ au/thor'/i/ty
 ____ con/sent'
 ____ con'/tract'
 ____ cov'/e/nant
 ____ ease'/ment
 ____ in/tent'
 ____ li'/cense
 ____ mal'/ice
 ____ no'/tice
 ____ ob'/li/ga'/tion
 ____ prom'/ise
 ____ rem'/e/dy
 ____ res'/er/va'/tion
 ____ war'/ran/ty
im/ply'
 im/plied'
 im/ply'/ing
im'/por'/ta'/tion
im'/port' let'/ter
im/port'
 im/port'/ed
 im/port'/ing
im'/por/tune'
 im'/por/tuned'
 im'/por/tun'/ing
im'/por/tu'/ni/ty
im/pose'
 im/posed'
 im/pos'/ing
im'/po/si'/tion
im/pos'/si/bil'/i/ty
im/pos'/si/ble
 ____ con'/tract'

im/pos'/tor *or* im/pos'/ter
im'/po/tence
im/pound'
 im/pound'/ed
 im/pound'/ing
im/prac'/ti/ca/bil'/i/ty
im/pre/scrip'/ti/bil'/i/ty
im/pre/scrip'/ti/ble rights
im/pres'/sion
im/press'/ment
im/prest' mon'/ey
im'/pre/ti/a'/bi/lis
im'/pri/ma'/tur
im/pri'/mis
im'/print'
im/pris'/on
 im/pris'/oned
 im/pris'/on/ing
im/pris'/on/ment
im/pris'/ti
im/prob'/a/ble
im/prop'/er
im'/pro/pri'/e/ty
im/prove'
 im/proved'
 im/prov'/ing
im/prove'/ment
im/prov'/i/dence
im/prov'/i/dent/ly
im/pru'/dence
im/pugn'
 im/pugned'
 im/pugn'/ing
im'/pulse'
im/pul'/sive

im/pu'/ni/ty
im/put'/a·bil'/i/ty
im/pute'
    im/put'/ed
    im/put'/ing
im/put'/ed
   ____ in'/come
   ____ knowl'/edge
   ____ neg'/li/gence
   ____ no'/tice
in/ad'/e/quate
   ____ con/sid'/er/
   a'tion
   ____ dam'/ag/es
   ____ rem'/e/dy
in'/ad/mis'/si/ble
in ad/ver'/sum
in'/ad/ver'/tence
in/a'li·en·a·ble
   ____ in'/ter/ests
   ____ rights
in a'li·o lo'/co
in am/big'/u·o
in/an'/i/mate
in a·per'/ta lu'/ce
in a·pic'/i/bus ju'/ris
in'/ar/tic'/u/late
in ar/ti'/cu/lo mor'/tis
in/au'/di/ble
in/au'/gu/ral
in/au'/gu/rate'
   in/au'/gu/rat'/ed
   in/au'/gu/rat'/ing
in/au'/gu/ra'/tion
in ban'/co

in be'/ing
in blank
in bo'/nis
in'/bound' com'/mons
in ca/hoots'
in cam'/er·a
in'/ca/pac'/i/tate'
   in'/ca/pac'/i/tat'/ed
   in'/ca/pac'/i/tat'/ing
in'/ca/pac'/i/ty
in cap'/i/ta
in cap'/i/te
in/car'/cer/ate'
   in/car'/cer/at'/ed
   in/car'/cer/at'/ing
in/car'/cer/a'/tion
in/cen'/di/ar'y
in/cep'/tion
in/cer'/tae per/so'/nae
in/ces'/sant
in'/cest
in/ces'/tu/o'/si
in/ces'/tu/ous
in'/char/ta'/re
in chief
in/cho'/ate
   ____ dow'/er
   ____ in'/stru/ment
   ____ in'/ter/est
   ____ lien
in'/ci/dent
in'/ci/den'/tal
   ____ ben'/e/fi'/cia/ry
   ____ dam'/ag/es
   ____ pow'/ers

in/ci/den//tal (contd.)
—— to ar/rest/
—— use
in/cin//er/ate/
in/cin//er/at/ed
in/cin//er/at//ing
in/cin//er/a//tion
in/cip//i/ent
in//ci/pit
in/ci//pi/tur
in/cite/
in/cit//ed
in/cit//ing
in/ci//vi/le
in/civ//ism
in//cli/na//tion
in/close/
in/closed/
in/clos//ing
in/clo//sure
in/clude/
in/clud//ed
in/clud//ing
in/clu//sive
—— sur//vey
in/co//la
in//come
—— av//er/ag/ing
—— ba//sis
—— ben//e/fi//cia/ry
—— prop//er/ty
—— tax de/fi//cien/cy
in com/men//dam
in com//mon

in com/mu//ni
in//com/mu//ni/ca/ble
in//com/mut//a·ble
in//com/pat//i/bil//i/ty
in//com/pat//i/ble
in/com//pe/tence
in/com//pe/ten/cy
in/com//pe/tent
ev//i/dence
in//con/clu//sive
in con/junc//tion with
in/con//se/quen//tial
in//con/sis//tent
—— pre/sump//tions
in//con/test/a·bil//i/ty
in//con/test/a·ble
in/con//ti/nence
in con/ti/nen//ti
in//con//tro/vert//i·ble
in//con/ve//nience
in//con/vert//i·ble
in/co//po/li//tus
in/cor//po/ra//mus
in/cor//po/rate/
in/cor//po/rat//ed
in/cor//po/rat//ing
in/cor//po/ra//tion
in cor//po/re/
in//cor/po//re/al
—— chat//tels
—— her//e/dit///
a/ments
—— prop//er/ty
in/cor//ri/gi/ble

in'/cor/rupt'/i·ble
in/crease'
    in/creased'
    in/creas'/ing
in'/cre/ment
in'/cre/men'/tum
in/crim'/i/nate'
    in/crim'/i/nat'/ed
    in/crim'/i/nat'/ing
in/crim'/i/nat'/ing
    _____ cir'/cum/stance
    _____ ev'/i/dence
in/crim'/i/na'/tion
in/crim'/i/na/to'/ry
in/cul'/pate'
    in/cul'/pat'/ed
    in/cul'/pat'/ing
in/cul'/pa/to'/ry
in/cum'/bent
in/cum'/brance
in/cur'
    in/curred'
    in/cur'/ring
in/cur'/a·ble
in/cur'/ra/men'/tum
in cus/to'/di·a le'/gis
in'/de
in/de'/bi/ta'/tus
in/debt'/ed/ness
in/de'/cen/cy
in/de'/cent
    _____ as/sault'
    _____ ex'/hi/bi'/tion
    _____ ex/po'/sure

in/de'/cent (contd.)
    _____ lib'/er/ties
    _____ pub'/li/ca'/tions
in'/de/fea'/si/ble
in/de/fen'/si/ble
in/def'/i/nite
    _____ fail'/ure of
    is'/sue
    _____ leg'/a/cy
in de/lic'/to
in/dem'/ni/fi/ca'/tion
in/dem'/ni/fi'/er
in/dem'/ni/fy'
    in/dem'/ni/fied'
    in/dem'/ni/fy'/ing
in/dem'/nis
in/dem'/ni/tee'
in/dem'/ni/tor'
in/dem'/ni/ty
    _____ a·gainst' li'/a/
    bil'/i/ty
    _____ con'/tract'
    _____ in/sur'/ance
    _____ pol'/i/cy
in/dent'
    in/dent'/ed
    in/dent'/ing
in/den'/ture
in'/de/pen'/dence
in'/de/pen'/dent
    _____ ad/just'/er
    _____ con'/tract'
    _____ con'/trac'/tor
    _____ sig/nif'/i/cance

in′/de/struc′/ti/ble
in′/de/ter′/min/a·ble
in′/de/ter′/mi/nate
   ob′/li/ga′/tion
   sen′/tence
in′/dex′
   an′/i/mi ser′/mo
In′/di/an
   a′gent
   dep′/re/da′/tions
   res′/er/va′/tion
   ti′/tle
in′/di/ca′/re
in′/di/ca′/tion
in/dic′/a/tive ev′/i/dence
in/di′/ci·a
in/di′/ci/um
in/dict′
   in/dict′/ed
   in/dict′/ing
in/dict′/a·ble
in/dict′/ment
in di′/em
in/dif′/fer/ent
in′/di/gent
   de/fen′/dant
   in/sane′ per′/son
in/dig′/ni/ty
in′/di/rect′
   at/tack′
   ev′/i/dence
in′/dis/creet′
in′/dis/crim′/i/nate
in′/dis/pens′/a·ble
   ev′/i/dence

in′/dis/pens′/a·ble (contd.)
   par′/ties
in′/dis/tan′/ter
in′/dis/tinct′
in′/dis/tin′/guish/a·ble
in′/di/vid′/u/al
   as′/sets
   pro/pri′/
e·tor/ship′
   sys′/tem of
lo/ca′/tion
in′/di/vid′/u/al/ly
in′/di/vis′/i/ble
in′/di/vi′/sum
in/dorse′
   in/dorsed′
   in/dors′/ing
in′/dors/ee′
in/dorse′/ment
in/dors′/er
in dor′/so
in du′/bi·o
in/du′/bi/ta/ble proof
in/duce′
   in/duced′
   in/duc′/ing
in/duce′/ment
in/du′/ci/ae
in/duct′
   in/duct′/ed
   in/duct′/ing
in′/duct′/ee′
in/duc′/tio
in/duc′/tion
in/dul′/gence

in/du′/ment
in du′/plo
in/dus′/tri/al
  ___ in/sur′/ance
  ___ re/la′/tions
in′/dus/try
in·e′/bri/ate
in′/ef/fec′/tive
in′/ef/fi′/cient
in′/e/gal′/i/tar′/i/an
in′/el′/i/gi/bil′/i/ty
in/el′/i/gi/ble
in′/e·qual′/i/ty
in′/eq′/ui/ty
in′/es/cap′/a·ble per′/il
in es′/se
in est de ju′/re
in′/es′/ti/ma/ble
in ev′/i/dence
in/ev′/i/ta/ble
  ___ ac′/ci/dent
in ex/cam′/bi·o
in ex′/e/cu′/tion and
  pur/su′/ance of
in ex′/i/tu
in ex/ten′/so
in ex/tre′/mis
in fa′/ci·e cu′/ri/ae′
in fa′/ci/en′/do
in fact
in fac′/to
in/fa′/mi·a
in′/fa/mous
  ___ crime
  ___ pun′/ish/ment

in′/fa/my
in′/fan/cy
in′/fans
in′/fant
in/fan′/ti/cide′
in fa/vo′/rem
  ___ lib′/er/ta′/tus
  ___ vi′/tae
in/fect′
  in/fect′/ed
  in/fect′/ing
in/fec′/tion
in fe/o′/do
in/fe·off′/ment
in′/fer/ence
  ___ on in′/fer/ence
in′/fer/en′/tial
in/fe′/ri/or
in/fe′/ri/or′/i/ty
in′/feu/da′/tion
in′/fi/del
in′/fi/del′/i/ty
in fi′/e·ri
in fi′/ne
in/firm′
in/fir′/ma/tive
  ___ con/sid′/er/
  a′tion
  ___ hy/poth′/e/sis
in/fir′/mi/ty
in/flam′/ma/ble
in/flam′/ma/to′/ry
in/fla′/tion
in/flict′
  in/flict′/ed

in/flict′ (contd.)
    in/flict′/ing
in′/flu′/ence
    in′/flu′/enced
    in′/flu′/enc/ing
in/for′/mal
    _____ con′/tract′
    _____ mar′/riage
    _____ pro/ceed′/ing
in′/for′/mal′/i/ty
in/for′/mant
in for′/ma pau′/per/is
in′/for/ma′/tion
in/formed′ con/sent′
in/form′/er
in fo′/ro
    _____ con′/sci/en′/ti/ae
    _____ con′/ten/ti·o′/so
    _____ sae′/cu/la′/ri
in′/fra
    _____ ae/ta′/tem
    _____ an′/nos nu/bil′/
es
    _____ an′/num luc′/tus
    _____ bra′/chi·a
    _____ civ′/i/ta′/tem
    _____ dig′/ni/ta′/tem
cu′/ri/ae
    _____ fu/ro′/rem
    _____ hos/pi′/ti/um
    _____ ju′/ris/dic′/ti/o′/
nem
    _____ me′/tas
    _____ prae/sid′/i·a
    _____ qua′/tu/or
ma′/ri·a

in/frac′/tion
in/fringe′
    in/fringed′
    in/fring′/ing
in/fringe′/ment
    _____ of cop′y/right′
    _____ of pat′/ent
    _____ of trade′/mark′
in/fring′/er
in fu′/tu/ro
in gen′/e/re
in′/ge/nu′/i/tas
in′/ge/nu′/i/ty
in/gen′/u/us
in/grat′/i/tude
in gre′/mi·o le′/gis
in′/gress′
in′/gros/sa′/tor
in/hab′/it
    in/hab′/it/ed
    in/hab′/it/ing
in/hab′/it/ant
in hac par′/te
in haec ver′/ba
in/here′
    in/hered′
    in/her′/ing
in/her′/ent
    _____ cov′/e/nant
    _____ pow′/er
in/her′/ent/ly dan′/
ger/ous
in/her′/e/trix′
in/her′/it
    in/her′/it/ed
    in/her′/it/ing

in/her′/it/a·ble
in/her′/i/tance
in/hib′/it
    in/hib′/it/ed
    in/hib′/it/ing
in′/hi/bi′/tion
in/hib′/i/tor *or*
in/hib′/it/er
in hoc
in/hu′/man treat′/ment
in i′is/dem ter′/mi/nis
in in′/di/vid′/u·o
in in′/fi/ni′/tum
in i·ni′/ti·o
in in/teg′/rum
in in/vid′/i/um
in in/vi′/tum
i·ni′/tial
    _____ car′/ri/er
    _____ sur′/plus
i·ni′/ti/ate′
    i·ni′/ti/at′/ed
    i·ni′/ti/at′/ing
i·ni′/ti/a′/tion
i·ni′/tia/tive
in/junc′/tion
in′/jure
    in′/jured
    in′/jur/ing
in ju′/re
    _____ al/ter′/i/us
    _____ pro′/pri·o
in/ju′′/ri·a
    _____ abs′/que
    dam′/no
    _____ non ex/cu′/sat

in/ju′′/ri·a (contd.)
    in/ju′′/ri/am
    _____ non prae/
sum′/i/tur
in/ju′′/ri/ous false′/hood
in′′/ju/ry
in/jus′/tice
in jus vo/ca′/re
in kind
in′/la/ga′/tion
in′/land
    _____ bill of ex/change′
    _____ nav′/i/ga′/tion
    _____ wa′/ters
in/law′
    in/lawed′
    in/law′/ing
in lec′/to mor/ta′/li
in lieu of
in li′/mi/ne
in li′/tem
in lo′/co
    _____ pa/ren′/tis
in ma/jo′/rem cau′/te/lam
in′′/mate′
in me′/di/as res
in med′/i/co
in mi/ser′i/cor′′/di·a
in mi/ti/o′′/ri sen′′/su
in mo′/dum as/si′′/sae
in mo′/ra
in mor′/tu·a ma′′/nu
inn
in/nav′/i/ga/ble
in′′/ner bar′′/ris/ter
inn′′/keep′/er

in'/no/cence
in'/no/cent
_____ a'gent
_____ mis/rep'/re/sen'/
ta'/tion
_____ pur'/chas/er
_____ tres'/pass/er
in/nom'/i/nate
_____ con'/tract'
in no'/tis
in'/no/va'/tion
in/nu/bi'/bus
in'/nu/en'/do
in nul'/li/us bo'/nis
in nul'/lo est er/ra'/tum
in/of/fi'/cious tes'/ta/ment
in/op'/er/a/tive
in/or'/di/na'/tus
in pais
in pa'/ri
_____ cau'/sa
_____ de/lic'/to
_____ e'le/mo'/si/nam
_____ ma/te'/ri·a
in pa/ti/en'/do
in pec'/to/re ju'/di/cis
in pe/jo'/rem par'/tem
in per'/pe/tu'/i·ty
in per'/son
in per/so'/nam
_____ ju'/ris/dic'/tion
in ple'/na vi'/ta
in ple'/no lu'/mi/ne
in pos'/se
in po/tes'/ta/te pa/ren'/tis

in prae/sen'/ti
in pren'/der
in pri'/mis
in prin/cip'/i·o
in promp'/tu'
in pro'/pri·a per/so'/na
in'/quest'
in/quire'
in/quired'
in/quir'/ing
in'/qui'/ry
in'/qui/si'/tion
in/quis'/i/tor
in/quis'/i/to'/ri/al
sys'/tem
in re
in re'/bus
in re/gard' to
in rem
in ren'/der
in re'/rum na/tu'/ra
in/sane'
in/san'/i/tar'y
in/san'/i/ty
in/scribe'
in/scribed'
in/scrib'/ing
in/scrip'/tion
in'/se/cure'
in'/se/cu'/ri/ty
in/sen'/si/ble
in sep'/a/ra'/li
in/sid'/er
in/sid'/i/ous
in/sig'/ni·a

in′/sig/nif′/i/cant
in sim′/i/li ma/te′/ri·a
in′/si/mul
in/sin′/u/ate′
    in/sin′/u/at′/ed
    in/sin′/u/at′/ing
in/sin′/u/a′/tion
in′/so/la′/tion
in′/so/lence
in so′/li/do
in so′/li/dum
in so′/lo
in/sol′/ven/cy
in/sol′/vent
in spe′/ci·e
in/spect′
    in/spect′/ed
    in/spect′/ing
in/spec′/ta/tor
in/spec′/tion
in/spec′/tor
in/spec′/tor/ship′
in/stall′
    in/stalled′
    in/stall′/ing
in′/stal/la′/tion
in/stall′/ment
    ____ cred′/it
    ____ meth′/od
in′/stance
in′/stant
in′/stan/ta′/ne·ous
in/stan′/ter
in′/stant/ly
in′/star′

in sta′/tu quo′
in′/sti/gate′
    in′/sti/gat′/ed
    in′/sti/gat′/ing
in′/sti/ga′/tion
in′/stir/pa′/re
in stir′/pes
in′/sti/tute′
    in′/sti/tut′/ed
    in′/sti/tut′/ing
in′/sti/tut′/ed ex/ec′/u/tor
in′/sti/tu′/tion
in′/sti/tu′/ti/o′/nes
in/struct′
    in/struct′/ed
    in/struct′/ing
in/struc′/tion
in′/stru/ment
    ____ of ap/peal′
    ____ of ev′/i/dence
in′/stru/men′/ta
in′/stru/men′/tal
in′/stru/men/tal′/i/ty
in′/sub/or′/di/na′/tion
in sub/sid′/i/um
in′/suf/fi′/cien/cy
in′/suf/fi′/cient
in′/su/la
in′/su/late′
    in′/su/lat′/ed
    in′/su/lat′/ing
in′/su/la′/tion
in/su′/per/a·ble
in′/sup/port′/a·ble
in/sur′/a·ble

in/sur′/ance
—— ad/just′/er
—— a′gent
—— com/mis′/sion/er
—— com′/pa/ny
—— pol′/i/cy
—— pre′/mi/um
—— rat′/ing
—— trust
in/sure′
in/sured′
in/sur′/ing
in/sur′/er
in/sur′/gen/cy
in/sur′/gent
in′/sur/rec′/tion
in/tan′/gi/ble
—— as′/set
—— prop′/er/ty
in tan′/tum
in′/te/ger
in′/te/grate′
in′/te/grat′/ed
in′/te/grat′/ing
in′/te/gra′/tion
in/teg′/ri/ty
in/tel′/li/gence
in/tel′/li/gi/bil′/i/ty
in/tel′/li/gi/ble
in/tem′/per/ance
in/tend′
in/tend′/ed
in/tend′/ing
in/tend′/ment of law
in/tent′

in/ten′/ti·o cae′/ca ma′/la
in/ten′/tion
in/ten′/tion/al
in′/ter
in′/ter a′li·a
in′/ter a′li/os
in′/ter a′pi/ces ju′/ris
—— ar′/ma si′/lent
le′/ges
in′/ter bra′/chi·a
in′/ter/cede′
in′/ter/ced′/ed
in′/ter/ced′/ing
in′/ter/cept′
in′/ter/cept′/ed
in′/ter/cept′/ing
in′/ter/cep′/tion
in′/ter/change′
in′/ter/change′/a·ble
in′/ter con′/ju/ges
in′/ter/course
in′/ter/dict′
in′/ter/dict′/ed
in′/ter/dict′/ing
in′/ter/dic′/tion
in′/ter/es′/se
—— ter′/mi/ni
in′/ter/est
—— e′qual/i·za′/tion
—— pol′/i/cy
—— up/on′
in′/ter/est
in′/ter/fere′
in′/ter/fered′
in′/ter/fer′/ing

in′/ter/fer′/ence
in′/ter/im
   ____ com/mit′/ti/tur
   ____ cu/ra′/tor
   ____ fi′/nanc′/ing
   ____ of′/fi/cer
   ____ or′/der
   ____ re/ceipt′
   ____ state′/ment
in′/ter/in/sur′/ance
in′/te′/ri/or
in′/ter/lin/e·a′/tion
in′/ter/lock′/ing
in′/ter/loc′/u/tor
in′/ter/loc′/u/to′/ry
   ____ ap/peal′
   ____ in/junc′/tion
   ____ judg′/ment
   ____ or′/der
in′/ter/lop′/er
in′/ter/mar′/riage
in′/ter/me′/di/ar′y
in′/ter/me′/di/ate
in ter′/mi/nis ter′/mi/
nan′/ti/bus
in′/ter/mit′/tent
ease′/ment
in′/ter/mix′/ture
in′/tern′
   in′/terned′
   in′/tern′/ing
in/ter′/nal
   ____ com′/merce
   ____ po/lice′
   ____ rev′/e/nue′

in/ter′/nal (contd.)
   ____ se/cu′/ri/ty
in′/ter/na′/tion/al
   ____ a·gree′/ment
   ____ ju′/ris/dic′/tion
in/tern′/ment
in′/ter pa′/res
in′/ter par′/tes
in′/ter/pel′/late
in′/ter/plea′
in′/ter/plead′/er
in/ter′/po/late′
   in/ter′/po/lat′/ed
   in/ter′/po/lat′/ing
in/ter′/po/la′/tion
in′/ter/po/si′/tion
in/ter′/pret
   in/ter′/pret/ed
   in/ter′/pret/ing
in/ter′/pre/ta′/tion
in/ter′/pret/er
in′/ter/ra′/cial
in′/ter re/ga′/li·a
in′/ter/reg′/num
in/ter′/ro/gate′
   in/ter′/ro/gat′/ed
   in/ter′/ro/gat′/ing
in/ter′/ro/·ga′/tion
in′/ter/rog′/a/to′/ry
in ter/ro′/rem
   ____ po′/pu/li
in′/ter/rup′/tion
in′/ter rus′/ti/cos
in′/ter/sec′/tion
in′/ter se

in'/ter se'/se
in'/ter/spous'/al im/
mu'/ni/ty
in'/ter/state'
_____ a·gree'/ment
_____ com'/merce
_____ com'/pact'
_____ ex'/tra/di'/tion
_____ ren/di'/tion
in'/ter/ven'/ing
_____ a'/gen/cy
_____ cause
_____ dam'/ag/es
in'/ter/ven'/or
in'/ter/ven'/tion
in'/ter vi'/rum et ux'/
o'/rem
in'/ter vi'/vos'
_____ trans'/fer
in/tes'/ta/ble
in/tes'/ta/cy
in/tes'/tate'
_____ suc/ces'/sion
in tes'/ti/mo'/ni/um
in'/ti/ma/cy
in'/ti/mate *adj*
in'/ti/mate' *v*
in'/ti/mat'/ed
in'/ti/mat'/ing
in'/ti/ma'/tion
in/tim'/i/date'
in/tim'/i/dat'/ed
in/tim'/i/dat'/ing
in/tim'/i/da'/tion
in'/to'

in/tol'/er/a·ble
in to'/to
in/tox'/i/cate'
in/tox'/i/cat'/ed
in/tox'/i/cat'/ing
in/tox'/i/ca'/tion
in'/tox/i'/me/ter
in'/tra
in'/tra an'/ni spa'/ti/um
in'/tra fi'/dem
in tra/jec'/tu
in'/tra/lim'/i/nal
in'/tra/mu'/ral
in/tran'/si/tive
_____ cov'/e/nant
in tran'/si/tu
in'/tra pa/ri/et'/es
in'/tra/state'
in'/tra vi'/res
in/trin'/sic
_____ ev'/i/dence
_____ val'/ue
in'/tro/duc'/tion
in/trude'
in/trud'/ed
in/trud'/ing
in/trud'/er
in/tru'/sion
in/trust'
in/trust'/ed
in/trust'/ing
in'/un/date'
in'/un/dat'/ed
in'/un/dat'/ing
in'/un/da'/tion

in/ure′
   in/ured′
   in/ur′/ing
in/ure′/ment
in ut/ro′/que ju′/re
in/val′/id
in/vade′
   in/vad′/ed
   in/vad′/ing
in/va′/sion
in/veigh′
   in/veighed′
   in/veigh′/ing
in/vent′
   in/vent′/ed
   in/vent′/ing
in/ven′/tion
in/ven′/tor
in′/ven/to′/ry
in ven′/tra sa mère
in/ven′/tus
in/vest′
   in/vest′/ed
   in/vest′/ing
in/ves′/ti/gate′
   in/ves′/ti/gat′/ed
   in/ves′/ti/gat′/ing
in/ves′/ti/ga′/tion
in/ves′/ti/ga′/tive
in/ves′/ti/ture′
in/vest′/ment
   ___ ad/vis′/er *or*
   ad/vi′/sor
   ___ com′/pa/ny
   ___ con′/tract′

in/vest′/ment (contd.)
   ___ se/cu′/ri/ty
in vin/cu′/lis
in/vi′/o/la/bil′/i/ty
in/vi′/o/la/ble
in′/vi/ta′/tion
in/vite′
   in/vit′/ed
   in/vit′/ing
in′/vi/tee′
in′/voice′
in/vol′/un/tar′y
   ___ a′li·en/a′/tion
   ___ con/fes′/sion
   ___ dis/con/tin′/
   u/ance
   ___ dis/mis′/sal
   ___ man′/slaugh′/ter
   ___ ser′/vi/tude′
   ___ trans′/fer
i·o′/ta
ip′/se
   ___ dix′/it
   ___ fac′/to
   ___ ju′/re
ir/ra′/tio/nal
ir′/re/but′/ta/ble
pre/sump′/tion
ir/rec′/on/cil′/a·ble
ir′/re/cu′/sa/ble
ir/reg′/u/lar
   ___ en/dorse′/ment
   suc/ces′/sion
ir/reg′/u/lar′/i/ty
ir/rel′/e/van/cy

ir/rel'/e/vant
ir'/re/me'/di/a·ble
ir'/re/mov'/a·ble
ir/rep'/a/ra/ble
_____ dam'/ag/es
_____ in'/ju/ry
ir'/re/peal'/a·ble
ir/re/plev'i/a·ble
ir'/re/sist'/i·ble
_____ im'/pulse'
ir'/re/triev'/a·ble
ir/rev'/o/ca/ble
_____ let'/ter
ir'/ri/gate'
    ir'/ri/gat'/ed
    ir'/ri/gat'/ing
ir'/ri/ga'/tion
ir'/ri/tant
ir'/ri/tate'
    ir'/ri/tat'/ed
    ir'/ri/tat'/ing
is'/land
i'so/late'
    i'so/lat'/ed
    i'so/lat'/ing
i'so/la'/tion
is'/su/a·ble
is'/sue
_____ pre/clu'/sion
i'tem
i'tem/i·za'/tion
i'tem/ize'
    i'tem/ized'
    i'tem/iz'/ing

i·tin'/er/ant
_____ ped'/dler
_____ ven'/dor
it/self'

J

ja'/cens
jac'/ti/ta'/tion
_____ of mar'/riage
jac'/ti'/vus
jac'/tus
jail
    jailed
    jail'/ing
jail'/break'
jail'/er *or* jail'/or
Ja'/nus-/faced
jay'/walk'
    jay'/walked'
    jay'/walk'/ing
jeo'/faile
jeop'/ar/dy
jet'/sam
jet'/ti/son
jet'/ty
jew'/el
jew'/el/ry
job'/ber
join
    joined

join (contd.)

    join′/ing

join′/der

    _____ in de/mur′/rer

    _____ in is′/sue

    _____ in plead′/ing

    _____ of ac′/tions

    _____ of er′/ror

    _____ of in/dict′/ments

    _____ of is′/sue

    _____ of of′/fens/es

    _____ of par′/ties

    _____ of rem′/e/dies

joint

    _____ ac/count′

    _____ ac′/tion

    _____ ad/ven′/ture

    _____ and sev′/er/al

    _____ au′/thor/ship′

    _____ cause of ac′/tion

    _____ con′/tract′

    _____ cov′/e/nant

    _____ debt′/ors

    _____ de/fen′/dants

    _____ en′/ter/prise′

    _____ es/tate′

    _____ ex/ec′/u/tors

    _____ fea′/sors in par′/ri de/lic′/to

    _____ in/dict′/ment

    _____ li′/a/bil′/i/ty

    _____ mort′/gage

    _____ neg′/li/gence

    _____ of/fense′

joint (contd.)

    _____ pol′/i/cy

    _____ stock in/sur′/ance com′/pa/ny

    _____ ten′/an/cy

    _____ tort′-/fea′sors

    _____ tri′/al

    _____ ven′/ture

    _____ ver′/dict′

joint′/ist

joint′/ly

    _____ ac/quired′ prop′/er/ty

    _____ and sev′/er/al/ly owned prop′/er/ty

join′/tress *or* join′/tur/ess

join′/ture

jok′/er

jour en banc

jour′/nal

jour′/nal/ist

jour′/ney

jour′/ney/man

jour′/neys ac/count′

joy′/ride′

joy′/rid/ing

ju/be′/re

ju′/dex

judge

    _____ ad′/vo/cate

    _____ de fac′/to

    _____ de′/le/ga′/tus

    _____ fis/ca′/lis

    _____ pro tem′/po/re

judge (contd.)

    —— tri′/al

judge′-/made law

judg′/ment *or* judge′/ment

    —— by de/fault′

    —— cred′/i/tor

    —— debt′/or

    —— dock′/et

    —— ex′/e/cu′/tion

    —— in per/so′/nam

    —— in rem

    —— in re/trax′/it

    —— in′/ter par′/tes

    —— of con/vec′/tion

    —— on mer′/its

    —— on plead′/ing

    —— on ver′/dict′

    —— pa′/per

    —— qua′/si′ in rem

    —— rec′/ord

ju′/di/ca′/re

ju′/di/ca/to′/ries

ju′/di/ca/ture′

ju′/di/ces

ju/di′/cial

    —— ac′/tion

    —— ad/mis′/sion

    —— and le′/gal

dis/cre′/tion

    —— au/thor′/i/ty

    —— bus′i/ness

    —— cir′/cuit

    —— cog′/ni/zance

    —— com′/i/ty

    —— cy pres

ju/di′/cial (contd.)

    —— de/ci′/sion

    —— dic′/tum

    —— doc′/u/ment

    —— du′/ty

    —— er′/ror

    —— es/top′/pel

    —— im/mu′/ni/ty

    —— knowl′/edge

    —— leg′/is/la′/tion

    —— mort′/gage

    —— no′/tice

    —— of′/fi/cer

    —— o·pin′/ion

    —— pow′/er

    —— pro/ceed′/ing

    —— ques′/tion

    —— re/prieve′

    —— sep′/a/ra′/tion

    —— sys′/tem

ju/di′/cia/ry

ju/di′/cious/ly

ju/di′/ci/um

juge de paix

jump

    jumped

    jump′/ing

ju′/nior

    —— cred′/i/tor

    —— ex′/e/cu′/tion

    —— in′/ter/est

    —— judg′/ment

    —— mort′/gage

    —— part′/ner

junk′/shop′

jun′/ta
ju′/ra
ju′/ral
ju′/ra/men′/tum
ju/ra′/re
ju′/rat
ju/ra′/tion
ju/ra′/tor
ju′/rats
ju′/re
_____ bel′/li
_____ ci′/vi/le
_____ di/vi′/no
_____ gen/ti′/um
_____ ux/o′/ris
ju/rid′/i/cal
ju/ri′/di/cus
ju′/ris
_____ pri/va′/ti
_____ pub′/li/ci
_____ u′trum
ju′/ris/con′/sult
ju′/ris/dic′/tion
_____ in per/so′/nam
_____ o′ver per′/son
_____ qua′/si in rem
ju′/ris/dic′/tion/al
_____ a·mount′
_____ dis/pute′
_____ lim′/its
ju′/ris/in/cep′/tor
ju′/ris/pru′/dence
ju′/rist
ju/ris′/tic
ju′/ror

ju′/ry
_____ box
_____ chal′/lenge
_____ com/mis′/sion/er
_____ in/struc′/tions
_____ list
_____ of good and
law′/ful men
_____ of ma′/trons
_____ pan′/el
_____ poll′/ing
_____ pro′/cess
_____ ques′/tions
_____ sum/ma′/tion
_____ tri′/al
_____ wheel
ju′/ry/man
ju′/ry/wom′/an
jus
_____ ab′/sti/nen′/di
_____ ab/u/ten′/di
_____ ac′/cre/scen′/di
_____ bel′/li
_____ ci′/vi/le
_____ com/mu′/ne
_____ co/ro′/nae
_____ da′/re
_____ di/ce′/re
_____ dis′/po/nen′/di
_____ dis′/tra/hen′/di
_____ di′/vi/den′/di
_____ du′/pli/ca′/tum
_____ e·di′/ce/re
_____ flu′/mi/num
_____ gen′/ti/um

jus (contd.)

_____ glad′/i·i
_____ ha/ben′/di
_____ hae/re′/di/ta′/tes
_____ im/mu′/ni/ta′/tis
_____ in′/cog/ni′/tum
_____ in′/di/vi′/du/um
_____ in per/so′/nam
_____ in re
_____ in re pro′/pri·a
_____ ju/ran′/dum
_____ le/gi′/ti/mum
_____ ma′/ri/ti
_____ na/tu′/rae
_____ na/tu/ra′/le
_____ nav′/i/gan′/di
_____ non scip′/tum
_____ per/so/na′/rum
_____ por′/tus
_____ pos/ses′/si/o′/nes
_____ pos′/si/den′/di
_____ pri/va′/tum
_____ pro/pri′/e/ta′/tis
_____ pub′/li/cum
_____ quae′/si/tum
_____ re′/cu/per/an′′/di
_____ re′/rum
_____ san′/gui/nis
_____ scrip′/tum
_____ so′/li
_____ spa′/ti/an′/di
_____ stric′/tum
_____ ter′/ti·i
_____ u·ten′′/di

just

_____ com′/pen/
sa′/tion
_____ ti′/tle
_____ val′/ue
jus′′/ta cau′′/sa
jus′′/tice
_____ court
_____ of the peace
jus′/ti′/cia/ble
_____ con′/tro/ver′/sy
jus′′/ti/fi′/a·ble
_____ ho′/mi/cide′
jus′′/ti/fi/ca′′/tion
jus′′/ti/fy′
jus′′/ti/fied′
jus′′/ti/fy′/ing
just′/ness
ju′′/ve/nile′
_____ court
_____ de/lin′′/quent
_____ of/fend′′/er
ju′′/ve/noc′′/ra/cy
jux′′/ta
_____ for′/mam
sta/tu′/ti
jux′′/ta/pose′
jux′′/ta/posed′
jux′′/ta/pos/′ing
jux′′/ta/po/si′/tion

K

kan′/ga/roo′ court
keep
kept

keep (contd.)
    keep′/ing
keep′/er
    ____ of a bawd′y
    house
    ____ of a gam′/bling
    house
    ____ of the for′/est
    ____ of the king's
    con′/science
    ____ of the priv′y seal
keep′/ing
    ____ a look′/out′
kelp′-/shore′
kempt
kernes
key′/age
key′/us
kick′/back′
kid′/der
kid′/nap
    kid′/napped
    kid′/nap/ping
kil′/der/kin
kill
    killed
    kill′/ing
kin
kind
kin′/dred
kin′/folk′
king′/dom
king's
    ____ ad′/vo/cate
    ____ cham′/bers

king's (contd.)
    ____ cor′/o/ner and
    at/tor′/ney
    ____ coun′/sel
    ____ proc′/tor
kings′-/at-/arms′
kins′/folk′
kin′/ship′
kins′/man
kins′/wom′/an
kin′/tal *or* kin′/tle
kiss
    kissed
    kiss′/ing
kite
    kit′/ed
    kit′/ing
klep′/to/ma′′/ni·a
klep′/to/ma′′/ni/ac
knack′/er
knave
knav′/er·y
knav′/ish
knight′/hood′
knight′-/mar′/shal
knight
    ____ bach′/e/lor
    ____ ban′/ner/et
    ____ of the this′/tle
    ____ ser′/vice
knock
    knocked
    knock′/ing
know
    knew

know (contd.)
  known
  know′/ing
know′/ing/ly
  _____ and will′/ful/ly
knowl′/edge
known
  _____ heirs
kow′/tow′
krem′/lin/ol′/o/gy
ku′/dos′

L

la′/bel
  la′/beled
  la′/bel/ing
la′/bor
  la′/bored
  la′/bor/ing
la′/bor
  _____ a ju′/ry
  _____ dis/pute′
  _____ or′/ga/ni/za′/
  tion
  _____ pick′/et/ing
  _____ sep′/a/ra′/tion
  _____ u′nion
la′/bor/er
la′/ches
lack
  _____ of ju′/ris/dic′/
  tion

lac′/ta
lad′/en in bulk
lad′/ing
la′/dy
lage day
lage′-/man′
lais′sez′-/faire′
lais′sez′-/pas′ser′
la′/it·y
lame duck ses′/sion
land
  _____ bound′/a·ries
  _____ cer/tif′/i/cate
  _____ con′/tract′
  _____ dam′/ag/es
  _____ de/part′/ment
  _____ de/scrip′/tions
  _____ dis′/trict′
  _____ gab′/el
  _____ grant
  _____ man′/age/ment
  _____ pat′/ent
  _____ rev′/e/nues
  _____ tax
  _____ ten′/ant
  _____ wait′/er
  _____ war′/rant
land′/ed
  _____ es/tate′
  _____ es/tates′ court
  _____ prop′/er/ty
  _____ pro/pri′/e/tor
  _____ se/cu′/ri/ties
land′/ing
land′/locked′

land'/lord'
land'/lord's' war'/rant
land'/mark'
land'-/poor'
lands, ten''/e/ments, and
her'/e/dit''/a/ments
lan'/guage
lap'/i/da''/tion
lap'/page
lapse *v*
    lapsed
    laps''/ing
lapse *adj*
    ____ pat'/ent
    ____ stat''/ute
lapsed
    ____ de/vise'
    ____ leg'/a/cy
    ____ pol'/i/cy
lar'/ce/nous
    ____ in/tent'
lar'/ce/ny
las/civ'/i/ous
    ____ car'/riage
    ____ co''/hab'/i/ta''/
    tion
last
    ____ an'/te/ce''/dent
    ____ clear chance
    ____ ill''/ness
    ____ re/sort'
    ____ sick''/ness
la''/ta cul''/pa
la''/ten/cy
la''/tens'

la'/tent
    ____ am'/bi/gu''/i·ty
    ____ de''/fect'
    ____ eq'/ui/ty
lat'/er/al
    ____ rail''/road'
    ____ sup/port'
la'/te/ra''/re
la''/ti fun'/dus
lat/ro''/ci/na''/tion
lat/ro''/ci/ny
lau''/da''/re
lau''/da''/tor
lau''/dum
launch
    launched
    launch''/ing
lau''/re/ate
law
    ____ ar'/bi/trar'y
    ____ court of ap/peals'
    ____ day
    ____ de/part'/ment
    ____ en/force''/ment
of''/fi/cer
    ____ mar'/tial
    ____ mer'/chant
    ____ of a gen''/er/al
na'/ture
    ____ of cap'/ture
    ____ of ev'/i/dence
    ____ of na''/tions
    ____ of na'/ture
    ____ of the land
    ____ of the sta''/ple

law (contd.)
　　　—— re/ports'
　　　—— re/view'
　　　—— spir'/i/tu/al
law'/ful
　　　—— au/thor'/i/ty
　　　—— dam'/ag/es
　　　—— de/pen'/dent
　　　—— dis'/charge'
　　　—— en'/try
　　　—— is'/sue
　　　—— mon'/ey
　　　—— rep'/re/sen'/ta/
tive
law'/less
law'/suit'
law'/yer
lay
　　　—— ad'/vo/cate
　　　—— cor'/po/ra'/tion
　　　—— dam'/ag/es
　　　—— in/ves'/ti/ture'
　　　—— peo'/ple
　　　—— sys'/tem
lay'/a·way'
laye
lay'/ing
　　　—— foun/da'/tion
　　　—— the ven'/ue
lay'/man
lay'/off'
lead
　　led
　　lead'/ing

lead coun'/sel
lead'/ing
　　　—— coun'/sel
　　　—— ob'/ject
　　　—— ques'/tion
league
leak'/age
le/al'
lean
　　leaned
　　lean'/ing
leap year
learn
　　learned
　　learn'/ing
lease
　　leased
　　leas'/ing
lease'/back'
lease'/hold'
　　　—— im/prove'/ments
　　　—— mort'/gage
lease'/hold'/er
leave *v*
　　left
　　leav'/ing
leave *n*
　　　—— and li'/cense
　　　—— of ab'/sence
　　　—— to de/fend'
lec/ca'/tur
lec'/tur/er
led'/ger
leet

leg′/a/cy
le′/gal
_____ a·cu′/men
_____ age
_____ aid
_____ as′/sets
_____ as/sis′/tant
_____ ca/pac′/i/ty to sue
_____ cap′/i/tal
_____ cause
_____ con/clu′/sion
_____ cru′/el/ty
_____ cus′/to/dy
_____ de/fense′
_____ de/mand′
_____ de/pen′/dent
_____ det′/ri/ment
_____ dis/cre′/tion
_____ dis/trib′/u/tee′
_____ du′/ty
_____ en′/ti/ty
_____ es/top′/pel
_____ eth′/ics
_____ ev′/i/dence
_____ ex/cuse′
_____ fic′/tion
_____ hol′/i/day′
_____ im/pos′/si/bil′/i/ty
_____ in′/ju/ry
_____ in/san′/i/ty
_____ in′/ter/est
_____ in/vest′/ment

le′/gal (contd.)
_____ is′/sue
_____ jeop′/ar/dy
_____ li′/a/bil′/i/ty
_____ mal′/ice
_____ mal′/prac′/tice
_____ mort′/gage
_____ neg′/li/gence
_____ no′/tice
_____ ob′/li/ga′/tion
_____ own′/er
_____ per′/son/al rep′/re/sen′/ta/tive
_____ pos/ses′/sor
_____ prej′/u/dice
_____ pre/sump′/tion
_____ priv′/i/ty
_____ pro/ceed′/ings
_____ rate of in′/ter/est
_____ rep′/re/sen′/ta/tive
_____ re/scis′/sion
_____ re/serve′
_____ res′/i/dence
_____ sep′/a/ra′/tion
_____ sub′/di/vi′/sion
_____ sub′/ro/ga′/tion
_____ suc/ces′/sion
_____ ten′/der
_____ ti′/tle
_____ u′su/fruct′
_____ vot′/er
le′/gal/ese′
le/ga′/lis ho′/mo

le′/gal/ism′

le′/gal/ist

le/gal′/i/ty

le/gal/i·za′/tion

le′/gal/ize′

   le′/gal/ized′

   le′/gal/iz′/ing

le′/gal/ly

   _____ a·dopt′/ed

   _____ com/mit′/ted

   _____ com′/pe/tent

   _____ con′/sti/tut′/ed

   court

   _____ li′/a/ble

   _____ re/side′

   _____ suf/fi′/cient

   ev′/i/dence

   _____ suf/fi′/cient

   ten′/der

le′/gal/ness

le/ga′/re

leg′/a/tar′y

le/gate′

   le/gat′/ed

   le/gat′/ing

leg′/a/tee′

leg′/a/tine′

le/ga′/tion

le/ga′/tor

leg′/a/to′/ry

le′/gem

leg′/end

le′/ges

leg′/is/late′

   leg′/is/lat′/ed

leg′/is/lat′/ing

leg′/is/la′/tion

leg′/is/la′/tive

   _____ ap/por′/tion/

   ment

   _____ as/sem′/bly

   _____ coun′/cil

   _____ de/part′/ment

   _____ dis′/trict′

   _____ di/vorce′

   _____ ex/pens′/es

   _____ func′/tion

   _____ in/tent′

   _____ in/ves′/ti/

   ga′/tion

   _____ ju′/ris/dic′/

   tion

   _____ of′/fi/cer

   _____ pow′/er

   _____ pur′/pose

leg′/is/la′/tor

leg′/is/la/to′/ri/al

leg′/is/la′/ture

le/git′/i/ma/cy

le/git′/i/mate *adj*

le/git′/i/mate′ *v*

   le/git′/i/mat′/ed

   le/git′/i/mat′/ing

le/git′/i/ma′/tion

leg/i′/time

le/git′/i/mism′

le/git′/i/mus

lei′/sure

lend

   lent

lend (contd.)

    lend′/ing

lend′-/lease′

lend′/er

lend′/ing mon′/ey

le′/nien/cy

le′/ni·ent

len′/i/ty

les′/bi/an

le′/sion

les/see′

less′/er of/fense′

les′/son

les′/sor′

    ____ of the plain′/tiff

lest

let

    let

    let′/ting

le′/thal

    ____ weap′/on

let′/ter

    ____ car′/ri/er

    ____ mis′/sive

    ____ of ad/vice′

    ____ of a·gree′/ment

    ____ of com′/ment

    ____ of cre′/dence

    ____ of cred′/it

    ____ of ex/change′

    ____ of in/tent′

    ____ of li′/cense

    ____ of re/call′

    ____ of re/cre/

den′/tials

let′/ter (contd.)

    ____ rul′/ing

let′/ters

    ____ of ad/min′/is/

tra′/tion

    ____ of guard′/i·an/

ship′

    ____ of marque

    ____ of re/quest′

    ____ pat′/ent

    ____ ro′/ga/to′/ry

    ____ tes′/ta/men′/

ta/ry

let′/ting out

let′/tre de ca′/chet′

lev′/ee dis′/trict′

lev′/el

lev′i/a·ble

lev′i/er

le′/vi/rate

lev′/i/ty

lev′y

    lev′/ied

    lev′/y/ing

lewd

    ____ and las/civ′/i/

ous co/hab′/i/ta′/tion

    ____ per′/son

lewd′/ness

lex

    ____ ac′/tus

    ____ a·mis′/sa

    ____ apos′/ta/ta

    ____ ap/par′/ens

    ____ bar′/ba/ra

lex (contd.)

    _____ co′/mi/ta′′/tus

    _____ com/mu′′/nis

    _____ do′′/mi/ci′′/li·i

    _____ fo′′/ri

    _____ ju′/di/ci/a′′/lis

    _____ lo′′/ci

    _____ lo′′/ci ac′′/tus

    _____ lo′′/ci ce′/le/
bra′/ti/o′/nis

    _____ lo′′/ci con/
trac′′/tus

    _____ lo′′/ci de/lic′′/ti

    _____ lo′′/ci do′′/mi/
ci′′/li·i

    _____ lo′′/ci re′i si′′/tae

    _____ lo′′/ci so/lu′′/ti/
o′′/nis

    _____ ma′′/ni/fes′′/ta

    _____ mer′/ca/to′′/ri·a

    _____ na′′/tu/ra′′/le

    _____ non co′′/git ad
im′′/pos/si/bil′′/ia

    _____ non cu′′/rat de
mi′′/ni/mis

    _____ sac/ra′′/men/ta′′/
lis

    _____ si′′/tus

    _____ ta′′/li/o′′/nis

    _____ ter′′/rae

ley

    _____ ga′′/ger

li′/a/bil′′/i/ty

    _____ cre/at′′/ed by
stat′/ute

li′/a/bil′i/ty (contd.)

    _____ for dam′′/ag/es

    _____ im/posed′ by law

    _____ in sol′′/i/do

    _____ in/sur′′/ance

li′/a/ble

    _____ to pen′′/al/ty

li′′/bel

    li′′/beled

    li′′/bel/ing

li′′/bel/ant

li′/bel/ee′

li′′/bel/ous

    _____ per quod

    _____ per se

li′′/ber

lib′′/er/al

    _____ con/struc′′/tion

    _____ in/ter′′/pre/
ta′′/tion

lib′′/er/al/ism′

lib′′/er/al′′/i/ty

lib′′/er/al/ize′

    lib′′/er/al/ized′

    lib′′/er/al/iz′′/ing

lib′′/er/ate′

    lib′′/er/at′/ed

    lib′′/er/at′/ing

lib′′/er/a′′/tion

lib′′/er/tar′′/i/an

lib′′/er/ti/cide′

lib′′/er/tine′

lib′′/er/ty

    _____ of con′′/science

    _____ of con′′/tract′

lib'/er/ty (contd.)
    ____ pole
li'/be/rum te'/ne/
men'/tum
li'/bra
    ____ nu'/me/ra''/ta
    ____ pen''/sa
li/brar''/i/an
li'/brar'y
li'/cense
    ____ cas''/es
    ____ in am''/or/ti/
za'/tion
li'/censed vict'/u·al
li'/cens/ee'
    ____ by in'/vi/ta''/tion
    ____ by per/mis''/sion
li'/cens/er *or* li'/cen/sor'
li'/cens/ing pow''/er
li'/cen/sure
li/cen''/tious
li/ce'/re
lic'/it
lie
    lied
    ly''/ing
liege
    ____ hom''/age
liege'/man
lien
    ____ ac/count'
    ____ cred'/i/tor
lien/ee'
lien'/or

lieu
    ____ co''/mus
lieu/ten'/ant
    ____ col'/o/nel
    ____ com/mand''/er
    ____ gen'/er/al
    ____ gov'/er/nor
life
    ____ an/nu''/i·ty
    ____ ben'/e/fi'/cia/ry
    ____ es/tate'
    ____ in be''/ing
    ____ in/sur''/ance
    ____ peer''/age
    ____ ta'/bles
    ____ ten''/an/cy
    ____ ten'/ant
life'/hold'
life'/land'
li/ga''/re
ligh''/ter/age
light'/house'
li/gi'/us
like
    ____ ben''/e/fits
    ____ char''/ac/ter
like'/li/hood
like'/ly
like'/wise
limb
lim'/it
    lim'/it/ed
    lim'/it/ing
lim'/i/ta''/tion
    ____ of as/size'

lim′/i/ta′/tion (contd.)
    ____ of dam′/ag/es
    ____ of li′/a/bil′/i/ty
    ____ of pros′/e/
cu′/tions
    ____ ti′/tle
lim′/it/ed
    ____ ad/min′/is/
tra′/tion
    ____ ad/mis′/si/
bil′/i/ty
    ____ ap/peal′
    ____ di/vorce′
    ____ ex/ec′/u/tor
    ____ guar′/an/ty
    ____ in/ter′/pre/
ta′/tion
    ____ ju′/ris/dic′/tion
    ____ li′/a/bil′/i/ty
    ____ own′/er
    ____ part′/ner/ship′
    ____ pol′/i/cy
    ____ pow′/er of
ap/point′/ment
    ____ pub′/li/ca′/tion
    ____ war′/ran/ty
line
    ____ of cred′/it
    ____ of du′/ty
    ____ of or′/di/nar′y
    high tide
lin′/e·a
    ____ ob/li′/qua
    ____ rec′/ta
    ____ trans′/ver/sa′/lis
lin′/e·age

lin′/e·al
    ____ con/san/
guin′/i/ty
    ____ de/scen′/dant
    ____ de/scent′
    ____ war′/ran/ty
lines and cor′/ners
line′/up′
liq′/uid
liq′/ui/date′
    liq′/ui/dat′/ed
    liq′/ui/dat′/ing
liq′/ui/dat′/ed
    ____ ac/count′
    ____ dam′/ag/es and
pen′/al/ties
    ____ de/mand′
liq′/ui/dat′/ing
    ____ dis′/tri/bu′/tion
    ____ part′/ner
liq′/ui/da′/tion
    ____ div′/i/dend
liq′/ui/da′/tor
li′/quor
    ____ deal′/er
    ____ shop
lis
    ____ al′i/bi′ pen′/dens
    ____ mo′/ta
    ____ pen′/dens
list
    list′/ed
    list′/ing
lis′/ten
    lis′/tened
    lis′/ten/ing

li′/te pen/den′′/te
li′/ter *or* li′/tre
li′/te/ra
lit′/er/a/cy
lit′/er/al
    ____ con/struc′/tion
    ____ con′/tract′
lit′/er/al/ism′
lit′/er/ar′y
    ____ com′/po/si′/tion
    ____ ex/ec′/u/tor
    ____ prop′/er/ty
    ____ work
lit′/er/ate
lit′/i/gant
lit′/i/gate′
    lit′/i/gat′/ed
    lit′/i/gat′/ing
lit′/i/ga′′/tion
li/ti′/gious
li′/tis aes′′/ti/ma′′/tio
lit′/ter
    lit′/tered
    lit′/ter/ing
lit′/te/rae′ hu/ma′′/ni/
o′′/res
lit′/to/ral
li/tu′′/ra
liv′/a·bil′′/i/ty
liv′/a·ble
live
    lived
    liv′/ing
live′/li/hood
liv′/er·y
    ____ con/vey′/ance

liv′/er·y (contd.)
    ____ of sei′′/sin
    ____ of′/fice
    ____ sta′′/ble
liv′/er·y/man
lives in be′/ing
live′/stock′
    ____ in/sur′/ance
live stor′/age
liv′/ing
    ____ a·part′
    ____ in o′pen and no/
to′/ri/ous a·dul′′/ter·y
    ____ sep′′/ar/ate and
a·part′
    ____ to/geth′′/er
    ____ trust
load
    load′/ed
    load′/ing
loan *n, adj*
    ____ as/so′/ci/a′′/tion
    ____ cer/tif′′/i/cate
    ____ com/mit′′/ment
    ____ for ex/change′
    ____ so/ci′′/et·y
loan *v*
    loaned
    loan′/ing
loaned em′/ploy/ee′
lob′/by
    lob′/bied
    lob′/by/ing
lob′/by/er
lob′/by/ist

lo′/cal
    ____ ac′/tion
    ____ af/fairs′
    ____ a′gent
    ____ and spe′/cial
leg′/is/la′/tion
    ____ as/sess′/ment
    ____ chat′/tel
    ____ con/cern′
    ____ gov′/ern/ment
    ____ im/prove′/ment
    ____ op′/tion
    ____ prej′/u/dice
    ____ stat′/ute
    ____ us′/age
lo/cal′/i/ty
lo′/cal/i·za′/tion
lo′/cal/ize′
    lo′/cal/ized′
    lo′/cal/iz′/ing
lo′/cate′
    lo′/cat′/ed
    lo′/cat′/ing
lo/ca′/tion
loc′/a/tive
lo′/ca′/tor
lo/ca′/tum
lock
    locked
    lock′/ing
lock′/out′
lock′/up′
lo′/co/mo′/tive
lo′/co pa/ren′/tis
lo′/cus
    ____ clas′/si/cus

loc′/us (contd.)
    ____ con/trac′/tus
    ____ crim′/i/nus
    ____ de/lic′/ti
    ____ in quo
    ____ par/ti′/tus
    ____ poen′/i/ten′/ti/ae
    ____ pub′/li/cus
    ____ re′/git ac′/tum
    ____ re′i si′/tae
    ____ stan′/di
lode
lodge
    lodged
    lodg′/ing
lodg′/er
lodg′/ings
log′/book′
log′/ging
lo′/gi·a
log′/ic
log′/i/cal
lo/gis′/tics
loi′/ter
    loi′/tered
    loi′/ter/ing
long
    ____ ac/count′
lon/gev′/i/ty
long′/shore/man
long′-/term′ fi′/nanc′/ing
look′/out′
lord
    ____ ad′/vo/cate
    ____ and vas′/sal
    ____ chief jus′/tice

lord (contd.)

    _____ high chan′′/cel/
lor

    _____ high stew′/ard

    _____ high treas′/ur/er

    _____ in gross

    _____ jus′′/tice clerk

    _____ keep′′/er

    _____ lieu/ten′′/ant

    _____ may′′/or

    _____ of a man′′/or

    _____ or′′/di/nar′y

    _____ par′′/a/mount

    _____ priv′y seal

lords

    _____ com/mis′′/sion/
ers

    _____ jus′′/tic/es of ap/
peal′

    _____ march′′/ers

    _____ of ap/peal′

    _____ of par′′/lia/ment

    _____ or/dain′′/ers

    _____ spir′/i/tu/al

    _____ tem′′/po/ral

lord′/ship′

lose

    lost

    los′′/ing

loss

    _____ lead′′/er

    _____ of con/sor′′/ti/
um

    _____ pay′′/a·ble

    _____ ra′′/tio

lot′′/ter·y

love and af/fec′′/tion

lov′′/er

low

    _____ dil′′/i/gence

    _____ wa′′/ter

low′′/est re/spon′′/si/ble
bid′′/der

low′-/wa′ter mark

loy′′/al

loy′′/al/ty

lu′′/cid

lu/cid′′/i/ty

lu′′/cra/tive

lu′′/cre

lu′′/cri cau′′/sa

lug′′/gage

lu′′/men

lu′′/mi/na′′/re

lump′′/ing sale

lump′-/sum′

    _____ al′′/i/mo′′/ny

    _____ dis′′/tri/bu′′/tion

    _____ pay′′/ment

    _____ set′′/tle/ment

lu′′/na/cy

lu′′/na/tic

lure

    lured

    lur′′/ing

lust

ly′′/ing

    _____ by

    _____ in fran′′/chise′

    _____ in grant

    _____ in wait

lynch
   lynched
   lynch′/ing

M

ma/ca′/bre
mac/ad′/am
Mace
mace′-/proof′
mach′/i/nate′
   mach′/i/nat′/ed
   mach′/i/nat′/ing
mach′/i/na′′/tion
ma/chine′
ma/chin′/er·y
ma/chin′/ist
made known
mad′/man
mad′/ness
mag′/a/zine′
ma/gis′/ter
   _____ li′/tis
   _____ na′/vis
mag′/is/te′/ri/al
   _____ pre′′/cinct
mag′/is/tra/cy
mag′/is/trate′
mag′/is/trate's′ court
mag′/is/tra′′/ture
mag′/na
   _____ cen′′/tum
   _____ cul′′/pa

mag′/na (contd.)
   _____ neg′′/li/gen′′/ti·a
mag′/na/nim′′/i/ty
mag′/nate′
mag′/ni/tude′
maid′/en
   _____ as/size′
mail
   _____ fraud
   _____ mat′′/ter
mail′/a·ble
mail′/box′
maim
   maimed
   maim′′/ing
main
   _____ chan′′/nel
   _____ line
   _____ pur′′/pose
main′-/a-/main′
main′′/land′
main′′/ly
main′′/per′′/na/ble
main′′/prise
   main′′/prised
   main′′/pris/ing
main/tain′
   main/tained′
   main/tain′/ing
main′′/te/nance
   _____ as/sess′/ment
maj′/es/ty
ma′′/jor
   _____ and mi′′/nor fault
   _____ an′′/nus

ma′/jor (contd.)
    _____ dis/pute′
    _____ gen′′/er/al
    _____ med′/i/cal in/
   sur′/ance
    _____ par′/ty
ma/jo′/ra re/ga′′/li·a
ma/jor′/i/ty
    _____ lead′′/er
    _____ of qual′/i/fied′
   e·lec′/tors
    _____ of stock′′/hold′/
   ers
ma′′/jus
make
   made
   mak′/ing
make
    _____ a con′′/tract′
    _____ an as/sign′′/ment
    _____ an a·ward′
    _____ de/fault′
    _____ o′ver
mak′′/er
ma′′/la
    _____ fi′′/des
    _____ in se
    _____ prax′/is
    _____ pro/hi′′/bi/ta
mal′/ad/just′′/ed
mal/ad/min′′/is/tra′′/tion
mal′/ap/por′′/tioned
mal′′/con′/duct
mal′′/con/tent′
mal′/dis′′/tri/bu′′/tion

male
mal′e/dic′′/tion
mal′e/fac′′/tion
mal′e/fac′/tor
ma/lev′′/o/lence
mal/fea′′/sance
mal′′/ice
    _____ a·fore′/thought′
    _____ pre′′/pense′
ma/li′′/cious
    _____ a·ban′′/don/ment
    _____ a·buse′ of le′′/gal
   pro′′/cess
    _____ ac′′/cu/sa′′/tion
    _____ ar/rest′
    _____ in′′/ju/ry
    _____ in/tent′
    _____ kill′′/ing
    _____ mis′′/chief
    _____ mo′′/tive
    _____ pros′/e/cu′′/tion
    _____ tres′′/pass
    _____ use of pro′′/cess
ma/li′′/cious/ly
ma/li′′/cious/ness
ma/lign′
   ma/ligned′
   ma/lign′′/ing
mal′′/le·a/ble
ma′′/lo
    _____ an′i/mo
    _____ gra′′/to
    _____ sen′′/su
mal/prac′′/tice
   mal/prac′′/ticed

mal/prac′/tice (contd.)
   mal/prac′/tic/ing
mal′/prac/ti′/tio/ner
mal/treat′/ment
ma′/lum
   —— in se
   —— pro/hi′/bi/tum
man′/a/cle
man′/age
   man′/aged
   man′/ag/ing
man′/age/ment
man′/ag/er
manche pre′/sent′
man′/ci/pate′
   man′/ci/pat′/ed
   man′/ci/pat′/ing
man/da′/mus
man′/da/tar′y
man′/date′
   man′dat′/ed
   man′/dat′/ing
man′/da/to′ry
   —— in/junc′/tion
   —— in/struc′/tion
   —— sen′/tenc/ing
   —— stat′/ute
man/da′/vi bal′/li/vo
man′-/day′
ma/neu′/ver
   ma/neu′/vered
   ma/neu′/ver/ing
man′/hood′
man′/hunt′
ma′/ni·a
ma′/ni/ac′

ma/ni′/a/cal
man′/ic
man′/i/fest′
   —— law
man′/i/fes/ta′/tion
man′/i/fes′/to
ma/nip′/u/late′
   ma/nip′/u/lat′/ed
   ma/nip′/u/lat′/ing
ma/nip′/u/la′/tion
man′/kind′
man′/ner
man′/ning
man/ni′/re
man of straw
man′/or
ma/no′/ri/al
manse
man′/ser
man′/sion
   —— house
man′/slaugh′/ter
man′/slay′/er
man′/steal′/ing
man/tic′/u/late′
   man/tic′/u/lat′/ed
   man/tic′/u/lat′/ing
man′/u/al
   —— de/liv′/er·y
   —— la′/bor
   —— rates
   —— train′/ing
man′/u/fac′/ture
   man′/u/fac′/tured
   man′/u/fac′/tur/ing
man′/u/fac′/tur/er

man′/u/fac′/tur/ers' li′/a/
bil′/i/ty
man′/u/mis′/sion
man′/u/mit′
    man′/u/mit′/ted
    man′/u/mit′/ting
man′u/script′
man′y
mar
    marred
    mar′/ring
mar′/a/thon′
ma/raud′
    ma/raud′/ed
    ma/raud′/ing
ma/raud′/er
march′/es
ma′/re
    _____ clau′/sum
    _____ li′/be/rum′
    _____ no′/strum
mar′/gin
    _____ ac/count′
    _____ prof′/it
    _____ trans/ac′/tion
mar′/gin/al
mar′/i/jua′/na
ma/ri/na′/ri/us
ma/ri′/na
ma/rine′
    _____ car′/ri/er
    _____ con′/tract′
    _____ in/sur′/ance
    _____ in′/ter/est
    _____ league
mar′/i/ner

mar′/i/tal
    _____ a·gree′/ment
    _____ co/er′/cion
    _____ de/duc′/tion
    _____ por′/tion
    _____ priv′/i/lege
    _____ rights and du′/
    ties
mar′/i/time′
    _____ con′/tract′
    _____ court
    _____ in′/ter/est
    _____ ju′/ris/dic′/tion
    _____ law
    _____ lien
    _____ prof′/it
    _____ ser′/vice
    _____ tort
mar′/i/tus
mark
    marked
    mark′/ing
mark′/down′ *n*
mar′/ket
    _____ geld
    _____ or′/der
    _____ o·vert′
    _____ price
    _____ quo/ta′/tions
    _____ re/search′
    _____ struc′/ture
    _____ val′/ue
mar′/ket/a·ble
    _____ se/cu′/ri/ties
    _____ ti′/tle
mar′/ket/er

mar′/ket/ing
mar′/ket/place′
marks′/man
marks′/wom′/an
mark′/up′ *n*
marque and re/pri′/sal
mar′/quis *or* mar′/quess
mar′/riage
_____ ar′/ti/cles
_____ bro′/ker
_____ cer′/e/mo′/ny
_____ cer/tif′/i/cate
_____ li′/cense
_____ no′/tice book
_____ of con/ve′/nience
_____ part′/ner
_____ per ver′/ba de
prae/sen′/ti
_____ por′/tion
_____ prom′/ise
_____ set′/tle/ment
_____ vows
mar′/ry
mar′/ried
mar′/ry/ing
mar′/shal
mar′/shal/ing
_____ as′/sets
_____ liens
_____ rem′/e/dies
_____ se/cu′/ri/ties
mar′/tial law
mar′/ti/net′
mas′/cu/line
mas′/och/ism′
mas′/sa

mass strike
mas′/ter
_____ a·gree′/ment
_____ and ser′/vant
_____ at com′/mon law
_____ in chan′/cer·y
mate
ma′/ter/fa/mil′/i/as
ma/te′/ri·a
_____ med′/i/ca
ma/te′/ri/al
_____ al′/le/ga′/tion
_____ al′/ter/a′/tion
_____ ev′/i/dence
_____ mis/rep′/re/sen′/
ta′/tion
_____ rep′/re/sen′/ta/′/
tion
_____ wit′/ness
ma/te′/ri/al/man
ma/ter′/nal
_____ line of de/scent′
_____ prop′/er/ty
ma/ter′/na ma/ter′/nis
ma/ter′/ni/ty
_____ leave
math′/e/mat′/i/cal
_____ ev′/i/dence
ma′/tri/arch′
ma′/tri/arch′/ate
ma′/tri/arch′/y
ma′/tri/cide′
ma/tric′/u/la
ma/tric′/u/late′
ma/tric′/u/lat′/ed
ma/tric′/u/lat′/ing

ma/tric′/u/la′/tion
ma′/tri/lin′′/e·al
mat′/ri/mo′′/ni·al
    _____ ac′/tion
    _____ caus′/es
    _____ co/hab′/i/ta′′/
tion
    _____ do′′/mi/cile′
mat′′/ri/mo′′/ny
ma/′′/trix, *pl* ma′/tri/ces′
or ma′/trix/es
ma′/tron
mat′′/ter
    _____ in con′/tro/ver′′/
sy
    _____ in dis/pute′
    _____ in is′/sue
    _____ of course
    _____ of form
    _____ of rec′/ord
    _____ of sub′′/stance
mat′′/ters of sub/sis′/tence
for man
mat′/u/ra′′/tion
ma/ture′
    ma/tured′
    ma/tur′′/ing
ma/tu′′/ri/ty
mau′/so/le′′/um
max′/im
max′/i/mal
max′i/min′
max′/i/mize′
    max′/i/mized′
    max′/i/miz′/ing
max′/i/mum

may′′/hem′
mayn
may′′/or
may′′/or/al/ty
may′′/or's court
mead′′/ow
mean
me/an′′/der
    me/an′′/dered
    me/an′′/der/ing
mean′′/ing
mean′′/ing/ful
mea′′/sure *n*
    mea′′/sured
    mea′′/sur/ing
mea′′/sure *v*
    _____ of dam′′/ag/es
    _____ of val′′/ue
mea′′/sur/er
mea′′/sur/ing mon′′/ey
me/chan′′/ic
me/chan′′/i/cal
    _____ draw′′/ing
    _____ e·quiv′/a/lent
    _____ move′′/ment
    _____ pro′′/cess
me/chan′′/ic's lien
mech′/a/nism′
med′′/dle
    med′′/dled
    med′′/dling
me′′/dia
    _____ con′/clu/den′′/di
me′′/di/an
me′′/di/ate′ *v*
    me′′/di/at′′/ed

me′/di/ate′ (contd.)
    me′/di/at′/ing
me′/di/ate *adj*
    _____ da′/tum
    _____ de/scent′
    _____ pow′/er
    _____ tes′/ti/mo′/ny
me′/di/a′/tion
me′/di/a′/tor
med′/i/cal
    _____ de/duc′/tion
    _____ ev′/i/dence
    _____ ex/am′/in/er
    _____ ju′/ris/pru′/
dence
    _____ mal/prac′/tice
    _____ ser′/vice
med′/i/ca′/tion
me/dic′/i/nal
med′/i/cine
med′/i/co/le′/gal
med/le′/tum
med′/ley
meet′/ing
meg′/a/lo/ma′/ni·a
meg′/a/lop′/o/lis
mein′/dre age
mel′/an/cho′/li·a
mel′/an/chol′y
me′/li/or
me′/li·o/ra′/tion
mem′/ber
mem′/ber/ship′
mem′/brum
me/men′/to
mem′/oir′

mem′/o/ra/ble
mem′/o/ran′/dum
    _____ ar′/ti/cles
    _____ clause
    _____ de/ci′/sion
    _____ in er′/ror
    _____ of al′/ter/a′/tion
    _____ of as/so′/ci/a′/
tion
me/mo′/ri/al
me/mo′/ri/ter′
mem′/o/ri/za′/tion
mem′/o/rize′
    mem′/o/rized′
    mem′/o/riz′/ing
mem′/o/ry
men′/ace
men/da′/cious
men/dac′·/i/ty
men′/di/cant
me′/nial
men of straw
mens
    _____ le′/ges
    _____ leg′/is/la/to′/ris
    _____ re′a
men′/sa
    _____ et tho′/ro
men/sa′/li·a
men′/sis
men′/sor
men′/tal
    _____ a′/li·en/a′/tion
    _____ an′/guish
    _____ ca/pac′/i/ty
    _____ com′/pe/tence

men′/tal (contd.)

_____ cru′′/el/ty

_____ de′′/fect

_____ de/fi′′/cien/cy

_____ dis/ease′

_____ in′/ca/pac′′/i/ty

_____ in/com′′/pe/

ten/cy

_____ res′/er/va′′/tion

_____ suf′′/fer/ing

men/tal′′/i/ty

men′/te cap′′/tus

men′′/tion

men′′/tioned

men′′/tion/ing

men/ti′′/ri

·men′′/ti′/tion

men′′/tor′

mer′′/ca/ble

mer′′/can/tile′

_____ a′gen/cy

_____ law

_____ pa′′/per

_____ part′′/ner/ship′

mer′/can/til/ism′

mer′′/cat

mer′′/ca/tive

mer/ca′′/tum

mer′′/ca/ture

mer′′/ce/dar′y

mer′′/ce/nar′y

mer′′/chan/dise′

_____ bro′′/ker

mer′′/chan/dis′′/ing

mer′′/chant

_____ ap/prais′′/er

mer′′/chant (contd.)

_____ sea′′/man

mer′′/chant/a·bil′′/i/ty

mer′′/chant/a·ble

mer′′/chant/man

mer′′/cia/ment

mer′′/cy

_____ kill′′/ing

mere

_____ ev′/i/dence

_____ li′′/cens/ee′

_____ mo′′/tion

_____ right

_____ stone

mere′/ly

mer′′/e/tri′′/cious

merge

merged

merg′′/ing

merg′′/er

me/rid′′/i/an

mer′′/it

_____ sys′′/tem

mer′′/i/toc′′/ra/cy

mer′′/i/to′′/ri/ous

_____ cause of ac′′/tion

_____ con/sid′′/er/

a′tion

_____ de/fense′

me′′/ro mo′′/tu

merx

mese

mes/nal′′/ty or mes/nal′′/i/

ty

mesne

_____ as/sign′′/ment

mesne (contd.)
     —— en/cum′/brance
     —— pro′/cess
     —— prof′/its
mes′/sage
mes′/sen/ger
mes′/suage
mes/ti′/zo
me′/ta
met′/a/bol′/ic
me/tab′/o/lism′
me/ta′/chro/nism′
me′/ter
meth′/od
me/thod′/i/cal
me′/tre
met′/ric sys′/tem
met′/ri/ca′/tion
me/trop′/o/lis
met′/ro/pol′/i/tan
     —— coun′/cil
me′/tus
mid′/day
mid′/dle
     —— line of main
     chan′/nel
     —— of the riv′/er
     —— term
     —— thread
mid′/dle/man
mid′/night′
mid′/point′
mid′/ship′/man
mid′/town′
mid′/way′
mid′/week′

mid′/wife′
mid′/wife′/ry
mid′/year′
mien
mi′/grant
mi′/grate′
     mi′/grat′/ed
     mi′/grat′/ing
mi/gra′/tion
mi′/gra/to′/ry
     —— di/vorce′
mile
mile′/age
mile′/stone′
mi/lieu′
mil′/i/tan/cy
mil′/i/tant
mil′/i/tar′/i/ly
mil′/i/ta/rism′
mil′/i/tar′y
     —— ap/peals′
     —— com/mis′/sions
     —— forc′/es
     —— gov′/ern/ment
     —— ju′/ris/dic′/tion
     —— of′/fi/cer
     —— po/lice′
     —— sci′/ence
     —— ser′/vice
     —— ten′/ure
     —— tes′/ta/ment
mil′/i/tate′
     mil′/i/tat′/ed
     mil′/i/tat′/ing
mi/li′/tia
mi/li′/tia/man

mill
    ____ priv''/i/lege
milled mon''/ey
mill''/ing in tran''/sit
min''/a·ble
mi/na''/re
mind and mem''/o/ry
min''/er
min''/er/al
    ____ dis''/trict'
    ____ land en''/try
    ____ lease
    ____ lode
    ____ right
    ____ roy''/al/ty
    ____ ser''/vi/tude'
min''/i/mal
min''/i/mum
    ____ sen''/tence
    ____ wage
min''/ing
    ____ claim
    ____ com''/pa/ny
    ____ dis''/trict'
    ____ lease
    ____ lo/ca''/tion
    ____ part''/ner/ship'
min''/is/ter
min''/is/te''/ri/al
    ____ du''/ty
    ____ of''/fice
    ____ of''/fi/cer
    ____ pow''/er
min''/is/ters plen'i/po/ten''/
ti·a/ry
min''/is/try

mi''/nor
    ____ de'/vi/a''/tion
    ____ dis/pute'
    ____ of/fense'
mi/nor''/i/ty
    ____ lead''/er
    ____ o·pin''/ion
    ____ stock'/hold''/er
mint
mint''/age
mi''/nus
min''/ute
mi/rage'
mir''/ror
mis'/ad/ven''/ture
mis'/al/lege'
    mis'/al/leged'
    mis'/al/leg''/ing
mis'/a·ligned'
mis'/al/li''/ance
mis'/al'/lo/ca''/tion
mis'/ap/pli/ca''/tion
mis'/ap''/pre/hen''/sion
mis'/ap/pro''/pri/a''/tion
mis'/be/hav''/ior
mis'/brand'
    mis'/brand'/ed
    mis'/brand'/ing
mis'/cal'/cu/late'
    mis'/cal'/cu/lat'/ed
    mis'/cal'/cu/lat'/ing
mis'/cal'/cu/la''/tion
mis/car''/riage
    ____ of jus''/tice
mis/car''/ry
    mis/carried'

mis/car′/ry (contd.)
    mis/car′/ry/ing
mis′/ce′/ge/na′/tion
mis′/cel/la′/ne·a
mis′/cel/la′/ne·ous
mis′/cel/la′/ny
mis′/chance′
mis/charge′
    mis/charged′
    mis/charg′/ing
mis′/chief
mis′/clas′/si/fy′
    mis′/clas′/si/fied′
    mis′/clas′/si/fy′/ing
mis/cog′/ni/zant
mis/con′/duct
mis′/con/tin′/u/ance
mis′/cre/ant
mis/date′
    mis/dat′/ed
    mis/dat′/ing
mis′/de/liv′/er·y
mis′/de/mean′/ant
mis′/de/mean′/or
mis′/de/scrip′/tion
mis′/di/rec′/tion
mise
mi′/ser
mis′/er/a·ble
mi′/se/re′/re
mi/ser′i/cor′/di·a
mis/fea′/sance
mis′/for′/tune
mis′/gov′/ern
    mis′/gov′/erned
    mis′/gov′/ern/ing

mis′/hap
mis′/i·den′/ti/fy′
    mis′/i·den′/ti/fied′
    mis′/i·den′/ti/fy′/ing
mis′/in/form′
    mis′/in/formed′
    mis′/in/form′/ing
mis′/in/ter′/pret
    mis′/in/ter′/pret/ed
    mis′/in/ter′/pret/ing
mis′/in/ter′/pre/ta′/tion
mis′/join′/der
mis′/judge′
    mis/judged′
    mis/judg′/ing
mis/lead′
    mis/led′
    mis/lead′/ing
mis′/man′/age
    mis′/man′/aged
    mis′/man′/ag/ing
mis′/man′/age/ment
mis′/no′·/mer
mi/sog′/a/mist
mi′/sog′/y/nist
mi/sol′/o/gy
mis/plead′/ing
mis/pri′/sion
    —— of fel′/o/ny
    —— of trea′/son
mis′/read′
    mis′/read′
    mis′/read′/ing
mis′/re/cit′/al
mis′/re/mem′/ber
    mis′/re/mem′/bered

mis′′/re/mem′′/ber (contd.)
    mis′′/re/mem′′/ber/ing
mis′′/re/port′
    mis′′/re/port′′/ed
    mis′′/re/port′′/ing
mis′′/rep′/re/sen′/ta′/tion
mis/rule′
    mis/ruled′
    mis/rul′/ing
mis′′/sion
mis′′/sion/ar′y
mis′′/sive
mis′′/state′
    mis′′/stat′/ed
    mis′′/stat′/ing
mis′′/state′/ment
mis/take′
    mis/took′
    mis/tak′′/en
    mis/tak′′/ing
mis′′/ter
mis′′/treat′′/ment
mis′·/tress
mis′′/tri′′/al
mis/us′′/age
mis′/ven′′/ture
mit′′/i/gate′
    mit′′/i/gat′′/ed
    mit′′/i/gat′′/ing
mit′′/i/gat′′/ing cir′′/
cum/stanc′/es
mit′′/i/ga′′/tion
    ____ of pun′′/ish/ment
mit′′/i/ga′′/tor
mi′′/ti/or sen′′/sus
mit/ter′

mit′′/ti/mus
mixed
    ____ con′′/tract′
    ____ es/tate′
    ____ in/sur′′/ance
    com′′/pa/ny
    ____ lar′′/ce/ny
    ____ mar′′/riage
    ____ pol′′/i/cy
    ____ ques′′/tion of law
    and fact
    ____ sub′′/jects of
    prop′′/er/ty
mix′′/tion
mix′′/ture
mob
    mobbed
    mob′′/bing
mo′′/bile
mo/bi′′/li·a
mo′′/bil/ize′
    mo′′/bil/ized′
    mo′′/bil/iz′/ing
mock
    mocked
    mock′′/ing
mock′′/er·y
mo′′/dal leg′′/a/cy
mode
mod′′/el
mod′′/er·/ate *adj*
mod′′/er·/ate′ *v*
    mod′′/er/at′′/ed
    mod′·/er/at′′/ing
mod′′/er/a′′/tion
mod′′/er/a′′/tor

mod'/i/fi/ca'/tion
mod'/i/fi'/er
mod'/i/fy'
    mod'/i/fied'
    mod'/i/fy'/ing
mo'/do et for'/ma
mo'/dus
   —— ha'/bi/lis
   —— o'pe/ran'/di
   —— te/nen'/di
   —— va/can'/di
   —— vi/ven'/di
moe'/ble
moer'/da
moi'/e·ty
mo/lest'
    mo/lest'/ed
    mo/lest'/ing
mo'/les'/ta'/tion
mo/lest'/er
mol'/li/fy'
    mol'/li/fied'
    mol'/li/fy'/ing
mo'/ment
mo/men'/tous
mo/men'/tum
mon'/arch/y
mon'/e/tar'y
   —— be/quest'
mon'/ey
   —— chang'/er
   —— claims
   —— de/mand'
   —— had and re/ceived'
   —— judg'/ment

mon'/ey (contd.)
   —— mar'/ket
   —— or'/der
mon'/ey/lend'/er
mon'/ger
mon'/ies
mon'/i/ment
mo/ni'/tion
mon'/i/tor
mon'/i/to'/ry
mo/noc'/ra/cy
mo/nog'/a/mist
mo/nog'/a/my
mo/nog'/y/nous
mo/nog'/y/ny
mon'o/ma'/ni·a
mo/nop'/o/list
mo/nop'/o/lize'
    mo/nop'/o/lized'
    mo/nop'/o/liz'/ing
mo/nop'/o/ly
mon'/strous
month
mon'/u/ment
moon'/shine'
moor'/age
moor'/ing
moot
   —— court
   —— hall
   —— point
moot'/ing
mo'/ra
mor'/al
   —— ac'/tions
   —— cer'/tain/ty

mor'/al (contd.)

    ____ con/sid'/er/
a'tion

    ____ du/ress'

    ____ ev'/i/dence

    ____ fraud

    ____ haz'/ard

    ____ in/san'/i/ty

    ____ ob'/li/ga'/tion

    ____ tur'/pi/tude'

mo/rale'

mo/ral'/i/ty

mo/rass'

mor'/a/to'/ri/um

mor'/bid

more/o'ver

mo'/res'

mor'/ga/nat'/ic mar'/riage

morgue

mor'/i/bund

morn'/ing

mo'/ron

mor'/phine'

mors

mor'/tal

mor/tal'/i/ty

    ____ ta'/ble

mort'/gage *n, adj*

    ____ bank'/er

    ____ bro'/ker

    ____ cer/tif'/i/cate

    ____ com/mit'/ment

    ____ com'/pa/ny

    ____ fore/clo'/sure

    ____ in/sur'/ance

mort'/gage *v*

    mort'/gaged

    mort'/gag/ing

mort'/gag/ee'

mort'/gag/or'

mor/ti'/cian

mor'/ti/fi/ca'/tion

mor'/tis cau'/sa

mort'/main

mor'/tu/ar'y

    ____ ta'/bles

mor'/tu/um va'/di/um

mor/tu'/us

most fa'/vored na'/tion
clause

mote

moth'/er

moth'er-/in-/law'

mo'/tion

    ____ for new tri'/al

    ____ to ad/vance'

    ____ to sup/press'

mo'/tive

mo'/tor/cy'/cle

mo'/tor ve'/hi/cle

    ____ in/sur'/ance

mourn'/ing

mouth of riv'/er

mov'/a·ble

    ____ es/tate'

    ____ free'/hold'

mov'/ant

move

    moved

    mov'/ing

move'/ment

mov′/ent
mug′/shot′
mu/lat′/to
mulct
mu′/li/er puis/ne′
mul′/ta
mul′/ti/cul′/tur/al
mul′/ti/dis′/trict′ lit′/i/
ga′/tion
mul′/ti/far′/i/ous
mul′/ti/na′/tion/al
mul′/ti/par′/tite′
mul′/ti/par′/ty
mul′/ti/ple
    _____ ac′/cess
    _____ ev′/i/dence
    _____ list′/ing
mul′/ti/plic′/i/ty
mul′/ti/ra′/cial
mul′/ti/tude′
mul′/ti/tu′/di/nous
mum′/mi/fi/ca′/tion
mum′/my
mu/nic′/i/pal
    _____ ac′/tion
    _____ af/fairs′
    _____ au/thor′/i/ty
    _____ char′/ter
    _____ cor′/po/ra′/tion
    _____ courts
    _____ do′/mi/cile′
    _____ e·lec′/tion
    _____ func′/tion
    _____ gov′/ern/ment
    _____ law

mu/nic′/i/pal (contd.)
    _____ lien
    _____ of′/fi/cer
    _____ or′/di/nance
    _____ pur′/pos/es
    _____ se/cu′/ri/ties
    _____ tax/a′/tion
    _____ war′/rants
mu/nic′/i/pal′/i/ty
mu′/ni/ment
mu/ni′/tion
mur′/der *n*
    _____ of the first de/
    gree′
    _____ of the sec′/ond
    de/gree′
    _____ with mal′/ice
    a·fore′/thought′
mur′/der *v*
    mur′/dered
    mur′/der/ing
mur′/drum
mu/se′/um
mus′/ter
    mus′/tered
    mus′/ter/ing
mu/ta′/tion
    _____ of li′/bel
mu/ta′/tis mu/tan′/dis
mute
mu′/ti/la′/tion
mu′/ti/nous
mu′/ti/ny
mu′/tu/al
    _____ af/fray′

mu′/tu/al (contd.)
_____ a·gree′/ment
_____ ben′/e/fit
_____ cov′/e/nant
_____ fund
_____ in/sur′/ance
_____ in′/ter/est con′/tract′
_____ mis/take′
_____ re/lief′ as/so′/ci/a′/tion
_____ re/serve′ com′/pa/ny
_____ tes′/ta/ment
mu′/tu/al′/i/ty
_____ of ob′/li/ga′/tion
_____ of rem′/e/dy
mu′/tu/ar′y
mu′/tu/um

N

nag
nagged
nag′/ging
na/ïve′ *or* na/ïfe′
na/ïve/té′
na′/ked
name
named
nam′/ing
name′/ly
nar/cot′/ic

nar′/rate′
nar′/rat′/ed
nar′/rat′/ing
nar/ra′/tion
nar′/ra/tive
nar′/ra′/tor
nar′/row
na′/tal
na′/tion
na′/tion/al
_____ cur′/ren/cy
_____ de/fense′
_____ e·mer′/gen/cy
_____ gov′/ern/ment
_____ mon′/u/ment
_____ or′/i/gin
na′/tion/al/ism′
na′/tion/al′/i/ty
na′/tion/al/ize′
na′/tion/al/ized′
na′/tion/al/iz′/ing
na′/tive
nat′/u/ral
_____ af/fec′/tion
_____ do′/mi/cile′
_____ eq′/ui/ty
_____ guard′/i·an
_____ mon′/u/ment
_____ pos/ses′/sion
_____ pre′/mi/um
_____ right
_____ suc/ces′/sion
nat′/u/ral/i·za′/tion
nat′/u/ral/ize′
nat′/u/ral/ized′

na′/tu/ral/ize′ (contd.)
    nat′/u/ral/iz′/ing
na′/tus
nau′/lage′
nau′/ti/cal
    _____ as/ses′/sors
    _____ mile
nau′/ti/ca pe/cu′/nia
na′/val
    _____ courts
    _____ of′/fi/cer
nav′/i/ga/ble
    _____ riv′/er
    _____ wa′/ters
nav′/i/gate′
    nav′/i/gat′/ed
    nav′/i/gat′/ing
nav′/i/ga′/tion
nav′/i/ga′/tion/al vis′/i/
bil′/i/ty
nav′/i/ga′/tor
na′/vy
    _____ de/part′/ment
neap tide
near mon′/ey
ne/ca′/tion
nec′/es/sar·ies
nec′/es/sar′/i/ly
nec′/es/sar′y
    _____ con/di′/tion
    _____ dam′/ag/es
    _____ dil′/i/gence
    _____ in′/fer/ence
ne/ces′/si/tous
ne/ces′/si/ty
nec′/ro/phil′/i·a

need′/ful
need′/less
need′y
ne ex′/e/at
    _____ reg′/no
    _____ re/pub′/li/ca
neg′/a/tive
    _____ a·ver′/ment
    _____ con/di′/tion
    _____ cov′/e/nant
    _____ ease′/ment
    _____ ev′/i/dence
    _____ mis/pri′/sion
    _____ preg′/nant
    _____ re/pri′/sal
ne/glect′
    ne/glect′/ed
    ne/glect′/ing
ne/glect′/ful
neg′/li/gence
neg′/li/gent
    _____ es/cape′
    _____ ho′/mi/cide′
    _____ of/fense′
    _____ man′/slaugh′/ter
    _____ mis/rep′/re/sen′/
ta′/tion
neg′/li/gen′/ti·a
neg′/li/gent/ly
neg′/li/gi/ble
ne/go′/tia/ble
    _____ doc′/u/ment
    _____ in′/stru/ment
ne/go′/ti/ate′
    ne/go′/ti/at′/ed
    ne/go′/ti/at′/ing

ne/go'/ti/a'/tion
neigh'/bor
neigh'/bor/hood'
nei'/ther par'/ty
ne'/mo
neph'/ew
nep'/o/tism'
ner'/vous/ness
ne'/science
net

   ____ as'/sets
   ____ bal'/ance
   ____ earn'/ings
   ____ es/tate'
   ____ in'/come
   ____ in'/ter/est
   ____ lev'/el an'/nu/al
   pre'/mi/um
   ____ op'/er/at'/ing
   loss
   ____ pre'/mi/um
   ____ price
   ____ pro'/ceeds
   ____ prof'/its
   ____ re/turn'
   ____ rev'/e/nues
   ____ sin'/gle pre'/
   mi/um
   ____ val'/ue
   ____ yield
ne un'/ques ac/cou'/ple
neu'/tral
neu/tral'/i/ty
   ____ proc'/la/ma'/tion
new
   ____ ac'/qui/si'/tion

new (contd.)
   ____ as'/sets
   ____ as/sign'/ment
   ____ cause of ac'/tion
   ____ mat'/ter
   ____ prom'/ise
   ____ tri'/al
new'/ly dis/cov'/ered ev'/
i/dence
news'/pa'/per
next
   ____ de/vi/see'
   ____ e·ven'/tu/al es/
   tate'
   ____ friend
   ____ of kin
   ____ pre'/sen/ta'/tion
nick'/name'
niece
ni/ent'
night mag'/is/trate'
night'/time'
ni'/hil
   ____ ca'/pi/at per
   bre'/ve
   ____ di'/cit
   ____ ha'/bet
   ____ ob'/stat'
ni'/hil'/ist
nil
   ____ de'/bet
nim'/mer
nine'/teenth'
ninth
ni'/si'
   ____ pri'/us

no/bil'/i/ty
no'/ble
no'/cent
noc/tur'/nal
no'/dus
no'-/fault'
     —— au'/to in/sur'/
ance
     —— di/vorce'
noise
no'/lens vo'/lens
nol'/le pro'/se/qui'
no'/lo con/ten'/de/re
no'/men
     —— col'/lec/ti'/vum
     —— gen'/er/al/is'/si/
mun
     —— ju'/ris
no'/men/cla'/ture
nom'/i/nal
     —— ac/count'
     —— cap'/i/tal
     —— con/sid'/er/a'
tion
     —— dam'/ag/es
     —— de/fen'/dant
     —— part'/ner
     —— par'/ty
     —— plain'/tiff
nom'/i/nate'
    nom'/i/nat'/ed
    nom'/i/nat'/ing
nom'/i/na'/tion
nom'/i/nee'
non
     —— as/sump'/sit

non (contd.)
     —— ce'/pit
     —— com'/pos men'/
tis
     —— con'/stat
     —— cul'/pa'/bi/lis
     —— dam'/ni/fi/ca'/
tus
     —— est fac'/tum
     —— in/ter'/fui'
     —— ob/stan'/te
ve/re/dic'/to
     —— pla'/cet
     —— pos'/su/mus
     —— pros
     —— pro/se'/qui/tur
     —— se'/qui/tur
non'/a·bil'/i/ty
non'/ac/cep'/tance
non/ac'/cess
non'/ad/mis'/sion
non'/age
non'/an/ces'/tral es/tate'
non'/ap/par'/ent ease'/
ment
non'/ap/pear'/ance
non'/as/sess'/a·ble
non/bail'/a·ble
non/can'/cel/a·ble
non/can'/di/date'
non'/claim'
non'/com/ba'/tant
non'/com/mis'·/sioned
of'/fi/cer
non'/com/pet'/i/tive
non'/con/for'/mance

non'/con/form'/ing use
non'/con/form'/ist
non'/con/test'/a·ble
non'/con/tin'/u/ous
ease'/ment
non'/cred'/it
non/cu'/mu/la'/tive div'/
i/dends
non'/de/duct'/i·ble
non'/de/liv'/e·ry
non'/de/script'
non'/de/tach'/a·ble fa/cil'/
i/ties
non'/di/rec'/tion
non'/dis/clo'/sure
none'/the/less'
non/fea'/sance
non/for'/feit/a·ble
non/func'/tion/al
non'/gov'/ern/men'/tal
non/in'/ter/course'
non/in'/ter/ven'/tion will
non'/in/volve'/ment
non/is'/su/a·ble pleas
non/join'/der
non/ju'/ror
non/lev'/i/a·ble
non/lit'/er/ate
non/mail'/a·ble
non/match'/ing
non/med'/i/cal pol'/i/cy
non/mer'/chant/a·ble
ti'/tle
non/mor'/al
non/nav'/i/ga/ble
non'/ne/go'/tia/ble

non/oc'/cu/pa'/tion/al
non/op'/er/at'/ing
in'/come
non/par'/ti/san
non/pay'/ment
non'/per/for'/mance
non'/prof'/it
non'/re'/course'
non'/re/fund'/a·ble
non/res'/i/dence
non/res'/i/dent
non/sane'
_____ mem'/o/ry
non'/sense'
non'/sig/nif'/i/cant
non'/suit'
non'/sup/port'
non'/u'nion
non'/us'/er
non'/vi'/o/lence
non'/waiv'/er a·gree'/ment
nor'/mal
nor'/mal/ly
north
north'/ern
nos'/trum
no'/ta
_____ be'/ne
no/tar'/i/al
no'/ta/ri/za'/tion
no'/ta/rize'
no'/ta/rized'
no'/ta/riz'/ing
no'/ta/ry pub'/lic
no/ta'/tion
_____ vot'/ing

note
 not'/ed
 not'/ing
notes
 ____ pay'/a·ble
 ____ re/ceiv'/a·ble
note'/wor'/thy
not ex/ceed'/ing
not guilt'y
no'/tice
 ____ in lieu of ser'/
 vice
 ____ of ap/peal'
 ____ of ap/pear'/ance
 ____ of judg'/ment
 ____ of lis pen'/dens'
 ____ of mo'/tion
 ____ of pro'/test'
 ____ of tri'/al
 ____ to ad/mit'
 ____ to cred'/i/tors
 ____ to pro/duce'
 ____ to quit
no'/ti/fi/ca'/tion
no'/ti/fy'
 no'/ti/fied'
 no'/ti/fy'/ing
no'/to/ri'/e·ty
no/to'/ri/ous
 ____ co'/hab'/i/ta'/
 tion
 ____ in/sol'/ven/cy
 ____ pos/ses'/sion
not sat'/is/fied
not trans/fer'/able

not'/with/stand'/ing
no'/va
 ____ cus'/tu/ma
no/va'/tion
nov'/el
 ____ as/sign'/ment
 ____ dis/sei'/sin
nov'/el/ty
no'/vus ho'/mo
no'/where'
nox'/ious
nu'/da
 ____ pa'/ti/en'/ti·a
 ____ pos/ses'/si·o
nude
 ____ con'/tract'
 ____ mat'/ter
 ____ pact
nu'/dum pac'/tum
nu'/ga/to'/ry
nui'/sance
 ____ per ac'/ci/dens'
nul
 ____ dis/sei'/sin
 ____ ti'/el rec'/ord
null
nul'/la bo'/na
nul'/li/fi/ca'/tion
nul'/lip'/a/rous
nul'/li/ty
 ____ of mar'/riage
nul'/li/us fi'/li/us
num'/bers game
nu'/mer/al
nu/mer'/i/cal

nu′/mis/mat′′/ics
nun′′/ci·o
nun′′/cu/pa′′/tive will
nup′′/tial
nur′′/ture
    nur′′/tured
    nur′′/tur/ing
nyc/them′′/er/on
nym′′/pho/ma′′/ni·a

O

oath
    ____ ex of/fi′′/ci·o
    ____ in li′′/tem
    ____ of al/le′′/giance
    ____ of cal′′/um/ny
ob con′′/tin/gen′′/ti/am
o·be′′/di/ence
o·be′/di/en′′/tial ob′′/li/ga′′/
tion
o′bit
    ____ si′′/ne pro′′/le
o′bi/ter dic′′/tum
ob/ject′ *v*
    ob/ject′′/ed
    ob/ject′′/ing
ob′′/ject *n*
    ____ of an ac′′/tion
    ____ of a stat′′/ute
ob/jec′′/tion
ob/jec′′/tive
ob/la′′/ti·o

ob/la′′/tion
ob′′/li/gate′
    ob′′/li/gat′′/ed
    ob′′/li/gat′′/ing
ob′′/li/ga′′/ti·o
ob′′/li/ga′′/tion
o·blig′′/a/to′′/ry
    ____ cov′′/e/nant
    ____ pact
    ____ writ′′/ing
ob′′/li/gee′
ob′′/li/gor′
o·blit′′/er/ate′
    o·blit′′/er/at′′/ed
    o·blit′′/er/at′′/ing
o·blit′′/er/a′′/tion
o·bliv′′/i/on
o·bliv′′/i/ous
ob′′/lo/quy
ob/nox′′/ious
ob/scene′
    ____ li′′/bel
ob/scen′′/i/ty
ob/scure′
ob/scu′′/ri/ty
ob/se′′/qui/ous
ob/ser/va′′/tion
ob/serve′
    ob/served′
    ob/serv′′/ing
ob/sig′′/na/to′′/ry
ob′′/so/les′′/cence
ob′′/so/les′′/cent
ob′′/so/lete′
ob/stan′′/te

ob'/sta prin'/ci'/pi/is
ob/stet'/rics
ob'/sti/nate de/ser'/tion
ob/strep'/er/ous
ob/stric'/tion
ob/struct'
 ob/struct'/ed
 ob/struct'/ing
ob/struct'/ing
 _____ an of'/fi/cer
 _____ jus'/tice
 _____ pro/ceed'/ings
 _____ pro'/cess
ob/struc'/tion
 _____ of jus'/tice
 _____ to nav'/i/ga'/tion
ob/tain'
 ob/tained'
 ob/tain'/ing
ob/test'
 ob/test'/ed
 ob/test'/ing
ob/tund'
 ob/tund'/ed
 ob/tund'/ing
ob/ven'/tion
ob'/vi/ous
 _____ dan'/ger
oc/ca'/sion
oc/ca'/sion/al/ly
oc/clude'
 oc/clud'/ed
 oc/clud'/ing
oc'/cu/pan/cy
oc'/cu/pant
oc'/cu/pa'/tion

oc'/cu/pa'/tion/al
 _____ dis/ease'
 _____ haz'/ard
 _____ safe'/ty
oc'/cu/pa'/tive
oc'/cu/pi'/er
oc'/cu/py'
 oc'/cu/pied'
 oc'/cu/py'/ing
oc'/cu/py'/ing claim'/ant
oc/cur'
 oc/curred'
 oc/cur'/ring
oc/cur'/rence
oc/cur'/rent
o'cean
och/loc'/ra/cy
oc'/u/list
odd lot
o'di/ous
o'di/um
oeu/vre
of coun'/sel
of/fend'/er
of/fense'
of/fen'/sive
 _____ lan'/guage
 _____ weap'/on
of'/fer *v*
 of'/fered
 of'/fer/ing
of'/fer *n*
 _____ of com'/pro/mise'
of'/fice
 _____ and ac/cep'/
 tance

of′/fice/hold′/er
of′/fi/cer
—— de fac′/to
—— de ju′/re
—— of jus′/tice
of/fi′/cial
—— fam′/i/ly
—— im/mu′/ni/ty
—— mis/con′/duct
of/fi′/cial/ism′
of/fi′/ci·al/i/ty
of/fi′/cious will
of force
off′/set′
    off′/set′
    off′/set′/ting
off′/spring′
of grace
of rec′/ord
of the blood
ol′i/gar′/chy
ol′i/gop′/o/ly
ol′/o/graph
ol′/o/graph′/ic tes′/
ta/ment
om′/buds′/man
o·mis′/sion
o·mit′
    o·mit′/ted
    o·mit′/ting
o·mit′/tance
om′/ni/bus
—— hear′/ing
om′/ni/um
on ac/count′
on de/fault′

on de/mand′
o′ner/ous
—— cause
—— con′/tract′
—— deed
—— ti′/tle
one′-/sid′ed
on or a·bout′
on or be/fore′
on′/set date
on the per′/son
on′/to′
o′nus
—— pro/ban′/di
on′/ward
o′pen
—— ac/count′
—— a com/mis′/sion
—— a judg′/ment
—— a high′/way
—— cred′/it
—— en′/try
—— let′/ter of cred′/
it
—— list′/ing
—— or′/der
—— pol′·/i/cy
—— sea′/son
—— the plead′/ings
o′pen-/end′
—— a·gree′/ment
—— con′/tract′
—— mort′/gage
—— trans/ac′/tion
o′pen/ing stat′ement
op′/er·a

op′/er/ate′
    op′/er/at′/ed
    op′/er/at′/ing
op′/er/at′/ing
    —— in′/come
    —— mar′/gin
    —— prof′/it
    —— sur′/plus
op′/er/a′′/tion
op′/er/a/tive
op′/er/a′/tor
o′pi/ate
o·pin′/ion
    —— ev′/i/dence
o′pi/um
op′/por/tun′/ism
op/pose′
    op/posed′
    op/pos′/ing
op′/po/site
    —— par′/ty
op′/po/si′/tion
op/press′
    op/pressed′
    op/press′/ing
op/pres′/sion
op/pres′/sor
op/pro′/bri/um
op/pugn′
    op/pugned′
    op/pugn′/ing
op′/ti/cal
op′/ti/mal
op′/ti/mum
op′/tion
op′/tion/al writ

op′/tion/or
op/tom′/e/tris
o′/pus
    —— lo/ca′/tum
o′ral
    —— ar′/gu/ment
    —— con/fes′/sion
    —— con′/tract′
    —— de′/po/si′/tion
    —— ev′/i/dence
    —— plead′/ing
or′/a/tor
or′/a/trix
or/ba′/tion
or/dain′
    or/dained′
    or/dain′/ing
or/deal′
or′/der
    —— ni′/si
    —— of dis/charge′
    —— of fil/i/a′/tion
    —— ju′/ris/dic′/tion
    —— of re/viv′/or
    —— to show cause
or′/der/ly
or′/ders
    —— of the day
or′/di/nance
or′/di/nar′y
    —— course of bus′/i/ness
    —— cred′/i/tor
    —— dil′./i/gence
    —— in′/come
    —— neg′/li/gence

or′/di/nar′y (contd.)
    ____ pro/ceed′/ing
    ____ re/pairs′
or′/di/na′/tion
ore′-/leave′
or/gan′/ic
or′/ga/ni/za′/tion
or′/ga/nize′
    or′/ga/nized′
    or′/ga/niz′/ing
o·rig′/i/nal
    ____ con′/trac′/tor
    ____ con/vey′/ance
    ____ doc′/u/ment
    ____ en′/try
    ____ ev′/i/dence
    ____ in/ven′/tor
    ____ is′/sue
    ____ ju′/ris/dic′/tion
    ____ plat
    ____ prom′/ise
    ____ writ
or′/phan
or′/phan/age
    ____ part
or′/phan′s court
os/ten′/si/ble
    ____ a′genc/cy
    ____ au/thor′/i/ty
    ____ part′′/ner
oth′/er/wise′
ought
oust
    oust′/ed
    oust′/ing
oust′/er

out′/age
out′/build′/ing
out′/cast′
out′/come′
out′/er
out′/fit′
out′/go′
out′/house′
out′/law′
out′/lawed′
out′/law′/ry
out′/lay′
out′/let′
out′/line′
out′/look′
out′/lot′
out′-/of-/court′ set′/
tle/ment
out′-/of-/pock′et loss
out′/part/ners
out′/put′
out′/rage′
out/ra′/geous
out′/rid′/er
out′/right′
out/side′
out/stand′/ing
    ____ and o′pen ac/
   count′
o′ver/bid′
    o′ver/bid′
    o′ver/bid′/ding
o′ver/buy′
    o′ver/bought′
    o′ver/buy′/ing

o′ver/charge′
   o′ver/charged′
   o′ver/charg′/ing
o′ver/come′
   o′ver/came′
   o′ver/com′/ing
o′ver/com′/pen/sa′/tion
o′ver/dose′
o′ver/draft′
o′ver/draw′
   o′ver/drew′
   o′ver/drawn′
   o′ver/draw′/ing
o′ver/due′
o′ver/haul′
   o′ver/hauled′
   o′ver/haul′/ing
o′ver/head′
o′ver/in/sur′/ance
o′ver/load′
   o′ver/load′/ed
   o′ver/load′/ing
o′ver/ly′/ing right
o′ver/rate′
   o′ver/rat′/ed
   o′ver/rat′/ing
o′ver/reach′/ing clause
o′ver/r̆ide′
   o′ver/rode′
   o′ver./rid′/den
   o′ver/rid′/ing
o′ver/rid′./ing roy′/al/ty
o′ver./rule′
   o′ver/ruled′
   o′ver/rul′/ing

o′vers
o′ver/state′/ment
o′ver/sub/scrip′/tion
o′vert′
   —— act
   —— word
o′ver/take′
   o′ver/took′
   o′ver/tak′/en
   o′ver/tak′/ing
o′ver/time′
o′ver/ture′
owe
   owed
   ow′/ing
ow′/el/ty
   —— of ex/change′
   —— of par/ti′/tion
   —— of ser′/vic/es
own
   owned
   own′/ing
own′/er
own′/er/ship′
oy′/er
   —— and ter′/mi/ner
oy′/ez

P

pa/ca′/re
pace
pa/cif′/ic

pac′/i/fi/ca′/tion
pac′/i/fist
pac′/i/fy′
 pac′/i/fied′
 pac′/i/fy′/ing
pack
 packed
 pack′/ing
pack′/age
 ____ mort′/gage
pack′/er
pact
 ____ de non a·li/en/
 an′/do
pac′/tion
pac′/tion/al
pac′/tum
 ____ com′/mis/so′/
 ri/um
pad′/der
pad′/dock
pain and suf′/fer/ing
pais *or* pays
pal′/ace
pa/la′/gi/um
pal′/i/mo′/ny
palm off
pal′/pa/ble
pam′/phlet
pan′/der
 pan′/dered
 pan′/der/ing
pan′/der/er
pan′/el
pan′/nel/la′/tion

pa′/per
 ____ block/ade′
 ____ hang′/ings
 ____ mon′/ey
 ____ pat′/ent
 ____ stan′/dard
par val′/ue
par′/age
par′a/graph
par/a′/gi/um
par′a/le′/gal
par′/al/lel′
pa/ral′/y/sis
pa/ram′/e/ter
par′/a/mount
 ____ eq′/ui/ty
 ____ ti′/tle
par′a/noi′a
par/a/pher/na′/li·a
par′a/pro/fes′/sion/al
pa/ra′/tum ha′/beo
par′/cel
par′/ce/nar′y
par′/ce/ner
parch′/ment
par de/lic′/tum
par′/don
 par′/doned
 par′/don/ing
par′/don/a·ble
par′/don/er
pa′/rens
 ____ pa′/tri/ae
par′/ent
pa/ren′/tal li′/a/bil′/i/ty

par′/ent/age
par′/en/te′/la
par′/en/thet′/i/cal
par′/ent/hood′
pa/ren′′/ti/cide′
pa′′/res
pa′′/ri
_____ cau′′/sa
_____ de/lic′′/to
_____ ma/te′′/ri·a
_____ mu′′/tu/el
_____ pas′′/su
par′/ish
pa/rish′′/io/ner
par′/i/ty
pa′′/ri/um ju/di′′/ci·um
park′/ing
park′/way′
par′/lia/ment
par′/lia/men′′/tar′/i/an
par′/lia/men′′/ta/ry
_____ a′gent
_____ com/mit′′/tee
_____ gov′′/ern/ment
_____ law
pa/ro′′/chi/al
par′/ol
_____ a·gree′′/ment
_____ con′′/tract′
_____ de/mur′′/rer
_____ ev′/i/dence
_____ prom′′/ise
pa/role′
_____ of′′/fi/cer
par′/ri/cide′

pars
_____ gra/va′′/ta
_____ re′′/a
par′/son
par′/son/age
par′/te in′′/au′′/di/ta
par′/tial
_____ ac/count′
_____ av′/er/age
_____ de/fense′
_____ de/pen′′/den/cy
_____ dis′/a·bil′′/i/ty
_____ e·vic′′/tion
_____ in/san′′/i/ty
_____ loss
_____ par′′/don
_____ pay′′/ment
_____ re/lease′
_____ ver′/dict′
par′/ti/ble
par/tic′/i/pate′
par/tic′/i/pat′′/ed
par/tic′/i/pat′′/ing
par/tic′/i/pa′′/tion
_____ mort′′/gage
par/tic′/i/pa/to′′/ry
par′/ti/cle
par/tic′′/u/lar
_____ mal′′/ice
par/tic′/u/lar′′/i/ty
par/tic′′/u/lars
_____ of crim′/i/nal
charg′/es
par′/ties
_____ and priv′/ies

par′/ties (contd.)
     _____ in in′/ter/est
par/ti′/tion
     _____ of a suc/ces′/sion
part′/ner
part′/ner/ship′
     _____ as′/sets
     _____ at will
     _____ debt
     _____ in com′/men/
     dam
par′/tu/ri′/tion
par′/ty
     _____ ag/grieved′
     _____ in′/jured
     _____ ju′/ry
     _____ struc′/ture
     _____ to be charged
     _____ wall
pa′/rum
pass
     passed
     pass′/ing
pas′/sage
pass′/book
pas′·/sen/ger
pas′·/sim
pas′·/sion
pas′·/sive
pass′·/port′
past
pas′/ture
pat′/ent
     _____ am′/bi/gu′/i·ty
     _____ ap/peals′

pat′/ent (contd.)
     _____ de′/fect′
     _____ of′/fice
     _____ pool′/ing
     _____ right deal′/er
     _____ rolls
     _____ suit
pat′/ent/a·ble
pat′/en/tee′
pat′/en/tor
pa′/ter
     pa′/tri/ae
pa′/ter/fa/mil′′/i/as
pa/ter′′/nal
     _____ line of de/scent′
     _____ pow′′/er
     _____ prop′′/er/ty
pa/ter′′/ni/ty
     _____ suit
pa/thol′′/o/gist
pa/thol′′/o/gy
pa′/ti/ens
pa′/tience
pa′/tient
pa′/tri·a
pa′/tri/arch′
pa′/tri/arch′′/y
pat′·/ri/cide′
pat′/ri/lin′′/e·al
pat′·/ri/mo′/ny
pa/trol′
     pa/trolled′
     pa/trol′′/ling
pa/trol′′/man
pa′/tron

pa'/tron/age
pa'/tron/ess
pa'/tron/ize'
    pa'/tron/ized'
    pa'/tron/iz'/ing
pat'/tern
pau'/per
pawn
    pawned
    pawn'/ing
pawn'/bro'/ker
pax re'/gis
pay
    paid
    pay'/ing
pay'/a·ble
    —— af'/ter sight
    —— on de/mand'
    —— to bear'/er
pay/ee'
pay'/er
pay'/ment
    —— guar'/an/teed'
    —— in'/to' court
pay'/off
pay/o'la
pay'/or
pay'/roll'
peace
peace'/a·ble
    —— pick'/et/ing
pec'/u/late'
    pec'/u/lat'/ed
    pec'/u/lat'/ing
pec'/u/la'/tion

pe/cu'/liar
pe/cu'/li·ar'/i/ty
pe/cu'/ni·a
pe/cu'/ni/ar'y
    —— ben'/e/fits
    —— be/quest'
    —— cause
    —— con/di'/tion
    —— dam'/ag/es
    —— for'/mu/la
    —— in'/ju/ry
    —— in'/ter/est
    —— leg'/a/cy
pedd'/ler
ped'/er/as'/ty
pe/des'/tri/an
ped'/i/gree'
pe'/dis pos/ses'/si·o
peer'/age
peer'/ess
peers
pe'/nal
    —— ac'/tion
    —— bond
    —— clause
    —— code
    —— in'/sti/tu'/tion
    —— ob'/li/ga'/tion
    —— ser'/vi/tude'
    —— stat'/ute
    —— sum
pen'/al/ty
pen'/ance
pen'/den/cy
pen'/dens

pen**'**/dent
    ____ ju**'**/ris/dic**'**/tion
pen/den**'**/te li**'**/te
pend**'**/ing
pen**'**/e/trate**'**
    pen**'**/e/trat**'**/ed
    pen**'**/e/trat**'**/ing
pen**'**/e/tra**'**/tion
pen**'**/i/ten**'**/tia/ry
pe/nol**'**/o/gy
pen**'**/sion
pen**'**/sion/er
pe/nu**'**/ri/ous
pen**'**/u/ry
pe**'**/on/age
peo**'**/ple
per
    ____ an**'**/num
    ____ au**'**/tre vie
    ____ cap**'**/i/ta
    ____ cen**'**/tum
    ____ con**'**/se/quens
    ____ con**'**/tra
    ____ di**'**/em
    ____ for**'**/mam do**'**/ni
    ____ frau**'**/dem
    ____ in/cu**'**/ri/am
    ____ in/dus**'**/tri/um
    ____ in/for/tu**'**/ni/um
    ____ mi**'**/nas
    ____ mis**'**/ad/ven**'**/ture
    ____ pro**'**/cu/ra**'**/tion
    ____ quod
    ____ se
    ____ stir**'**/pes

per (contd.)
    ____ to**'**/tam cu**'**/ri/
    am
per/am**'**/bu/late**'**
    per/am**'**/bu/lat**'**/ed
    per/am**'**/bu/lat**'**/ing
per/am**'**/bu/la**'**/tion
per/ceiv**'**/a·ble risk
percent**'**
per/cent**'**/age
perch
per**'**/co/late**'**
    per**'**/co/lat**'**/ed
    per**'**/co/lat**'**/ing
per**'**/di**'**/da
per/du**'**/ra/bil**'**/i/ty
per/du**'**/ra/ble
per/emp**'**/tion
per/emp**'**/to/ry
    ____ chal**'**/lenge
    ____ de/fense**'**
    ____ ex/cep**'**/tion
    ____ in/struc**'**/tion
    ____ pa**'**/per
    ____ un**'**/der/tak**'**/ing
per**'**/fect
    ____ at**'**/tes/ta**'**/tion
    clause
    ____ eq**'**/ui/ty
per**'**/fi/dy
per/form**'**
    per/formed**'**
    per/form**'**/ing
per/for**'**/mance
per/form**'**/er

pe/ri′/cu/lum
per′/il
pe′/ri/od
pe′/ri/od′/ic ten′/an/cy
pe′/ri/od′/i/cal
pe/riph′/ert
pe/riph′/ra/sis
per′/ish
per′/ish/a·ble
_____ com/mod′/i/ty
_____ goods
per′/jure
   per′/jured
   per′/jur/ing
per′/jur/er
per/ju′/ri/ous
per′/ju/ry
perk
per′/ma/nent
_____ a·bode′
_____ dis′/a·bil′/i/ty
_____ em/ploy′/ment
_____ in/junc′/tion
_____ nui′/sance
per/mis′/sion
per/mis′/sive
_____ join′/der
_____ waste
per/mit′
   per/mit′/ted
   per/mit′/ting
per′/mu/ta′/tion
per′/nan/cy
per/ni′/cious

per′/pe/trate′
   per′/pe/trat′/ed
   per′/pe/trat′/ing
per′/pe/tra′/tor
per/pet′/u/al
_____ in/junc′/tion
_____ stat′/ute
per/pet′/u/at/ing tes′/ti/
mo′/ny
per′/pe/tu′/i·ty
per/plexed′
per′/qui/site
per′/son
per/so′/na
_____ gra′/ta
_____ non gra′/ta
per′/son/a·ble
per′/son/al
_____ con′/tract′
_____ cred′/it
_____ de/fense′
_____ ef/fects′
_____ judg′/ment
_____ li′/a/bil′/i/ty
_____ lib′/er/ty
_____ ob′/li/ga′/tion
per′/son/al/ly
per′/son/ate′
   per′/son/at′/ed
   per′/son/at′/ing
per/suade′
   per/suad′/ed
   per/suad′/ing
per/sua′/sion

per/tain′
    per/tained′
    per/tain′/ing
per′/ti/nent
per/turb′
    per/turbed′
    per/turb′/ing
per′/tur/ba′/tion
per/verse′
pet′/it
    _____ ju′/ry
    _____ lar′/ce/ny
pe/tite′ as/size′
pe/ti′/ti·o prin/ci′/pi·i
pe/ti′/tion
    _____ in bank′/rupt/cy
pe/ti′/tion/er
pe/ti′/tion/ing cred′/i/tor
pet′/i/to′/ry ac′/tion
pet′/ti/fog′
    pet′/ti/fogged′
    pet′/ti/fog′/ging
pet′/ti/fog′/ger
pet′/ty
    _____ ju′/ry
    _____ lar′/ce/ny
    _____ of/fense′
    _____ of′/fi/cers
phar′/ma/cy
pho′/to/graph′
pho′/to/graph′/ic
pho/tog′/ra/phy
phy′/la/sist

phys′/i/cal
    _____ cru′/el/ty
    _____ de/pre′/ci/a′/
tion
    _____ dis′/a·bil′/i/ty
    _____ im/pos′/si/bil′/i/
ty
    _____ in′/ju/ry
    _____ ne/ces′/si/ty
phy/si′/cian
pick′/et
    pick′/et/ed
    pick′/et/ing
pick′/pock′/et
piece′/work′
pie/pou′/dre
pier
pierce
    pierced
    pierc′/ing
pig′/nus
pil′/fer
    pil′/fered
    pil′/fer/ing
pil′/fer/age
pil′/fer/er
pil′/lage
    pil′/laged
    pil′/lag/ing
pil′/lo/ry
pimp
pin′/point′
    pin′/point′/ed
    pin′/point′/ing

pi'/o/neer' pat'/ent
pi'/ous
pi'/ra/cy
pi'/rate
pis'/ca/ry
pis'/tol
plac'/ard
pla'/cate'
    pla'/cat'/ed
    pla'/cat'/ing
place
    ____ of bus'/i/ness
    ____ of con'/tract'
    ____ of de/liv'/er·y
    ____ of em/ploy'/ment
plac'/er
    ____ lo/ca'/tion
pla'/cit
pla'/ci/ta ju'/ris
pla'/ci/ta'/re
pla'/ci/tum
pla'/gia/rism'
pla'/gia/rize'
    pla'/gia/rized'
    pla'/gia/riz'/ing
pla'/gia/ry'
plague
plaint
plain'/tiff
    ____ in er'/ror
plan
    planned
    plan'/ning
plan/ta'/tion

plat
    plat'/ted
    plat'/ting
plat'/form'
plau'/si/bil'/i/ty
plau'/si/ble
plea
    ____ a·gree'/ment
    ____ bar'/gain
    ____ in a·bate'/ment
    ____ in bar
    ____ in dis/charge'
    ____ of guilt'y
    ____ of no'/lo con/ten'/de/re
    ____ of priv'/i/lege
    ____ of re/lease'
plead *v*
    plead'/ed
    plead'/ing
plead *n*
    ____ is'/su/a·bly
    ____ o'ver
plead'/er
ple/be'/i·an
pleb'/i/scite'
pledge
    pledged
    pledg'/ing
pledg/ee'
pled'/gor
ple'/nar·y
    ____ ac'/tion
    ____ con/fes'/sion

ple′/nar·y (contd.)
    ____ ju′/ris/dic′/tion
    ____ ses′/sion
ple′/ne
    ____ com′/pu/ta′/vit
plen′i/po/ten′/tia/ry
ple′/num
ple′/vin
pli′/a·ble
plight
plot
plot′/tage
plow
    plowed
    plow′/ing
plun′/der
    plun′/dered
    plun′/der/ing
plun′/der/age
plu′/ral
    ____ mar′/riage
plu′/ral/ism′
plu/ral′/i/ty
plu′/ries sum′/mons
poach
    poached
    poach′/ing
pock′/et
    ____ sher′/iff
    ____ ve′/to
point
    ____ re/served′
    ____ sys′/tem
point′/ed

poi′/son
poi′/son/ous
po′/lar star rule
po/lice′
    ____ ju′/ry
    ____ mag′/is/trate′
    ____ of′/fi/cer
    ____ pow′/er
    ____ reg′/u/la′/tions
    ____ su′/per/vi′/sion
pol′/i/cy
pol′/i/cy/hold′/er
po/lit′/i/cal
    ____ cor′/po/ra′/tion
    ____ lib′/er/ty
    ____ of′/fice
    ____ par′/ty
    ____ ques′/tion
    ____ rights
    ____ sub′/di/vi′/sion
pol′/i/tics′
pol′/i/ty
poll
    ____ mon′/ey
    ____ tax
poll′/ing the ju′/ry
polls
pol/lute′
    pol/lut′/ed
    pol/lut′/ing
pol′y/an′/dry
po/lyg′/a/my
pol′y/gar′/chy
pol′y/graph′

pool'/ing
     —— as'/sets
     —— con'/tracts'
poor
pop'/u/lace
pop'/u/lar
pop'/u/late'
     pop'/u/lat'/ed
     pop'/u/lat'/ing
pop'/u/la'/tion
por/nog'/ra/pher
por'/no/graph'/ic
por/nog'/ra/phy
port
     —— au/thor'/i/ty
     —— charg'/es
     —— of de/liv'/er·y
     —— of de/par'/ture
     —— of des'/ti/na'/
tion
     —— of dis/charge'
     —— of en'/try
     —— risk
     —— toll
por'/ter
por'/ter/age
port/fo'/li·o
por'/tion
po/si'/tion
pos'/i/tive
     —— ev'/i/dence
     —— mis/pri'/sion
     —— re/pri'/sals
     —— wrong

po/si/ti'/vi ju'/ris
pos'/se
     —— co'/mi/ta'/tus
pos/sess'
     pos/sessed'
     pos/sess'/ing
pos/ses'/sion
pos/sess'/or
     —— bo'/na fide
     —— ma'/la fide
pos/ses'/so/ry
     —— ac'/tion
     —— in'/ter/est
     —— judg'/ment
     —— war'/rant
pos'/si/bil'/i/ty
pos'/si/ble
post
     post'/ed
     post'/ing
post
     —— di'/em
     —— dis/sei'/sin
     —— ex/change'
     —— fac'/to
     —— hac
     —— mor'/tem
     —— na'/tus
     —— o'/bit
     —— of'/fice
     —— ter'/mi/num
post'/age
post'/al
     —— cur'/ren/cy

post′/al (contd.)
    ____ sav′/ings de/
    pos′/i/to′/ries
post′/date′
    post′/dat′/ed
    post′/dat′/ing
pos/te′/ri/or
pos/te′/ri/or′/i/ty
pos/ter′/i/ty
post′/hu/mous
post′/man
post′/mark′
post′/mas′/ter
    ____ gen′′/er/al
post/nup′/tial
    ____ set′/tle/ment
post/pone′
    post/poned′
    post/pon′′/ing
po′/ta/ble
po′/ten/tate′
po/ten′′/tia pro/pin′′/qua
po/ten′′/tial
pound
pound′′/age
pow′/er
    ____ of ap/point′′/
    ment
    ____ of at/tor′′/ney
    ____ of dis′/po/si′′/
    tion
    ____ of re′/vo/ca′′/tion
    ____ of ter′/mi/na′′/
    tion

pow′/er (contd.)
    ____ of vis′′/i/ta′′/tion
prac′/ti/ca/ble
prac′/ti/cal
prac′/tice
    prac′/ticed
    prac′/tic/ing
prac/ti′′/tio/ner
prae′/ci/pe′
prae′/di/al
    ____ ser′′/vi/tude′
prae/fa′′/tus
prae/fec′′/tus vil′′/lae
prae′/mi/um
prae′/no/men
prae′/tor
prae/to′′/ri/an law
prae/var′/i/ca/tor
prag/mat′′/ic
prai′′/rie
prax′/is
prayer
pre′/am′/ble
pre′/ap/point′′/ed
pre/au′′/di/ence
pre/car′′/i/ous
    ____ cir′/cum/stanc′/
    es
    ____ loan
    ____ pos/ses′′/sion
    ____ trade
prec′/a/to′′/ry
pre/cau′′/tion
pre/cau′′/tion/ar′y

pre/cede′
  pre/ced′/ed
  pre/ced′/ing
pre/ce′/dence
pre/ce′/dent *adj*
prec′/e/dent *n*
prec′/e/dents sub si/len′/ti·o
pre′/ce par′/ti/um
pre′/cept′
  ____ of at/tach′/ment
pre′/cinct′
pre′/ci/pe
prec′/i/pice
pre/cip′/i/ta′/tion
pre/cise′
pre/clude′
  pre/clud′/ed
  pre/clud′/ing
pre′/cog/ni′/tion
pre′/con/ceived′ mal′/ice
pre/con′/tract
pred′/a/to′/ry in/tent′
pre′/de/ces′/sor
pre/des′/tined in/ter′/pre/ta′/tion
pre′/di/al
  ____ ser′/vi/tude′
pred′/i/cate′
  pred′/i/cat′/ed
  pred′/i/cat′/ing
pre/dom′/i/nant
pre/emp′/tion
  ____ claim′/ant
  ____ en′/try

pre/emp′/tion (contd.)
  ____ right
pre/emp′/tion/er
pre′/fect′
pre/fer′
  pre/ferred′
  pre/fer′/ring
pref′/er/a·ble
pref′/er/ence
pref′/er/en′/tial
  ____ as/sign′/ment
  ____ div′/i/dend
  ____ tar′/iff
pre/ferred′
  ____ debt
  ____ div′/i/dend
  ____ dock′/et
preg′/nan/cy
preg′nant neg′/a/tive
prej′/u/dice
prej′/u/di′/cial
  ____ er′/ror
  ____ pub/lic′/i/ty
prel′/ate
pre/lim′/i/nar′y
  ____ com/plaint′
  ____ ex/am′/i/na′/tion
  ____ hear′/ing
  ____ in/junc′/tion
pre/med′/i/tate′
  pre/med′/i/tat′/ed
  pre/med′/i/tat′/ing
pre/med′/i/ta′/tion
pre/mier′
prem′/is/es

pre′/mi/um
pren/der′ *or* pren′/dre
pre′/no′/men
prep′/a/ra′/tion
pre/pare′
    pre/pared′
    pre/par′/ing
pre/pense′
pre/pon′/der/ance
pre/rog′/a/tive
pres
pres′/by/ter
pre/scribe′
    pre/scribed′
    pre/scrib′/ing
pre/scrip′/tion
pre/scrip′/tive
pres′/ence
    _____ of an of′/fi/cer
    _____ of de/fen′/dant
    _____ of the tes′/ta/tor
pre/sent′ *v*
    pre/sent′/ed
    pre/sent′/ing
pres′/ent *n, adj*
    _____ con/vey′/ance
    _____ dan′/ger
    _____ en/joy′/ment
    _____ es/tate′
    _____ in′/ter/est
pre/sen′/ta′/tion
pre/sen′/ta/tive ad/vow′/
son
pre/sent′/er
pres′/ent/ly

pre/sent′/ment
pres′/er/va′/tion
pre/serve′
    pre/served′
    pre/serv′/ing
pre/side′
    pre/sid′/ed
    pre/sid′/ing
pres′/i/den/cy
pres′/i/dent
pres′/i/den′/tial
pre/sid′/i/al
pre/sid′/i/um
pre/sum′/a·bly
pre/sume′
    pre/sumed′
    pre/sum′/ing
pre/sump′/tion
    _____ of in′/no/cence
    _____ of le/git′/i/
    ma/cy
    _____ of sur/vi′/vor/
    ship′
pre/sump′/tive
    _____ ev′/i/dence
pre/tend′
    pre/tend′/ed
    pre/tend′/ing
pre/tend′/er
prête′-/nom′
pre′/tens′
pre′/ter le′/gal
pre′/ter/mis′/sion
pre′/ter/mit′
    pre′/ter/mit′/ted

pre′/ter/mit′ (contd.)
    pre′/ter/mit′/ting
pre′/ter/mit′/ted
    _____ de/fense′
    _____ heir
pre′/text′
pre′/ti/um
    _____ af′/fec/ti′o′/nis
    _____ pe′/ric/u′/li
pre/vail′
    pre/vailed′
    pre/vail′/ing
pre/vail′/ing par′/ty
pre/var′/i/cate′
    pre/var′/i/cat′/ed
    pre/var′/i/cat′/ing
pre/var′/i/ca′/tion
pre/vent′
    pre/vent′/ed
    pre/vent′/ing
pre/ven′/tion
pre/ven′/tive
    _____ in/junc′/tion
    _____ jus′/tice
pre′/vi/ous
    _____ ques′/tion
pre′/vi/ous/ly
price
    _____ cur′/rent
    _____ dis/crim′/i/na′/
tion
    _____ ex/pec′/tan/cy
    _____ in′/dex
    _____ sup′/ports

pri′/ma fa′/cie
    _____ ev′/i/dence
pri′/mal
pri′/ma′/ry
    _____ al′/le/ga′/tion
    _____ ben′/e/fi′/cia/ry
    _____ boy′/cott
    _____ e·lec′/tion
    _____ ev′/i/dence
    _____ li′/a/bil′/i/ty
    _____ ob′/li/ga′/tion
    _____ pow′/ers
    _____ pur′/pose
pri′/mate′
prime
    _____ con′/trac′/tor
    _____ mak′/er
    _____ min′/is/ter
prim′/er
    _____ e·lec′/tion
    _____ sei′/sin
prim′/i/tive
    _____ ob′/li/ga′/tion
pri′/mo/gen′/i/tor
pri′/mo/gen′/i/ture
prince
prin′/cess
prin′/ci/pal
    _____ and sur′e/ty
    _____ cov′/e/nant
    _____ cred′/i/tor
    _____ of′/fice
    _____ of the house
prin′/ci/ple

print
    print'/ed
    print'/ing
pri'/or
    ____ cred'/i/tor
    ____ jeop'/ar/dy
    ____ pe'/tens
    ____ re/straint'
pri/or'/i/ty
prise
pris'/on
    ____ break'/ing
pris'/on/er
    ____ at the bar
    ____ of war
pri'/va/cy
pri'/vate
    ____ at/tor'/ney
    ____ ease'/ment
    ____ ex/am'/i/na'/tion
    ____ foun/da'/tion
    ____ nui'/sance
    ____ per'/son
    ____ rul'/ing
    ____ stat'/ute
pri'/va/teer'
pri/va'/tion
priv'/ies
priv'/i/lege
    ____ ab'/so/lute'
    ____ from ar/rest'
    ____ of tran'/sit
    ____ tax

priv'/i/leged
    ____ com/mu'/ni/ca'/
tion
    ____ cop'y/hold'
    ____ ev'/i/dence
    ____ ves'/sel
priv'/i/ty
    ____ of con'/tract'
    ____ of es/tate'
priv'y
    ____ coun'/cil
    ____ coun'/cil/or
    ____ purse
    ____ sig'/net
    ____ to'/ken
    ____ ver'/dict'
prize
    ____ courts
    ____ mon'/ey
pro and con
prob'/a/bil'/i/ty
prob'/a/ble
    ____ cause hear'/ing
    ____ con'/se/quence
    ____ fu'/ture pay'/
ments
prob'/a/bly
pro'/bate'
    ____ du'/ty
    ____ home'/stead'
    ____ ju'/ris/dic'/tion
    ____ pro/ceed'/ing
pro'/bate'
    pro'/bat'/ed

pro′/bate′ (contd.)
   pro′/bat′/ing
pro/ba′/tion
   _____ of′/fi/cer
pro/ba′/tion/ar′y
pro/ba′/tion/er
pro′/ba/tive
pro′/ba/to′/ry
prob′/lem
pro bo′/no
   _____ et ma′/lo
   _____ pub′/li/co
pro′/ce/den′/do
pro/ce′/dur/al
pro/ce′/dure
pro/ceed′
   pro/ceed′/ed
   pro/ceed′/ing
pro/ceed′/ings
   _____ in bank′/rupt/cy
pro′/ceeds′
pro′/cess
   _____ a′gent
   _____ pat′/ent
   _____ serv′/er
pro/ces′/sion
pro/ces′/sion/ing
pro/chein′
   _____ a·mi′ *or* a·my′
   _____ a·void′/ance
pro/claim′
   pro/claimed′
   pro/claim′/ing
proc′/la/ma′/tion
proc′/la/ma/tor

pro con/fes′/so
pro′/cre/ate′
   pro′/cre/at′/ed
   pro′/cre/at′/ing
pro′/cre/a′tion
proc′/tor
proc′/u/ra/cy
proc′/u/ra′/tion
proc′/u/ra′/tor
   _____ li′/tis
proc′/u/ra′/trix′
pro/cure′
   pro/cured′
   pro/cur′/ing
pro/cure′/ment
pro/cur′/er
pro/cur′/ing cause
pro de′/fen/den′/te
prod′/i/gal
pro/di′/tion
pro/di′/tor
pro/duce′ *v*
   pro/duced′
   pro/duc′/ing
pro′/duce′ *n*
pro/duc′/er
prod′/uct
pro/duc′/tion
pro fac′/to
pro/fane′
pro/fane′/ly
pro/fan′/i/ty
pro/fess′
   pro/fessed′
   pro/fess′/ing

pro/fes'/sion
pro/fes'/sion/al
pro/fes'/sor
prof/fered' ev'/i/dence
pro'/file
prof'/it
_____ and loss state'/
    ment
prof'/i/teer'/ing
pro for'/ma
prog/no'/sis
pro'/gram'
prog'/ress *n*
pro/gress' *v*
    pro/gressed'
    pro/gress'/ing
pro/gres'/sion
pro/gres'/sive tax
pro hac vi'/ce
pro/hib'/it
    pro/hib'/it/ed
    pro/hib'/it/ing
pro'/hi/bi'/tion
pro/hib'/i/tive
pro in'/ter/es'/se su'o
pro lae'/si/o'/ne fi/de'i
pro le/ga'/to
pro'/les
pro'/le/tar'/i/at
pro'/le/ta'/ri/us
pro'/li/cide'
pro/lif'/ic
pro/lix'/i/ty
pro/loc'/u/tor
pro'/logue'

pro/long'
    pro/longed'
    pro/long'/ing
pro/lon'/ga'/tion
pro ma'/jo/ri cau'/te/la
prom'/ise
prom'/is/ee'
prom'/i/sor'
prom'/is/so'/ry
    _____ es/top'/pel
    _____ note
    _____ rep'/re/sen'/
    ta/tive
    _____ war'/ran/ty
pro/mote'
    pro/mot'/ed
    pro/mot'/ing
pro/mot'/er
pro/mo'/tion
prompt
    _____ de/liv'/er·y
    _____ ship'/ment
prompt'/ly
pro'/mul/gate'
    pro'/mul/gat'/ed
    pro'/mul/gat'/ing
pro'/mul/ga'/tion
pro non scrip'/to
pro'/no'/ta/ry
pro/nounce'
    pro/nounced'
    pro/nounc'/ing
pro/nounce'/ment
pro/nun'/ci/a/men'/to
pro/nun'/ci/a'/tion

proof
_____ be/yond′ a rea′′/
son/a·ble doubt
_____ ev′/i/dent
_____ of ser′′/vice
pro′/pa/gan′′/da
prop′/a/gate′
prop′/a/gat′/ed
prop′/a/gat′/ing
prop′/a/ga′′/tion
pro par′′/ti/bus lib′/er/
an′′/dis
prop′′/er
_____ en/dorse′′/ment
_____ look′′/out′
_____ par′′/ty
prop′′/er/ty
_____ set′′/tle/ment
_____ tort
pro/pin′′/qui/ty
pro/po′/nent
pro/por′′/tion/al
_____ rep′′/re/sen/ta′′/
tion
pro/pos′′/al
pro/pose′
pro/posed′
pro/pos′′/ing
prop′/o/si′′/tion
pro pos′′/ses/so′′/re
pro/pound′
pro/pound′′/ed
pro/pound′′/ing
pro/pri′′/e·tar′y
_____ ar′′/ti/cles
_____ du′′/ties

pro/pri′′/e·tar′y (contd.)
_____ in′′/ter/est
pro/pri′′/e/tas
pro/pri′′/e·tor
pro/pri′′/e·ty
pro′′/pri·o vi/go′′/re
prop′′/ter
_____ af/fec′′/tum
_____ de/fec′′/tum
_____ de/fec′′/tum
san/gui′′/nis
_____ de/lic′′/tum
_____ im′′/po/ten′′/
ti/am
pro ra′′/ta
pro/rate′
pro/rat′′/ed
pro/rat′′/ing
pro/ra′′/tion
pro re na′′/ta
pro′/ro/ga′′/tion
pro/rogue′
pro/rogued′
pro/rogu′′/ing
pro sa/lu′′/te an′′/i/mae
pro/scribe′
pro/scribed′
pro/scrib′′/ing
pro/scrip′′/tion
pro se
pros′/e/cute′
pros′/e/cut′/ed
pros′/e/cut′/ing
pros′/e/cut′/ing at/tor′′/
ney
pros′/e/cu′′/tion

pros′/e/cu′/tor
pros′/e/cu′/trix
pro/se′/qui
pro/se′/qui/tur
pro sol′/i/do
pro/spec′/tive
pro/spec′/tus
pros′/per/ous
pros′/ti/tute′
pros′/ti/tu′/tion
pro tan′/to
pro/tect′
    pro/tect′/ed
    pro/tect′/ing
pro/tec′/tion
pro/tec′/tive
    _____ cus′/to/dy
    _____ tar′/iff
pro/tec′/tor
pro/tec′/tor/ate
pro tem/po′/re
pro′/test′ *n*
pro/test′ *v*
    pro/test′/ed
    pro/test′/ing
pro′/tes/tan′/do
pro′/tes/ta′/tion
pro/tho′/no/ta′/ry
pro′/to/col
prov′/a·ble
prove
    proved
    proved *or* prov′/en
    prov′/ing
pro/vide′
    pro/vid′/ed

pro/vide′ (contd.)
    pro/vid′/ing
prov′/ince
pro/vin′/cial
pro/vi′/sion
pro/vi′/sion/al
    _____ in/junc′/tion
    _____ rem′/e/dy
pro/vi′/so
pro/vi′/so/ry
prov′/o/ca′/tion
pro/voke′
    pro/voked′
    pro/vok′/ing
pro′/vost′
    _____ court
    _____ mar′/shal
prox′/i/mate
    _____ cause
    _____ con′/se/quence′
    _____ dam′/ag/es
    _____ re/sult′
prox/im′/i/ty
prox′y
    _____ mar′/riage
pru′/dence
pru′/dent
pru′/ri/ent
pseu′/do
pseu′/do/cy/e′/sis
psy/chol′/o/gy
psy′/cho/neu/ro′/sis
psy′/cho/path′
psy/cho′/sis
psy′/cho/ther′/a/py
pto′/maine

pu′/ber/ty
pub′/lic
_____ ad′/vo/cate
_____ at/tor′/ney
_____ ap/point′/ment
_____ char′/ac/ter
_____ con/ve′/nience
_____ cor′/po/ra′/tion
_____ de/fend′/er
_____ do/main′
_____ ease′/ment
_____ en′/ti/ty
_____ fig′/ure
_____ in/de′/cen/cy
_____ in′/ter/est
_____ mar′/ket
_____ nui′/sance
_____ of/fense′
_____ of′/fice
_____ pas′/sage
_____ rec′/ord
_____ se/cu′/ri/ties
_____ ser′/vice
_____ tri′/al
_____ trust′/ee′
_____ u/til′/i/ty
_____ ves′/sel
_____ wel′/fare′
pub′/li/can
pub′/li/ca′/tion
pub′/li/ci ju′/ris
pub′/li/cist
pub/lic′/i/ty
pub′/lic/ly
pub′/lish
pub′/lished

pub′/lish (contd.)
pub′/lish/ing
pub′/lish/er
pu/dic′/i/ty
pu′/er/ile
pu′/er/il′/i/ty
puis′/ne
pull
pulled
pull′/ing
pul/sa′/re
pul′/sa′/tor
punc′/til′/i/ous
punc′/tu/al
punc′/tu/ate′
punc′/tu/at′/ed
punc′/tu/at′/ing
punc′/tu/a′/tion
punc′/tum tem/po′/ris
punc′/ture
punc′/tured
punc′/tur/ing
pun′/ish
pun′/ished
pun′/ish/ing
pun′/ish/a·ble
pun′/ish/ment
pu/ni′/tion
pu′/ni/tive
_____ dam′/ag/es
_____ pow′/er
_____ stat′/ute
pu′/pil
pur′/chase
pur′/chased
pur′/chas/ing

pur′/chase
    _____ a·gree′/ment
    _____ mon′/ey
    _____ or′/der
pur′/chas/er
pure′/bred′
pur′/ga′/tion
purge
    purged
    purg′/ing
pu′/ri/ty
pur′/lieu
pur/loin′
    pur/loined′
    pur/loin′/ing
pur′/part
pur/port′
    pur/port′/ed
    pur/port′/ing
pur′/pose
pur′/pose/ful
pur′/pose/ly
purs′/er
pur/su′/ance
pur/su′/ant to
pur/sue′
    pur/sued′
    pur/su′/ing
pur/suit′
pu′/rus id′/i/o′/ta
pur/vey′/ance
pur/vey′/or
pur′/view′
pu′/ta/tive
    _____ mar′/riage
pyr′/a′mid′

pyr′/a/mid′/ed
pyr′/a/mid′/ing
py′/ro/ma′/ni·a
py′/ro/ma′/ni/ac′

Q

qua
quack
qua/cun′/que vi′a da′/ta
quad′/rant
quad′/ri/par′/titē
quad′/ri/par/ti/tus
quae est ea′dem
quae ni′/hil frus′/tra
quae′/re
quae′/rens
quaes′/ti′o
quaes′/tus
qual′/i/fi′a·ble
qual′/i/fi/ca′′/tion
qual′/i/fied′
    _____ ac/cep′/tance
    _____ es/tate′
    _____ pen′/sion plan
qual′/i/fi′/er
qual′/i/fy′
    qual′/i/fied′
    qual′/i/fy′/ing
qual′/i/ta′/tive
qual′/i/ty
    _____ con/trol′
    _____ of es/tate′
qualm

quam diu
quan′/da/ry
quan′/do
quan′/ti mi/no′/ris
quan′/ti/ty
quan′/tum
    ____ me′/ru/it
    ____ va/le′/bant
quar′/an/tin′/a·ble
quar′/an/tine′
    quar′/an/tined′
    quar′/an/tin′/ing
qua′/re
    ____ clau′/sum fre′/git
quar′/rel
    quar′/reled
    quar′/rel/ing
quar′/ry
quar′/ter
    ____ ses′/sion
quar′/ter/ly
    ____ courts
quash
qua′/si
    ____ ad/mis′/sion
    ____ con′/tract′
    ____ con/trac′/tus
    ____ ease′/ment
    ____ es/top′/pel
    ____ ju/di′/cial
    ____ of/fense′
    ____ pur′chase
    ____ sei′/sin
quay
queen's
    ____ bench

queen's (contd.)
    ____ coun′/sel
    ____ pris′/on
que es/tate′
que est le mesme
que/re′/la
que′/rens
que′/rist
quer′/u/lous
que′/ry
    que′/ried
    que′/ry/ing
ques′/ta
ques′/tion
ques′/tion/a·ble
ques′/tion/naire′
qui′a ti′/met
quib′/ble
    quib′/bled
    quib′/bling
quick
    ____ as′set ra′/ti·o
quick′/en/ing
qui′/dam
quid pro quo
qui′/et
    ____ en/joy′/ment
    ____ po/ses′/sion
    ____ ti′/tle
qu′/e/ta′/re
qui/e′tus
quit
    quit
    quit′/ting
qui tam ac′/tion
quit′/claim

quit**′**/claim (contd.)
    ____ deed
quod com**′**/pu/tet
quod re/cu**′**/per/et
quod vi**′**/de
quon**′**/dom
quo**′**/rum
quo**′**/ta
quo/ta**′**/tion
quote
    quot**′**/ed
    quot**′**/ing
quo/tid**′**/i/an
quo**′**/tient ver**′**/dict**′**
quo war/ran**′**/to

R

rab**′**/bi**′**
rab**′**/ble
race
    raced
    rac**′**/ing
rack**′**/et
rack**′**/e/teer**′**
rad**′**/i/cal
ra**′**/di/us
raf**′**/fle
rail**′**/road**′**
rail**′**/way
raise
    raised
    rais**′**/ing

raise
    ____ an is**′**/sue
    ____ a pre/sump**′**/tion
    ____ rev**′**/e/nue
range
rang**′**/er
rank
rank**′**/ing
ran**′**/som
rape
    raped
    rap**′**/ing
rap**′**/id tran**′**/sit
rap**′**/ine
rap**′**/proche**′**/ment**′**
ra**′**/sure
rat**′**/a·ble
rate
    rat**′**/ed
    rat**′**/ing
rate
    ____ fix**′**/ing
    ____ of re/turn**′**
rat**′**/i/fi/ca**′**/tion
rat**′**/i/fy**′**
    rat**′**/i/fied**′**
    rat**′**/i/fy**′**/ing
ra**′**/ti·o
    ____ de**′**/ci/den**′**/di
    ____ le**′**/gis
ra**′**/tio/nal
    ____ ba**′**/sis
    ____ doubt
    ____ pur**′**/pose
ra**′**/ti/o**′**/ne
    ____ im**′**/po/ten**′**/ti/ae

ra/′/ti/o′/ne (contd.)
____ ma/te′/ri/ae
____ per/so′/nae
____ priv′/i/le′/gi·i
____ so′/li
____ ten′/u/rae
ra/vine′
rav′/ish
rav′/ished
rav/ish/ing
rav′/ish/ment
raze
razed
raz′/ing
re
re′/ac/quire′
re′/ac/quired′
re′/ac/quir′/ing
re/act′
re/act′/ed
re/act′/ing
re/ac′/tion
re/ac′/tion/ar′y
re/ac′/tor
read′/er
read′y and will′/ing
real
____ con′/tract′
____ cov′/e/nant
____ es/tate′
____ ev′/i/dence
____ in′/ju/ry
____ prop′/er/ty
re/al′/i/ty
re′/al/i·za′/tion
re′/al/ize′

re′/al/ize′ (contd.)
re′/al/ized′
re′/al/iz′/ing
realm
re′/al/ty
re′/ap/por′/tion
re′/ap/por′/tioned
re′/ap/por′/tion/ing
re′/ap/por′/tion/ment
re′/ap/prais′/er
rear
re/ar′/gu/ment
rea′/son
rea′/soned
rea′/son/ing
rea′/son/a·ble
____ and prob′/a·ble
cause
____ be/lief′
____ crea′/ture
____ dil′/i/gence
____ doubt
____ no′/tice
____ sus/pi′/cion
re′/as/sess′/ment
re′/as/sur′/ance
re′/at/tach′/ment
re′/bate′
reb′/el *n*
re/bel′ *v*
re/belled′
re/bel′/ling
re/bel′/lion
re/bel′/lious
re/but′
re/but′/ted

re/but′ (contd.)
    re/but′/ting
re/but′/ta/ble pre/sump′/
tion
re/but′/tal
re/but′/ter
re/but′/ting ev′/i/dence
re/call′
    re/called′
    re/call′/ing
re/call′ e·lec′/tion
re/cant′
    re/cant′/ed
    re/cant′/ing
re/cap′/i/tal/i·za′/tion
re/cap′/tion
re/cap′/ture
    re/cap′/tured
    re/cap′/tur′/ing
re/ceiv′/a·ble
re/ceive′
    re/ceived′
    re/ceiv′/ing
re/ceiv′/er
    _____ pen/den′/te li′/te
re/ceiv′/er/ship′
re/ceiv′/ing sto′/len goods
re′/cess′
re/ces′/sion
re/cid′/i/vism′
re/cid′/i/vist
re/cip′/ro/cal
    _____ con′/tract′
    _____ in/sur′/ance
    _____ neg′/a/tive ease′/
    ment

re/cip′/ro/cal (contd.)
    _____ wills
re/cip′/ro/cate′
    re/cip′/ro/cat′/ed
    re/cip′/ro/cat′/ing
re/cip′/ro/ca′/tion
rec′/i/proc′/i/ty
re/ci′/sion
re/cit′/al
re/cite′
    re/cit′/ed
    re/cit′/ing
reck
reck′/less
    _____ dis′/re/gard′
    _____ driv′/ing
    _____ ho′/mi/cide′
reck′/on
    reck′/oned
    reck′/on/ing
re/claim′
    re/claimed′
    re/claim′/ing
rec′/la/ma′/tion
re/clu′/sion
rec′/og/ni′/tion
re/cog′/ni/tor
re/cog′/ni/zance
rec′/og/nize′
    rec′/og/nized′
    rec′/og/niz′/ing
re/cog′/ni/zee′
re/cog′/ni/zor
rec′/ol/lect′
    rec/ol/lect′/ed
    rec/ol/lect′/ing

rec'/ol/lec'/tion
rec'/om/mend'
   rec'/om/mend'/ed
   rec'/om/mend'/ing
rec'/om/men/da'/tion
rec'/om/men'/da/to'/ry
rec'/om/pense'
   rec'/om/pensed'
   rec'/om/pens'/ing
rec'/on/cil'/a·ble
rec'/on/cile'
   rec'/on/ciled'
   rec'/on/cil'/ing
rec'/on/cil'/i/a'/tion
re'/con/duc'/tion
re'/con/struct'
   re'/con/struct'/ed
   re'/con/struct'/ing
re'/con/struc'/tion
re'/con/tin'/u/ance
re'/con/ver'/sion
re'/con/vey'/ance
re/cord' *v*
   re/cord'/ed
   re/cord'/ing
rec'/ord *n*
re'/cor/da'/re
re/cord'/er
re/coup'
   re/couped'
   re/coup'/ing
re/coup'/ment
re'/course'
re/cov'/er
   re/cov'/ered
   re/cov'/er/ing

re/cov'/er/ee'
re'/cov'/er/er
re/cov'/er·y
rec'/re/ant
re/crim'/i/nate'
   re/crim'/i/nat'/ed
   re/crim'/i/nat'/ing
re/crim'/i/na'/tion
re/crim'/i/na/to'/ry
re/cruit'
re/cruit'/ing
rec'/ti/fi/ca'/tion
rec'/ti/fi'/er
rec'/ti/fy'
   rec'/ti/fied'
   rec'/ti/fy'/ing
rec'/ti/tude'
rec'/tor
rec'/to/ry
rec'/tum
   _____ es'/se
   _____ ro/ga'/re
rec'/tus in cu'/ri·a
re'/cu/pe/ra'/ti·o
re/cu'/per/a'/tion
rec'/u/sa'/tion
red/den'/dum
re/deem'
   re/deemed'
   re/deem'/ing
re/deem'/a·ble
re'/de/liv'/e·ry
re'/de/mise'
   re'/de/mised'
   re'/de/mis'/ing
re/demp'/tion

re/demp'/tion (contd.)
    ____ pe'/ri/od
red'-/hand'ed
red'/hi/bi'/tion
re'/dis/se'/sin
re/dis'/tri/bu'/tion
re/di'/tus
    ____ al'/bi
    ____ nig'/ri
re'/draft'
re/dress'
   re/dressed'
   re/dress'/ing
re/duce'
   re/duced'
   re/duc'/ing
re/duc'/i·ble fel'/o/ny
re/duc'/ti·o ad ab/sur'/dum
re/duc'/tion
    ____ of cap'/i/tal
    ____ to pos/ses'/sion
re/dun'/dan/cy
re/dun'/dant
re'/en/act'
   re'/en/act'/ed
   re'/en/act'/ing
re'/en'/try
re'/es/tab'/lish/ment
re'/ex/am'/i/na'/tion
re'/ex/am'/ine
   re'/ex/am'/ined
   re'/ex/am'/in/ing
re/fer'
   re/ferred'
   re/fer'/ring

ref'/er/ee'
    ____ in bank'/rupt/cy
ref'/er/ence
ref'/er/en'/dum
re'/fi'/nance'
   re'/fi'/nanced'
   re'/fi'/nanc'/ing
re/fine'/ment
re/form'
   re/formed'
   re/form'/ing
ref'/or/ma'/tion
re/for'/ma/to'ry
re/fresh'/ing
    ____ the mem'/o/ry
re/fund' *v*
   re/fund'/ed
   re/fund'/ing
re'/fund' *n*
re/fus'/al
re/fuse' *v*
   re/fused'
   re/fus'/ing
ref'/use' *n*
re/ga'/li·a
    ____ fa'/ce/re
re/gard'
re'/gen/cy
re'/gent
reg'/i/cide'
re/gime' *or* ré/gime'
re/gi'/na
re'/gion
reg'/is/ter
    ____ in bank'/rupt/cy
    ____ of land of'/fice

reg′/is/ter (contd.)
    _____ of pat′/ents
    _____ of the trea′/sur·y
reg′/is/tered
    _____ bond
    _____ rep′/re/sen′/
ta/tive
    _____ trade′/mark
    _____ vot′/ers
reg′/is/trant
reg′/is/trar
reg′/is/tra′/tion
reg′/is/try
reg′/nal
reg′/nant
reg′/num
re′/grant′
    re′/grant′/ed
    re′/grant′/ing
re/gress′
    re/gressed′
    re/gress′/ing
re/gres′/sion
reg′/u/la
reg′/u/lar
    _____ ar′/my
    _____ course of bus′i/
ness
    _____ e·lec′/tion
    _____ en/dorse′/ment
reg′/u/lar/ly
reg′/u/late′
    reg′/u/lat′/ed
    reg′/u/lat′/ing
reg′/u/la′/tion

re′/ha/bil′/i/tate′
    re′/ha/bil′/i/tat′/ed
    re′/ha/bil′/i/tat′/ing
re′/ha/bil′/i/ta′/tion
    _____ of crim′/i/nal
    _____ of wit′/ness
re/hear′/ing
re/hears′/al
re/hearse′
    re/hearsed′
    re/hears′/ing
reif
re′/im/burse′
    re′/im/bursed′
    re′/im/burs′/ing
re′/in/state′
    re′/in/stat′/ed
    re′/in/stat′/ing
re′/in/state′/ment
re′/in/sur′/ance
re′/in/sur′/er
re′/is′/sued pat′/ent
re/join′
    re/joined′
    re/join′/ing
re/join′
    _____ gra′/tis
re/join′/der
re/late′
    re/lat′/ed
    re/lat′/ing
re/la′/tion
re/la′/tion/ship′
rel′/a/tive
re/la′/tor

re/la′/trix′
re/lax′/a/re
re/lax/a′/ti·o
re/lease′ *v*
   re/leased′
   re/leas′/ing
re/lease′ *n*
   _____ by way of en′/try
   and fe·off′/ment
   _____ by way of ex/tin′/
   guish/ment
   _____ of dow′/er
re′-/lease′
   re′-/leased′
   re′-/leas′ing
re/leas′/er
rel′/e/gate′
   rel′/e/gat′/ed
   rel′/e/gat′/ing
rel′/e/ga′/tion
rel′/e/van/cy
rel′/e/vant
   _____ ev′/i/dence
   _____ mar′/ket
re/li′/a·ble
re/li′/ance
rel′/ict
re/lic′/tion
re/lief′
re/lieve′
   re/lieved′
   re/liev′/ing
re/li′/gion
re/li′/gious
   _____ free′/dom

re/li′/gious (contd.)
   _____ lib′/er/ty
re/lin′/quish
   re/lin′/quished
   re/lin′/quish/ing
re/lin′/quish/ment
re/liq′/ui/ae′
re′/lo/ca′/tion
re/lo′/cate′
   re/lo′/cat′/ed
   re/lo′/cat′/ing
re/luc′/tance
re/ly′
   re/lied′
   re/ly′/ing
re/main′/der
re/main′/der/man
re/mand′
   re/mand′/ed
   re/mand′/ing
re/mark′
re/me′/di/al
   _____ ac′/tion
   _____ law
   _____ stat′/ute
rem′/e/dy
re/mem′/ber
   re/mem′/bered
   re/mem′/ber/ing
re/mise′
   re/mised′
   re/mis′/ing
re/miss′
re/mis′/sion
re/miss′/ness

re/mit′
    re/mit′′/ted
    re/mit′′/ing
re/mit′′/tance
re/mit′′/tit dam′′/na
re/mit′′/ti/tur
    _____ dam′′/na
    _____ of rec′′/ord
rem′/nant
re/mod′′/el
    re/mod′′/eled
    re/mod′′/el/ing
re/mon′/e/ti/za′′/tion
re/mon′/strance
re/morse′
re/mote′
    _____ dam′/ag/es
    _____ pos′′/si/bil′′/i/ty
re/mote′/ness
re/mov′′/al
    _____ from of′′/fice
    _____ with/out′ prop′′/
    er cause
re/move′
    re/moved′
    re/mov′′/ing
re/mu′′/ner/a′′/tion
ren/con/tre *or* ren/coun′′/
ter
ren′′/der *v*
    ren′′/dered
    ren′′/der/ing
ren′′/der *n*
    _____ an ac/count′
    _____ judg′′/ment
    _____ ver′′/dict′

ren′′/dez/vous′
re/nege′
    re/neged′
    re/neg′′/ing
re′/ne/go′′/ti/ate′
    re′/ne/go′′/ti/at′′/ed
    re′/ne/go′′/ti/at′′/ing
re′/ne/go′′/ti/a′′/tion
re/new′
    re/newed′
    re/new′′/ing
re/new′′/al
re/nounce′
    re/nounced′
    re/nounc′′/ing
re′/no/va′′/re
re/nown′
rent
    rent′′/ed
    rent′′/ing
re/nun′/ci/a′′/tion
re′o ab/sen′′/te
re/o′pen
    re/o′pened
    re/o′pen/ing
re/or′′/ga/ni/za′′/tion
re/pair′
    re/paired′
    re/pair′′/ing
rep′/a/ra′′/tion
re′/par′/ti′/tion
re/pa′/tri/a′′/tion
re/pay′
    re/paid′
    re/pay′′/ing
re/peal′

re/peal' (contd.)
    re/pealed'
    re/peal'/ing
re/peat'
    re/peat'/ed
    re/peat'/ing
re/peat'/er
rep'/e/ti'/tion
re/place'
    re/placed'
    re/plac'/ing
re/plead'
    re/plead'/ed
    re/plead'/ing
re/plead'/er
re/ple/gi'/a/re
re/plev'/in
re/plev'y
    re/plev'/ied
    re/plev'y/ing
rep'/li/ca
rep'/li/cant
rep'/li/ca'/tion
re/ply'
    re/plied'
    re/ply'/ing
re/port'
re/port'/er
re'/pos/ses'/sion
rep'/re/hend'
    rep'/re/hend'/ed
    rep'/re/hend'/ing
rep'/re/hen'/sion
rep'/re/sent'
    rep'/re/sent'/ed
    rep'/re/sent'/ing

rep'/re/sen'/ta'/tion
rep'/re/sen'/ta/tive
    _____ ac'/tion
re/press'
    re/pressed'
    re/press'/ing
re/prieve'
    re/prieved'
    re/priev'/ing
rep'/ri/mand'
    rep'/ri/mand'/ed
    rep'/ri/mand'/ing
re/pri'/sal
re/proach'
re/pub'/lic
re/pub'/li/can
re/pub'/li/ca'/tion
re/pu'/di/ate'
    re/pu'/di/at'/ed
    re/pu'/di/at'/ing
re/pu'/di/a'/tion
re/pug'/nance
rep'/u/ta/ble
rep'/u/ta'/tion
re/put'/ed
re/quest'
    re/quest'/ed
    re/quest'/ing
re/quire'
    re/quired'
    re/quir'/ing
re/quire'/ment con'/tract'
req'/ui/si'/tion
re/quite'
    re/quit'/ed
    re/quit'/ing

res
    —— ad/ju′/di/ca′/ta
    —— de/re/lic′/ta
    —— ges′/tae
    —— in′/teg/ra
    —— in′/ter a′li/os
    ac′/ta
    —— ip′/sa lo′/qui/tur
    —— ju′/di/ca′/ta
    —— no′/va
    —— pu′/bli/cae
    —— quo/tid′/i/a′/nae
    —— re/li′/gi/o′/sae
re′/sale
re/scind′
    re/scind′/ed
    re/scind′/ing
re/scis′/sion
re′/script′
res′/cue
res′/cu/er
re/scyt′
re/search′
    re/searched′
    re/rearch′/ing
res′/er/va′/tion
re/serve′
    re/served′
    re/serv′/ing
re/served′ sur′/plus
res′/er/voir′
re/set′
    re/set′
    re/set′/ting
re/set′/tle/ment

re/side′
    re/sid′/ed
    re/sid′/ing
res′/i/dence
res′/i/den/cy
res′/i/dent
res′/i/den′/tial
re/sid′/u/al
re/sid′/u/ar′y
    —— ac/count′
    —— be/quest′
    —— de/vise′
    —— es/tate′
    —— leg′/a/cy
    —— leg′/a/tee′
res′/i/due′
re/sid′/u/um
re/sign′
    re/signed′
    re/sign′/ing
res′/ig/na′/tion
re/sil′/ience
re/sist′
    re/sist′/ed
    re/sist′/ing
re/sis′/tance
re/sist′/ing an of′/fi/cer
res′/o/lu′/tion
re/sort′
    re/sort′/ed
    re/sort′/ing
re′/sourc′/es
re/spec′/tive
re′/spite
re/spond′

re/spond′ (contd.)
    re/spond′/ed
    re/spond′/ing
re/spon′/de/at
    _____ oust′/er
    _____ su/pe′/ri/or
re/spon′/dent
re′/spon/den′/ti·a
re/sponse′
re/spon′/si/bil′/i/ty
re/spon′/si/ble
re/spon′/sive
res/seis/er′
rest
    rest′/ed
    rest′/ing
res′/ti/tute′
    res′/ti/tut′/ed
    res′/ti/tut′/ing
res′/ti/tu′/tion
re/strain′
    re/strained′
    re/strain′/ing
re/strain′/ing or′/der
re/straint′
    _____ of mar′/riage
    _____ of trade
    _____ on a′li·en/a′tion
re/strict′
    re/strict′/ed
    re/strict′/ing
re/stric′/tion
re/stric′/tive
    _____ cov′/e/nant
    _____ en/dorse′/ment

re/sult′
    re/sult′/ed
    re/sult′/ing
re/sum′/mons
re/sump′/tion
re′/tail′
re′/tail′/ing
re/tain′
    re/tained′
    re/tain′/ing
re/tain′/er
re/tal′/i/ate′
    re/tal′/i/at′/ed
    re/tal′/i/at′/ing
re/tal′/i/a′/tion
re/tal′/ia/to′/ry e·vic′/tion
re/ten′/tion
re/tire′
    re/tired′
    re/tir′/ing
re/tire′/ment
re/tort′
    re/tort′/ed
    re/tort′/ing
re/tor′/tion
re/tract′
    re/tract′/ed
    re/tract′/ing
re/trac′/tion
re/trax′/it
re/treat′ to the wall
ret′/ri/bu′/tion
re/triev′/a·ble
ret′/ro
ret′/ro/ac′/tive

ret′/ro/spect′
ret′/ro/spec′/tive
re/turn′
    re/turned′
    re/turn′/ing
re/turn′/a·ble
re′/us
re/val′/u/a′/tion sur′/plus
rev′/el
    rev′/eled
    rev′/el/ing
re/venge′
rev′/e/nue′
re/ver′/sal
re/verse′
    re/versed′
    re/vers′/ing
re/vers′/i·ble
re/ver′/sion
re/ver′/sion/ar′y
    _____ in′/ter/est
    _____ lease
re/ver′/sion/er
re/vert′
    re/vert′/ed
    re/vert′/ing
re/vert′/er
re/vest′
    re/vest′/ed
    re/vest′/ing
re/view′
    re/viewed′
    re/view′/ing
re/vise′
    re/vised′
    re/vis′/ing

re/vi′/sion
re/viv′/al
    _____ of ac′/tion
re/vive′
    re/vived′
    re/viv′/ing
re/viv′/er
re′/vo/ca′/tion
re/voke′
    re/voked′
    re/vok′/ing
re/volt′
    re/volt′/ed
    re/volt′/ing
rev′/o/lu′/tion
rev′/o/lu′/tion/ar′y
re/volv′/ing
    _____ cred′/it
    _____ fund
re/ward′
rex
rhe/tor′/i/cal ques′/tion
rid′/er
ri/en′
    _____ dulp
    _____ dit
right
    _____ of ac′/tion
    _____ of en′/try
    _____ of first re/fu′/sal
    _____ of hab′/i/ta′/tion
    _____ of pos/ses′/sion
    _____ of pri′/va/cy
    _____ of re/demp′/tion
    _____ of rep′/re/sen/
    ta′/tion

right (contd.)

    ____ to be/gin′

    ____ to re/deem′

rig′/or mor′/tis

ring

ri′/ot

ri′/ot/er

ri′/ot/ous as/sem′/bly

ri′/ot/ous/ly

ri/par′/i/an

    ____ na′/tions

    ____ own′/er

    ____ pro/pri′/e·tor

    ____ rights

ripe for judg′/ment

rise

    rose

    ris′/en

    ris′/ing

risk

    ____ cap′/i/tal

    ____ pre′/mi/um

rite

riv′/er

road′/bed′

rob

    robbed

    rob′/bing

rob′/ber

rob′/ber·y

ro/ga′/re

ro′/ga/to′/ry let′/ters

rogue

roll

    rolled

    roll′/ing

rood of land

room′/er

root of de/scent′

ros′/ter

ro′/ta′

rot′/ten clause

rout

    rout′/ed

    rout′/ing

route

roy′/al

    ____ as/sent′

    ____ bo′/nus

    ____ pre/rog′/a/tive

roy′/al/ty

rub′/ber check

ru′/bric

rule

    ruled

    rul′/ing

rule

    ____ ab′/so/lute′

    ____ a·gainst′ per′/pe/tu′/i·ties

    ____ dis/charged′

    ____ ni′/si

    ____ of ap/por′/tion/ment

    ____ of len′/i/ty

    ____ of ne/ces′/si/ty

    ____ of pre/sump′/tion

rules

    ____·of prac′/tice

    ____ of pro/ce′/dure

rul′/ing

ru′/mor
run
    ran
    run′/ning
run′/ning
    —— ac/count′
    —— days
    —— with the re/ver′/
    sion
rus′/ti/cum ju/di′/ci/um
rus′/tler
ruth′/ful
ruth′/less
rut′/tish

S

sab′/bath
sab′/o/tage′
sab′/o/teur′
sac′/ra/men′/tum
sac′/ri/lege
sa′/dism′
sae/ve′/ti·a
safe
    —— con′/duct′
    —— de/pos′/it box
    —— com′/pa/ny
safe′/ty
said
sail
    sailed
    sail′/ing

sail′/or
sal′/a·ble
sal′/a/ry
sale
    —— and lease′/back′
    —— and re/turn′
    —— by sam′/ple
    —— on ap/prov′/al
    —— on cred′/it
    —— with right of
    re/demp′/tion
sales′/man
sa′/line
sa/loon′
sa/loon′/keep′/er
sa′/lus
sa/lute′
    sa/lut′/ed
    sa/lut′/ing
sal′/vage
    —— ser′/vice
    —— val′/ue
sal′/vo
sal′/vor
sal′/vus ple′/gi/us
same
    —— in/ven′/tion
    —— of/fense′
sam′/ple
san′/a/to′/ri/um
sanc′/tion
sanc′/tu/ar′y
sane
san′/guine
san′/i/tar′/i/um

san′/i/tar′y
san′/i/ta′/tion
san′/i/ty
_____ hear′/ing
_____ tri′/al
sat′/is/fac′/tion
sat′/is/fac′/to/ry
_____ ev′/i/dence
sat′/is/fy′
sat′/is/fied′
sat′/is/fy′/ing
save
saved
sav′/ing
sav′/ings bank
sa′/vour
scab
scalp′/er
scan′/dal
scan′/dal/ous mat′/ter
sched′/ule
sched′/uled
sched′/ul/ing
scheme
schemed
schem′/ing
schism
school
_____ board
_____ dis′/trict′
_____ di/rec′/tors
_____ pur′/pos/es
_____ teach′/er
school′/mas′/ter
sci/en′/ter

sci′/li/cet′
scin/til′/la
_____ ju′/ris
_____ of ev′/i/dence
_____ sci′/re fa′/ci·as
scold
scold′/ed
scold′/ing
scope of au/thor′/i/ty
scorn
scoun′/drel
scram′/ble
scram′/bled
scram′/bling
scri′/ba
scrip
script
scrip′/tum
scriv′/en/er
scroll
scur′/ri/lous
seal
_____ of′/fice
_____ pa′/per
sealed
_____ and de/liv′/ered
_____ in′/stru/ment
_____ ver′/dict
seal′/ing
sea′/man
search
_____ and sei′/zure
_____ of ti′/tle
_____ war′/rant
search′/er

sea'/shore'
sea'/son/al em/ploy'/ment
sea'/wor'/thi/ness
sea'/wor'/thy
se/cede'
    se/ced'/ed
    se/ced'/ing
se/ces'/sion
se/clu'/sion
sec'/ond
   ____ de/liv'/er·y
   ____ dis/tress'
   ____ lien
   ____ mort'/gage
   ____ of/fense'
sec'/ond/ar'y
   ____ boy'/cott
   ____ dis'/tri/bu'/tion
   ____ ease'/ment
   ____ ev'/i/dence
   ____ li'/a/bil'/i/ty
   ____ ob'/li/ga'/tion
   ____ strike
se'/cre/cy
se'/cret
   ____ com/mit'/tee
   ____ part'/ner/ship'
sec'/re/tar'y
se/crete'
    se/cret'/ed
    se/cret'/ing
sect
sec/tar'/i/an
sec'/tion
sec'/tor

sec'/u/lar
se/cun'/dum
   ____ ar'/tem
   ____ bo'/nos mo'/res
   ____ for'/mam char'/
tae
   ____ le'/gem com/
mu'/nem
   ____ nor'/mam le'/gis
   ____ reg'/u/lam
se/cure'
    se/cured'
    se/cur'/ing
se/cured' cred'/i/tor
se/cu'/ri/ties
   ____ ex/change'
se/cu'/ri/ty
   ____ a·gree'/ment
   ____ coun'/cil
   ____ de/pos'/it
   ____ in'/ter/est
se'/cus
se/da'/to an'/i/mo
sed'/i/ment
se/di'/tion
se/di'/tious li'/bel
sed per cu'/ri/am
sed quae'/re
se/duce'
    se/duced'
    se/duc'/ing
se/duc'/tion
sed vi'/de
seg'/re/gate'
    seg'/re/gat'/ed

seg′/re/gate′ (contd.)
    seg′/re/gat′/ing
seg′/re/ga′/tion
sei/gnior′
sei′/gnior/age *or*
sei′/gnor/age
sei′/gnior·y *or* sei′/gnor·y
sei′/sin *or* sei′/zin
seize
    seized
    seiz′/ing
sei′/zure
se/lect′
    se/lect′/ed
    se/lect′/ing
se/lec′/tion
se/lec′/tive
se/lect′/man
self′-/deal′ing
self′-/de·fense′
self′-/de·struc′tion
self′-/em·ployed′
self′-/ex′e·cut′ing
self′-/help′
self′-/in·crim′i·na′tion
self′-/serv′/ing dec′/la/
ra′/tion
sell
    sold
    sell′/ing
sell′/er
sem′/blance
sem′/ble
    sem′/bled
    sem′/bling

sem′i/do/mes′/ti/cat′/ed
sem′/i/nar′y
sem′i/pub′/lic
sem′/per pa/ra′/tus
sen′/ate
sen′/a/tor
sen′/a/to′/ri/al
    _____ dis′/trict′
send
    sent
    send′/ing
se′/nile
se/nil′/i/ty
se′/nior
    _____ coun′/sel
    _____ judge
    _____ mort′/gage
se/nior′/i/ty
sen′/sus
sen′/tence
    sen′/tenced
    sen′/tenc/ing
sep′/a/ra/bil′/i/ty
sep′/a/ra/ble con′/tro/
ver′/sy
sep′/a/rate′ *v*
    sep′/a/rat′/ed
    sep′/a/rat′/ing
sep′/a/rate *adj*
    _____ cov′/e/nant
    _____ main′/te/nance
sep′/a/ra′/tion
    _____ a men′/sa et
tho′/ro
    _____ of pat′/ri/mo′/ny

sep′/a/ra′′/tion (contd.)
    ——— of pow′′/ers
    ——— of wit′′/ness/es
sep′/a/rat/ist
sep′/ul/cher *or*
sep′/ul/chre
se/quel′a
se′/quence
se/ques′′/ter
    se/ques′′/tered
    se/ques′′/ter/ing
se′/ques/tra′′/tion
se′/qui/tur
serf
ser′/geant
se′/ri/ate′
se′/ri/a′′/tim
se′/ries
se′/ri/ous
ser′/rat′/ed
ser′/vant
serve
    served
    serv′′/ing
ser′/vice
    ——— by pub′/li/ca′′/
    tion
    ——— con′′/tract′
    ——— es/tab′′/lish/ment
    ——— of pro′′/cess
ser′/vi/ent
    ——— es/tate′
    ——— ten′′/e/ment
ser′/vi/tude′
ser′′/vi/tus
ser′/vus

sess
ses′/sion
set
    ——— a·side′
set′-/off′ *n*
set′/tle
    set′/tled
    set′/tling
set′/tle/ment
    ——— op′/tion
    ——— state′/ment
set′/tler
set′/tlor
sev′/en/teenth′
sev′/enth
sev′/er
    sev′/ered
    sev′/er/ing
sev′/er/a·bil′′/i/ty
sev′/er/a·ble
    ——— con′/tract′
    ——— cov′′/e/nant
    ——— ten′′/an/cy
sev′/er/al
sev′/er/al/ty
sev′/er/ance
    ——— dam′′/ag/es
se/vere′
sew′/age
sew′/er
sex
sex′/u/al
    ——— in′′/ter/course′
shall
sham
    ——— de/fense′

share
_____ cer/tif′/i/cate
_____ of cor′/po/rate
stock
share′/hold′/er
sharp
shave
shaved
shav′/ing
shel′/ter
shel′/tered
shel′/ter/ing
sher′/iff
shift′/ing
_____ clause
_____ in′/come
_____ risk
_____ sev′/er/al/ty
_____ the bur′/den of
proof
shill
ship
_____ bro′/ker
_____ chan′/dler·y
_____ chan′/nel
_____ mas′/ter
_____ mon′/ey
ship′/ment
_____ con′tract′
ship′/per
ship's
_____ hus′/band
_____ pa′/pers
ship′/wreck′
shire
shock

shop
shop′/book′ rule
shop′/keep′/er
shore′/line′
short
_____ cov′/er/ing
_____ no′/tice
_____ po/si′/tion
should
show
showed
shown
show′/ing
show′/er
shrub′/ber·y
shy′/ster
sic
sick′/ness
side′-/bar′ rules
side re/port′
side′/walk′
sight
_____ draft
sign
signed
sign′/ing
sig′/nal
sig′/na/to′/ry
sig′/na/ture′
sig′/net
sig′/ni/fi/ca′/tion
sig′/ni/fy′
sig′/ni/fied′
sig′/ni/fy′/ing
si′/lence
sil′/ver plat′/ter doc′/trine

sim′/i/lar
sim′/i/lar′/i/ty
si/mil′/i/ter
sim′/ple
    ____ con′/tract′
    ____ lar′/ce/ny
    ____ ob′/li/ga′/tion
    ____ rob′/ber·y
sim′/plex dic′/tum
sim/pli′/ci/ter
sim′/u/late′
   sim′/u/lat′/ed
   sim′/u/lat′/ing
sim′/u/la′/tion
si′/mul cum
si′/mul/ta′/ne·ous
since
si′/ne
    ____ an′/i/mo
   re/ver/ten′/di
    ____ di′e
    ____ nu′/me/ro
    ____ pro′/le
    ____ qua non
sin′/gle
    ____ a·dul′/ter·y
sin′gle-/name′ pa′/per
sin′/gu/lar
sink′/ing fund
sis′/ter
sis′/ter-/in-/law′
sit
   sat
   sit′/ting
sit′/tings in cam′/er·a

sit′/u/ate′
   sit′/u/at′/ed
   sit′/u/at′/ing
sit′/u/a′/tion
si′/tus
six′-/day′ li′/cense
sixth
six′/teenth′
skel′/e/ton
    ____ bill
skid
   skid′/ded
   skid′/ding
skill
skilled wit′/ness
slan′/der
   slan′/dered
   slan′/der/ing
slan′/der/er
slan′/der/ous per se
slave
slav′/er·y
slay
   slew
   slain
   slay′/ing
sledge
slight
slip *v*
   slipped
   slip′/ping
slip *adj*
    ____ de/ci′/sion
    ____ o·pin′/ion
slope

slough
slow′/down′
sluice′/way′
slum
slush fund
small claims court
smart mon′/ey dam′/ag/es
smelt′/ing
smut
soak′/age
so′/ber
so/bri′/e·t·y
so′/cial con′/tract′
so′/cial/ism′
so/ci′/e/tal
so/ci/é/té′
so/ci′/e·t·y
so′/ci·o/path′/ic
sod′/om/ite′
sod′/om·y
soil
soit
so′/journ′
   so′/journed′
   so′/journ′/ing
so′/lar
so/la′/ti/um
sold note
sol′/dier
sole
   ____ ac′/tor
sol′/emn
so/lem′/ni/ty
sol′/em/nize′
   sol′/em/nized′

sol′/em/nize′ (contd.)
   sol′/em/niz′/ing
sole′/print′
so/lic′/it
   so/lic′/it/ed
   so/lic′/it/ing
so/lic′/i/ta′/tion
so/lic′/i/tor
   ____ gen′/er/al
sol′/id
so/lid′/i/ty
sol′/i/tar′y con/fine′′/ment
so/lu′/tion
sol′/ven/cy
sol′/vent
sol′/vit
som/nam′/bu/lism′
son
son′-/in-/law′
soon
sound *v*
   sound′/ed
   sound′/ing
sound *adj*
   ____ and dis/pos′/ing
   mind and mem′/o/ry
   ____ health
   ____ ju/di′/cial
   dis/cre′/tion
sound′/ing
   ____ in dam′/ag/es
sound′/ness
source
south
south′/ern

sov′/er/eign
_____ im/mu′/ni/ty
_____ peo′/ple
_____ pow′/er
_____ pre/rog′/a/tive
sov′/er/eign/ty
speak
    spoke
    spo′/ken
    speak′/ing
speak′/er
speak′/ing
_____ de/mur′/rer
_____ mo′/tion
_____ or′/der
spe′/cial
_____ con′/tract
_____ dil′/i/gence
_____ e·lec′/tion
_____ en/dorse′/ment
_____ er′/rors
_____ ex/am′/in/er
_____ ex/cep′/tion
_____ ex/ec′/u/tor
_____ in/junc′/tion
_____ ju′/ris/dic′/tion
_____ ju′/ry
_____ leg′/a/cy
_____ lim′/i/ta′/tion
_____ mal′/ice
_____ mat′/ter
_____ oc′/cu/pant
_____ pa′/per
_____ per′/mit
_____ plead′/ing

spe′/cial (contd.)
_____ priv′/i/lege
_____ reg′/is/tra′/tion
_____ re/pri′/sals
_____ ses′/sion
_____ ver′/dict′
spe′/cial/ist
spe′/cial/ty
spe′/cie
spe/cif′/ic
_____ be/quest′
_____ cov′/e/nant
_____ de/ni′/al
_____ de/vise′
_____ in/tent′
_____ leg′/a/cy
_____ per/for′/mance
spe/cif′/i/cal/ly
spec′/i/fi/ca′/tion
spec′/i/fy′
    spec′/i/fied′
    spec′/i/fy′/ing
spec′/i/men
spec′/u/late′
    spec′/u/lat′/ed
    spec′/u/lat′/ing
spec′/u/la′/tion
spec′/u/la/tive dam′/ag/es
spec′/u/lum
speed′y
_____ ex′/e/cu′/tion
_____ rem′/e/dy
_____ tri′/al
spell′/ing
spend′/thrift′ trust

spe'/rate
spin'-/off'
spin'/ster
spir'/it/u/al
spir'/its
spit'/al
spite fence
split
   _____ in'/come
   _____ sen'/tence
split'/ting a cause of
ac'/tion
spoil
   spoiled
   spoil'/ing
spo'/li/a'/tion
spo'/li/a'/tor
spon'/sion
spon'/sor
spon/ta'/ne/ous
   _____ com/bus'/tion
   _____ ex'/cla/ma'/tion
spon'/te
sport'/ing house
spouse
spread
spring'-/branch'
spring'/ing use
spu'/ri/ous
   _____ class ac'/tion
spy
   spied
   spy'/ing
square
squat'/ter

squire
sta'/bi/lize'
   sta'/bi/lized'
   sta'/bi/liz'/ing
sta'/ble
stake
stake'/hold'/er
stale
   _____ check
   _____ claim
   _____ de/mand'
stall'/age
stamp
   _____ du'/ties
stance
stand
   stood
   stand'/ing
stan'/dard
   _____ de/duc'/tion
   _____ mort'/gage
stand'/ing
   _____ a·side' ju'/rors
   _____ in lo'/co pa/
ren'/tis
   _____ or'der
sta'/ple
star'/board'
star'-/cham'ber
sta'/re
   _____ de/ci'/sis
   _____ in ju/di'/ci·o
state *v*
   stat'/ed
   stat'/ing

state *n, adj*
    ____ of'/fice
    ____ rev'/e/nue
    ____ sov'/er/eign/ty
stat'/ed
    ____ cap'/i/tal
    ____ meet'/ing
state'/ment
    ____ of ac/count'
    ____ of af/fairs'
    ____ of claim
    ____ of con/fes'/sion
    ____ of de/fense'
    ____ of par/tic'/u/lars
state's ev'/i/dence
states'/man
sta'/tion
stat'/ism'
stat'/ist
sta/tis'/tic
sta'/tus
stat'/ute
    ____ of dis'/tri/bu'/
    tions
    ____ of frauds
    ____ of la'/bor/ers
    ____ of lim'/i/ta'/
    tions
    ____ of us'/es
stat'/u/to'/ry
    ____ con/struc'/tion
    ____ dam'/ag/es
    ____ ded'/i/ca'/tion
    ____ deed
    ____ ex'/po/si'/tion
    ____ fore/clo'/sure

stat'/u/to'/ry (contd.)
    ____ lien
    ____ pen'/al/ty
    ____ pre/sump'/tion
    ____ rape
    ____ re/lease'
    ____ sta'/ple
    ____ suc/ces'/sor
sta/tu'/tum
stay *v*
    stayed
    stay'/ing
stay *n*
    ____ laws
    ____ of ex'/e/cu'/tion
    ____ of pro/ceed'/ings
stead'y
steal
    stole
    sto'/len
    steal'/ing
stealth
steam'/ship'
steer'/er
ste/nog'/ra/pher
ste/nog'/ra/phy
step'/broth'/er
step'/child'
step'/daugh'/ter
step'/fa'/ther
step'/moth'/er
step'/par'/ent
step'/sis'/ter
step'/son'
ster'/ile
ste/ril'/i/ty

stet pro/ces//sus
ste//ve/dore/
stew//ard
stick//ler
sti//fle
    sti//fled
    sti//fling
still//born/
stim//u/lant
stint
sti//pend/
sti/pen//di/ar/y
stip//u/late/
    stip//u/lat//ed
    stip//u/lat//ing
stip//u/la//tion
stir//·pes
stock
    ____ as/so//ci/a//tion
    ____ bro//ker
    ____ cer/tif//i/cate
    ____ cor//po/ra//tion
    ____ div//i/dend
    ____ ex/change/
    ____ job//ber
    ____ law dis//trict/
    ____ life in/sur//ance
    com//pa/ny
    ____ op//tions
    ____ re/demp//tion
    ____ split
stock//hold//er
stock//hold//er's
    ____ de/riv//a/tive
    ____ eq//ui/ty
    ____ li//a/bil//i/ty

stock//hold//er's (contd.)
    ____ rep//re/sen//ta/
    tive ac//tion
stop
    ____ or//der
    ____ pay//ment
stop//page
    ____ in tran//si/tu
stor//age
store
    stored
    stor//ing
store//house/
store//room/
storm
stow//age
stow//a·way/
strad//dle
    strad//dled
    strad//dling
strag//gler
straight/-/line/
    ____ de/pre//ci/
    a//tion
    ____ mort//gage
stra/min//e/us ho//mo
strand
    strand//ed
    strand//ing
strang//er
strat//a/gem
straw
    ____ bond
    ____ man
    ____ par//ty
stray

stream of com'/merce
street
strict
    ____ fore/clo'/sure
    ____ in/ter'/pre/
    ta'/tion
    ____ li'/a/bil'/i/ty
stric'/ti ju'/ris
stric/tis'/si/mi ju'/ris
strict'/ly
    ____ con/strued'
    ____ min'/is/te'/ri/al
    du'/ty
stric'/to ju'/ri
stric'/tum jus
strike
strike'/break'/er
strik'/ing
    ____ a ju'/ry
    ____ off the roll
strip'-/min'/ing
strong hand
struck ju'/ry
stuc'/tur/al al'/ter/a'/tion
struc'/ture
strum'/pet
stul'/ti/fy'
    stul'/ti/fied'
    stul'/ti/fy'/ing
stump'/age
su'/a·ble
su'a spon'/te
sub
sub'/a'gent
sub/al'/tern
sub co/lo'/re ju'/ris

sub/con'/tract'
sub/con'/trac'/tor
sub cu'/ri·a
sub'/di/vide'
    sub'/di/vid'/ed
    sub'/di/vid'/ing
sub'/di/vi'/sion
sub'/ir'/ri/gate'
    sub'/ir'/ri/gat'/ed
    sub'/ir'/ri/gat'/ing
sub'/ja'/cent
    ____ sup/port'
sub'/ject *n*
sub/jec'/tion
sub ju'/di/ce
sub'/lease'
sub'/let'
    sub'/let'
    sub'/let'/ting
sub/mer'/gence
sub/mis'/sion
sub/mit'
    sub/mit'/ted
    sub/mit'/ting
sub mo'/do
sub/mort'/gage
sub nom
sub no'/mi/ne
sub/or'/di/nate'
    sub/or'/di/nat'/ed
    sub/or'/di/nat'/ing
sub/or'/di/na'/tion
sub/orn'
    sub/orned'
    sub/orn'/ing
sub'/or'/na'/tion of

per′/ju/ry
sub/orn′/er
sub/poe′/na *v*
    sub/poe′/naed
    sub/poe′/na/ing
sub/poe′/na *n*
    _____ ad tes′/ti/fi/can′/
    dum
    _____ du′/ces te′/cum
sub po/tes/ta′/te
sub/ro/ga′/tion
sub/ro/gee
sub/scribe′
    sub/scribed′
    sub/scrib′/ing
sub/scribed′ cap′/i/tal
sub/scrib′/er
sub/scrib′/ing wit′/ness
sub/scrip′/tion
sub′/se/quent
    _____ con/di′/tion
    _____ cred′/i/tor
sub/ser′/vi/ent
sub/sid′/i·ar·y
sub′/si/dy
sub si/len′/ti·o
sub/sis′/tence
sub′/stance
sub/stan′/tial
    _____ com/pli′/ance
    _____ dam′/ag/es
    _____ er′/ror
    _____ jus′/tice
    _____ per/for′/mance
sub/stan′/tial/ly
sub/stan′/ti/ate′

sub/stan′/ti/ate′ (contd.)
    sub/stan′/ti/at′/ed
    sub/stan′/ti/at′/ing
sub/stan′/ti/a′/tion
sub′/stan/tive
    _____ ev′/i/dence
    _____ fel′/o/ny
    _____ of/fense′
sub′/sti/tute′
    sub′/sti/tut′/ed
    sub′/sti/tut′/ing
sub′/sti/tut′/ed
    _____ ex/ec′/u/tor
    _____ ser′/vice
sub′/sti/tu′/tion
sub′/sti/tu′/tion/ar′y
sub′/ten′/ant
sub′/ter/fuge′
sub′/ter/ra′/ne·an wa′/ters
sub/tract′
    sub/tract′/ed
    sub/tract′/ing
sub/trac′/tion
sub/ver′/sion
sub/ver′/sive ac/tiv′/i/ties
suc/cess′
suc/ces′/sion
suc/ces′/sive
suc/ces′/sor
    _____ trust′/ee′
suc/cinct′
such
sud′/den
    _____ af/fray′
    _____ e·mer′/gen/cy
    _____ heat of pas′/sion

sud′/den (contd.)
    _____ in′/ju/ry
    _____ per′/il
sue
    sued
    su′/ing
suf′/fer
    suf′/fered
    suf′/fer/ing
suf′/fer/ance
suf/fi′/cient
    _____ cause
    _____ ev′/i/dence
suf′/fo/cate′
    suf′/fo/cat′/ed
    suf′/fo/cat′/ing
suf′/fo/ca′/tion
suf′/frage
sug/gest′
    sug/gest′/ed
    sug/gest′/ing
sug/ges′/tion
    _____ of er′/ror
sug/ges′/tive
    _____ in/ter′/ro/ga′/
    tion
su′i/cid′/al
su′i/cide
sui ge′/ner/is
sui ju′/ris
suit
suit′/a·ble
suite
suit′/or
sum
    _____ in gross

sum (contd.)
    _____ pay′/a·ble
    _____ re/ceiv′/a·ble
sum/mar′i/ly
sum′/ma/ry
    _____ con/vic′/tion
    _____ judg′/ment
    _____ ju′/ris/dic′/tion
    _____ pro/ceed′/ing
    _____ pro′/cess
sum/ma′/tion
sum′/ming up
sum′/mon
    sum′/moned
    sum′/mon/ing
sum′/mum jus
sump′/tu/ar′y
sun′/dries
sun′/dry
sun′/shine
su′o no′/mi/ne
su′o pe/ri′/cu/lo
su′/per
su/per′/flu/ous
su′/per/in/tend′
su′/per/in/ten′/dent
su/pe′/ri/or
su/pe′/ri/or′/i/ty
su′/per/nu′/mer/ar′y
su′/per/sede′
    su′/per/sed′/ed
    su′/per/sed′/ing
su′/per/se′/de/as
su′/per/sti′/tion
su′/per/vene′
    su′/per/vened′

su'/per/vene' (contd.)
    su'/per/ven'/ing
su'/per/vise'
    su'/per/vised'
    su'/per/vis'/ing
su'/per/vi'/sion
su'/per/vi'/sor
su'/per/vi'/so/ry
su'/per vi'/sum cor'/po/ris
sup'/ple/ment
sup'/ple/men'/tal
    —— af'/fi/da'/vit
    —— an'/swer
    —— com/plaint'
    —— plead'/ing
sup'/ple/men'/ta/ry
    —— pro/ceed'/ings
sup'/pli/ant
sup/pli'/er
sup/ply'
sup/port'
    sup/port'/ed
    sup/port'/ing
sup/pose'
    sup/posed'
    sup/pos'/ing
sup'/po/si'/tion
sup/pos'/i/ti'/tious
sup/press'
    sup/pressed'
    sup/press'/ing
su'/pra
su'/pra/ri/par'/i/an
su/prem'/a/cy
su/preme'
sur'/charge

sur'e/ty
sur'/face
sur'/geon
sur'/ger·y
sur/mise'
    sur/mised'
    sur/mis'/ing
sur'/name'
sur'/plus
    —— earn'/ings
sur'/plus/age
sur/prise'
    sur/prised'
    sur/pris'/ing
sur'/re/but'/ter
sur'/re/join'/der
sur/ren'/der *v*
    sur/ren'/dered
    sur/ren'/der/ing
sur/ren'/der *n, adj*
    —— of char'/ter
    —— of cop'y/hold'
    —— val'/ue
sur/ren'/der/ee'
sur/ren'/der/or
sur'/rep/ti'/tious
sur'/ro/gate'
sur/round'
    sur/round'/ed
    sur/round'/ing
sur'/tax'
sur/veil'/lance
sur/vey' *v*
    sur/veyed'
    sur/vey'/ing
sur'/vey' *n*

sur/vey'/or
sur/viv'/al stat'/utes
sur/vive'
    sur/vived'
    sur/viv'/ing
sur/vi'/vor/ship'
sus/cep'/ti/bil'/i/ty
sus/cep'/ti/ble
sus'/pect' *n, adj*
sus/pect'
    sus/pect'/ed
    sus/pect'/ing
sus/pense'
sus/pi'/cion
sus/pi'/cious
sus/tain'
    sus/tained'
    sus/tain'/ing
sus'/te/nance
sus'/ten/ta'/tion
swear
    swore
    sworn
    swear'/ing
sweat'/ing
sweat'/shop'
sweep'/ing
sweep'/stakes'
swin'/dle
    swin'/dled
    swin'/dling
switch'/yard' doc'/trine
sworn
syl'/la/bus
syl'/lo/gism'

sym/bol'/ic de/liv'/er•y
sym'/me/try
sym'/pa/thet'/ic
sym'/pa/thy strike
syn'/al/lag/mat'/ic con'/tract'
syn'/chro/ni/za'/tion
syn'/dic
syn'/di/cal/ism'
syn'/di/cate *n*
syn'/di/cate' *v*
    syn'/di/cat'/ed
    syn'/di/cat'/ing
syn'/di/ca'/tion
syn'/od
syn/on'/y/mous
syn/op'/sis
syph'/i/lis
sys'/tem

T

ta'/ble
    ____ of cas'/es
tab'/u/la
    ____ in nau/fra'/gi•o
    ____ ra'/sa
tac'/it
    ____ ac/cept'/ance
    ____ ded'/i/ca'/tion
    ____ mort'/gage
    ____ re/lo/ca'/tion
tack

tack (contd.)
    tacked
    tack′/ing
tail
    ____ fe′′male′
    __ gen′′er/al
    ____ male
    ____ spe′/cial
taint
    taint′/ed
    taint′/ing
take
    took
    tak′/en
    tak′/ing
take
    ____ a·way′
    ____ back
    ____ by stealth
    ____ ef/fect′
    ____ o′/ver
tak′/er
ta′/les′
ta′/les/man
tal′/lage
tal/la′/gi/um
tal′/ley *or* tal′/ly
tal′/weg′
tame
    tamed
    tam′/ing
ta′/men
tam′/per
    tam′/pered
    tam′/per/ing

tam quam
tan′/gi/ble
    ____ ev′/i/dence
    ____ prop′/er/ty
tap
    tapped
    tap′/ping
tar′/get
tar′/iff
tau/tol′/o/gy
tav′/ern
    ____ keep′/er
tav′/ern/er
tax
    taxed
    tax′/ing
tax
    ____ an/tic′/i/pa′/tion
    war′/rants
    ____ as/sess′/ment
    ____ au′/dit
    ____ a·void′/ance
    ____ cer/tif′/i/cate
    ____ cred′/it
    ____ de/duc′/tion
    ____ deed
    ____ e·va′/sion
    ____ ex/emp′/tion
    ____ fer′/ret
    ____ fore/clo′/sure
    ____ im′/pli/ca′/tions
    ____ lease
    ____ lev′y
    ____ pref′/er/ence
    ____ pur′/chas/er

tax (contd.)

    ———— re′′/bate

    ———— re/turn′

    ———— shel′′/ter

    ———— sur′′/charge′

    ———— ta′′/ble

    ———— ti′′/tle

tax′/a·ble

tax/a′′/tion

tax′/es

tax′i/cab

tax′′/pay′′/er

teach

    taught

    teach′′/ing

teach′′/er

team

team′′/ster

tear′/ing of will

tech′′/ni/cal

tel′e/gram′

tel′e/graph′

tel′e/phone′

tel′e/scope′

tel′e/vi′/sion

tell′′/er

tem′′/per/a/ment

tem′′/per/ance

tem′′/pest

tem′/po/ra′′/lis

tem′/po/ral′′/i/ties

tem′/po/ral′′/i/ty

tem′/po/ral lords

tem′/po/rar′i/ly

tem′/po/rar′y

tem′′/po/rar′y (contd.)

    ———— ad/min′/is/tra′′/

tion

    ———— dam′′/ag/es

    ———— dis′/a·bil′′/i/ty

    ———— in/junc′′/tion

    ———— re/strain′/ing

or′/der

tem′′/po/re′

tem′′/pus

    ———— u′ti/le

ten′′/an/cy

    ———— at suf′′/fer/ance

    ———— by the en/tire′′/ty

    ———— in com′′/mon

ten′′/ant

    ———— at suf′′/fer/ance

    ———— at will

    ———— by the cur′′/te/sy

    ———— by the man′′/ner

    ———— for life

    ———— from year to year

    ———— in com′′/mon

    ———— in dow′′/er

    ———— in fee sim′′/ple

    ———— in sev′′/er/al/ty

    ———— in tail

    ———— in tail ex pro′′/

vi/si/o′′/ne vi′′/ri

    ———— of the de/mesne′

    ———— par′′/a/vaile′

tend

    tend′′/ed

    tend′′/ing

ten′′/der

ten′/e/ment
te/ne′/re
te′/net
ten′/or
ten′/ta/tive
tenth
ten′/u/it
ten′/u/ra
ten′/ure
    ____ in of′/fice
term
    ____ for de/lib′/er/at′/ing
    ____ in gross
    ____ in/sur′/ance
    ____ of court
    ____ of lease
    ____ of of′/fice
    ____ pro′/ba/to′/ry
ter′/mi/na/ble
ter′/mi/nal
ter′/mi/nate′
    ter′/mi/nat′/ed
    ter′/mi/nat′/ing
ter′/mi/na′/tion
    ____ of em/ploy′/ment
ter′/min/er
ter′/mi/ni
ter′/mi/nus
    ____ ad quem
    ____ a que
ter′/ra
    ____ af′/fir/ma′/ta
    ____ cul′/ta
    ____ in′/cog′/ni′/ta

ter′/ra (contd.)
    ____ no′/va
ter′/ri/er
ter′/ri/to′/ri/al
    ____ court
    ____ ju′/ris/dic′/tion
ter′/ri/to/ri/al′/i/ty
ter′/ri/to′/ry
ter′/ror
test *v*
    test′/ed
    test′/ing
test *adj.*
    ____ case
    ____ oath
test′/a·ble
tes′/ta/cy
tes′/ta/ment
tes′/ta/men′/ta/ry
    ____ ca/pac′/i/ty
    ____ class
    ____ dis′/po/si′/tion
    ____ guard′/i·an
    ____ in′/stru/ment
    ____ pa′/per
    ____ suc/ces′/sion
    ____ trust′/ee′
tes′/tate′
tes/ta′/tion
tes′/ta/tor
tes/ta′/trix
tes′/te of a writ
tes′/tes
tes′/ti/fy′
    tes′/ti/fied′

tes'/ti/fy' (contd.)
    tes'/ti/fy'/ing
tes'/ti/mo'/ni/al
tes'/ti/mo'/ny
tes'/tis
text'/book'
the'/a·ter *or* the'/a·tre
theft
theme
the'/o/ret'/i/cal
the'/o/ry
there'/a·bout'
there/af'/ter
there/by'
there/for'
there'/fore'
there/in'
there'/in/af'/ter
there/to'
there/un'/der
there/un'/to
there'/u·pon'
thief
thiev'/er·y
things of val'/ue
third par'/ty
thir'/teenth'
thir'/ty
thor'/ough/fare'
thread
threat
threat'/en
    threat'/ened
    threat'/en/ing
through

throw'/back'
thrust'/ing
tick'/et
tid'/al
tide'/land'
tide'/mark'
tides'/men'
tide'/wa/ter
tide'/way'
tie
    tied
    ty'/ing
tierce
tight
till'/age
tim'/ber
time
    _____ bar'/gain
    _____ char'/ter
    _____ de/pos'/it
    _____ draft
    _____ im'/me/mo'/ri/al
    _____ is of the es'/sence
    _____ pol'/i/cy
time'/ta'/ble
tip'/staff'
tith'/a·ble
tithe
tith'/er
ti'/tle
    _____ by ad/verse' pos/ses'/sion
    _____ by de/scent'
    _____ by lim'/i/ta'/tion

ti′/tle (contd.)

    ____ by pre/scrip′/ tion

    ____ de/fec′/tive in form

    ____ doc′/u/ment

    ____ guar′/an/ty

    ____ in/sur′/ance

    ____ of a cause

    ____ of cler′/gy/man

    ____ of dec′/la/ra′/ tion

    ____ of en′/try

    ____ re/ten′/tion

    ____ search

    ____ trans/ac′/tion

    ____ to or′/ders

to have and to hold

to′/ken

tol′/er/ant

tol′/er/ate′

    tol′/er/at′/ed

    tol′/er/at′/ing

tol′/er/a′/tion

toll

    ____ bridge

    ____ gath′/er/er

    ____ road

    ____ thor′/ough

    ____ tra′/verse

toll′/age

toll′/er

tomb

tomb′/stone′

ton

ton′/nage

    ____ du′/ty

    ____ rent

ton′/sure

took and car′/ried a·way′

to/pog′/ra/phy

tor′/rent

tor/ren′/tial

tor/pe′/do doc′/trine

tort

tort′-/fea′sor

tor′/tious

tor′/ture

    tor′/tured

    tor′/tur/ing

to′/tal

    ____ de/pen′/den/cy

    ____ dis′/a·bil′/i/ty

    ____ e·vic′/tion

    ____ loss

Tot′/ten trust

touch and stay

tour′/na/ment

tout

    ____ temps prist

    ____ un sound

tow′/age

to/ward′

to wit

town

    ____ clerk

    ____ cri′/er

    ____ com/mis′/sion/er

    ____ meet′/ing

    ____ trea′/sur·y

town (contd.)

    _____ war′/rant

town′/ship′

town′/site′

tox′/ic

tox′/i/cant

tox′/i/cate′

    tox′/i/cat′/ed

    tox′/i/cat′/ing

tox′/i/col′/o/gy

tox′/in

trace

    traced

    trac′/ing

tract

trade

    _____ ac/cept′/ance

    _____ a·gree′/ment

    _____ dis/pute′

    _____ li′/bel

    _____ se′/cret

    _____ u′nion

    _____ us′/age

trade′/mark′

trad′/er

trades′/man

trad′/ing

    _____ cor′/po/ra′/tion

    _____ part′/ner/ship′

    _____ voy′/age

tra/di′/ti·o

    _____ bre′/vi ma′/nu

    _____ lon′/ga ma′/nu

tra/di′/tion

tra/di′/tion/ar′y

traf′/fic

    _____ reg′/u/la′/tion

trail′/er

train

trai′/tor

trai′/tor/ous

tra′/jec/ti′/ti·a pe/cu′/ni·a

tramp

trans/act′

    trans/act′/ed

    trans/act′/ing

trans/ac′/tion

tran/scribe′

    tran/scribed′

    tran/scrib′/ing

tran′/script

tran/scrip′/tion

trans/fer′ *v*

    trans/ferred′

    trans/fer′/ring

trans′/fer′ *n*

    _____ in con′/tem/pla′/

    tion of death

    _____ of a cause

    _____ pay′/ment

    _____ tick′/et

trans/fer′/a·ble

trans′/fer/ee′

trans′/fer′/ence

trans′/fer/or′

trans/ship′/ment

tran′/sience

tran′/sient

    _____ per′/son

trans/i′/re

tran'/sit
    ____ in rem ju'/di/ca'/
    tam
tran'/si/tive
    ____ cov'/e/nant
tran'/si/to'/ry
    ____ ac'/tion
trans/late'
    trans/lat'/ed
    trans/lat'/ing
trans/la'/tion
tran/mis'/sion
trans/mit'
    trans/mit'/ted
    trans/mit'/ting
trans/port' *v*
    trans/port'/ed
    trans/port'/ing
trans'/port' *n*
tran'/por/ta'/tion
trap
    trapped
    trap'/ping
trau'/ma
trau/mat'/ic
tra/vail'
trav'/el
    trav'/eled
    trav'/el/ing
trav'/el/er
trav'/el/ing sales'/man
tra'/verse
    ____ ju'/ry
tra/vers'/er
tra/vers'/ing note

treach'/er·y
trea'/son
    ____ fel'/o/ny
trea'/son/a·ble
trea'/son/ous
trea'/sure
trea'/sur/er
trea'/sur·y
    ____ cer/tif'/i/cate
    ____ note
    ____ se/cu'/ri/ties
    ____ stock
treat'/ment
trea'/ty
tre'/ble
    ____ costs
    ____ dam'/ag/es
tres'/pass
    tres'/passed
    tres'/pass/ing
tres'/pass
    ____ de bo'/nis as'/
    por/ta'/tis
    ____ for mesne prof'/
    its
    ____ qua'/re clau'/
    sum fre'/git
    ____ to land
    ____ to try ti'/tle
    ____ vi et ar'/mis
tres'/pass/er
tri'/al
    ____ a·mend'/ment
    ____ at bar
    ____ at ni'/si pri'/us

tri′/al (contd.)
  ____ bal′/ance
  ____ by grand as/size′
  ____ by ju′/ry
  ____ by wa′/ger of
bat′/tle
  ____ cal′/en/dar
  ____ de no′/vo
trib′/al lands
tribe
tri/bu′/nal
trib′/u/tar′y
trib′/ute
trick′/er·y
tri/en′/ni/al
tri/fur′/cat′/ed tri′/al
tri′/or
tri/par′/tite′
tri′/ple
triv′/i/al
troop
tro′/phy
tro′/ver
troy weight
tru′/an/cy
tru′/ant
truce
true
  ____ ad/mis′/sion
  ____ bill
  ____ cop′y
  ____ val′/ue
  ____ ver′/dict′
trust
  ____ al/lot′/ment

trust (contd.)
  ____ cer/tif′/i/cate
  ____ de/pos′/it
  ____ es/tate′
  ____ ex de/lic′/to
  ____ ex mal′/e/fi′/ci·o
  ____ in/den′/ture
  ____ in in/vi′/tum
  ____ leg′/a/cy
  ____ of′/fi/cer
  ____ ter′/ri/to′/ry
trust′/ee′
  ____ ex mal′/e/fi′/ci·o
  ____ in bank′/rupt/cy
  ____ pro′/cess
truth
try
  tried
  try′/ing
tu/i′tion
tu/mul′/tu/ous
tun
tun′/nage
tur′/ba/ry
turn′/coat′ wit′/ness
turn′/key′
turn′/out′
turn′/pike′
tur′/pis
  ____ cau′/sa
  ____ con/trac′/tus
tur′/pi/tude′
tu′/te/lage
tu′/tor
tu′/tor/ship′

tu'/trix'
twelfth
twelve'-/month' bond
twice
typ'/i/cal
tyr'/an/ny
ty'/rant
ty'/ro

U

u·biq'/ui/tous
u·biq'/ui/ty
ul'/lage
ul'/te'/ri/or
ul'/ti/ma ra'/ti·o
ul'/ti/mate
_____ is'/sue
ul'/ti/ma'/tum
ul'/ti/mo'
ul'/tra
_____ ma'/re
_____ re/pris'/es
_____ vi'/res
um'/brel'/la pol'/i/cy
in/sur'/ance
um'/pir'/age
um'/pire'
un'/a'ble
un'/ac/crued'
un'/am/big'/u/ous
u'na/nim'/i/ty
u·nan'/i/mous

un'/an'/swer/a·ble
un'/ap/peal'/a·ble
un'/au'/thor/ized' use
u'na vo'/ce
un'/a·void'/a·ble
un'/born' child
un/bro'/ken
un'/cer'/tain/ty
un'/chal'/lenge/a·ble
un'/chas'/ti/ty
un'/cle
un'/clean' hands
un'/con/di'/tion/al
par'/don
un/con'/scio/na·ble
_____ con'/tract'
un'/con'/scious
un'/con'/sti/tu'/tion/al
un'/con/trol'/la/ble
un'/de/fend'/ed
un'/der
un'/der/cov'/er a'gent
un'/der/cur'/rent
un'/der/ground
un'/der/hand'/ed
un'/der/in/sured'
un'/der/lease'
un'/der/neath'
un'/der/rep'/re/sen'/ta'/tion
un'/der/signed'
un'/der/stand'
un'/der/stood'
un'/der/stand'/ing
un'/der/take'

un′/der/take′ (contd.)
    un′/der/took′
    un′/der/tak′/en
    un′/der/tak′/ing
un′/der/tak′/er
un′/der/ten′′/ant
un′/der/write′
    un′/der/wrote′
    un′/der/writ′/ten
    un′/der/writ′/ing
un′/dis/closed′ prin′/ci/pal
un′/dis/put′′/ed fact
un′/di/vid′′/ed
un/due′ in′′/flu/ence
un′/earned′
    _____ in′′/come
    _____ in′′/cre/ment
un′/ed′′/u/cat′′/ed
un′/em/ploy′/ment
un′/en/closed′ place
un/e′qual
un′/e·quiv′′/o/cal
un′/err′′/ing
un′/es/sen′′/tial
un′/eth′′/i/cal
un′/ex/cep′′/tion/a·ble
un′/ex/cep′′/tion/al
un′/ex/pect′′/ed
un′/ex/pired′ term
un′/fair
    _____ com′′/pe/ti′′/tion
    _____ hear′′/ing
    _____ la′′/bor prac′′/tice
un/faith′′/ful
un/fin′′/ished

un/fit′
un′/fore/seen′
un/harmed′
un′/i·den′′/ti/fied′
u′ni/fac′′/tor/al ob′/li/ga′′/
tion
u′ni/form′
u′ni/for′′/mi/ty
u′ni/fy′
    u′ni/fied′
    u′ni/fy′/ing
u′ni/lat′′/er/al
    _____ con′′/tract′
    _____ mis/take′
un′/im/peach′′/a·ble wit′′/
ness
un′/im/proved′ land
un′/in/cor′′/po/rated′
un′/in/fect′′/ed
un′/in/sured′
un′/in/tel′′/li/gi/ble
u′nion
    _____ cer′/ti/fi/ca′′/tion
    _____ con′′/tract′
    _____ mort′′/gage
u′nit
u·nite′
    u·nit′′/ed
u·nit′′/ing
u′ni/trust′
u′ni/ty
    _____ of in′′/ter/est
    _____ of pos/ses′′/sion
    _____ of sei′/sin *or* sei′/
    zin

u′ni/ty (contd.)
    _____ of ti′/tle
u′ni/ver′/sal
    _____ a′/gent
    _____ leg′/a/cy
u′ni/ver′/si/ty
un/just′
    _____ en/rich′/ment
un/law′/ful
    _____ as/sem′/bly
    _____ de/tain′/er
    _____ en′/try
    _____ pick′/et/ing
    _____ search
un/law′/ful/ly
un/less′
un′/lim′/it/ed
un′/liq′/ui/dat′/ed
    _____ dam′/ag/es
    _____ de/mand′
un/liv′/er·y
un/mar′/ket/a·ble ti′/tle
un/mar′/ried
un′/nat′/u/ral of/fense′
un′/nec′/es/sar′y
    _____ hard′/ship
u′no ac′/tu
un′/oc′/cu/pied′
un′/prec′/e/dent′/ed
un′/prej′/u/diced
un′/pro/fes′/sion/al
    _____ con′/duct′
un′/prof′/it/a·ble
un′/ques′/tion/a·ble
un′/rea′/son/a·ble

un′/rea′/son/a·ble (contd.)
    _____ com′/pen/sa′/
    tion
    _____ re/straint′ of
    trade
un′/re/strict′/ed in/ter′/
pre/ta′/tion
un′/rul′y
un′/safe′
un′/sta′/ble
un′/suit′/a·ble
un′/thrift′y
un/til′
un′/to′/ward
un′/true′
un′/u′su/al
un′/val′/ued
un′/whole′/some
un′/wor′/thy
un′/writ′/ten
    _____ con′/sti/tu′/tion
    _____ law
up′/keep′
up′/lands′
up′/per bench
up′/set′ price
ur′/ban
ure
us′/age
us′/ance
use *v*
    used
    us′/ing
use *n*
    _____ and hab′/i/ta′/

use (contd.)

    tion

    ———— and oc''/cu/pa''/

    tion

    ———— im/mu''/ni/ty

    ———— plain''/tiff

    ———— var'i/ance

use''/ful life

use''/ful/ness

us''/er

us''/que

u'su/al

    ———— cov''/e/nant

u'su/fruct'

u'su/fruc''/tu/ar'y

u·su''/ri/ous

u'su/ry

u'ter/ine'

ut hos''/pi/tes

u·til''/i/ty

ut''/most'

ut''/ter

    ut''/tered

    ut''/ter/ing

ut''/ter/ance

ux''/or

ux'/o''/ri/al

ux'/or''/i/cide

V

va''/can/cy

va''/cant

    ———— suc/ces''/sion

va''/cate'

    va''/cat''/ed

    va''/cat''/ing

va/ca''/tion

    ———— of judg''/ment

va/ca''/tur

vac''/il/late'

    vac''/il/lat''/ed

    vac''/il/lat''/ing

va''/cu·a pos/ses''/si·o

va/cu''/i·ty

vac''/u/um

va''/di/um

    ———— mor''/tu/um

    ———— po''/ne/re

    ———— vi''/vum

vag'/a/bond'

va''/gran/cy

va''/grant

vague

vague'/ness

va/len''/ti·a

va''/let

val''/id

val''/i/date'

    val''/i/dat''/ed

    val''/i/dat''/ing

val'/i/da''/tion

va/lid''/i/ty

    ———— of a stat''/ute

    ———— of a trea''/ty

    ———— of a will

val''/ley

val''/or

val'u/a·ble

    ———— con/sid'/er/a'

val'u/a·ble (contd.)
   tion
     _____ im/prove'/ment
     _____ pa'/pers
val'/u/a'/tion
val'/ue
val'/ued pol'/i/cy
val'/ue/less
val'u/er
van'/dal
van'/dal/ism'
var'i/a·ble
var'i/ance
var'i/a'/tion
va/sec'/to/my
vas'/sal
vas'/sal/age
vas'/tum
ve'/hi'/cle
ve/hic'/u/lar
     _____ ho'/mi/cide'
vein
ve'/jours
vel non
ve'/nal
ve/na'/ri·a
ve/na'/ti·o
vend
   vend'/ed
   vend'/ing
vend/ee'
vend'/er
ven/det'/ta
ven/di'/tion
ven'/di/trix'
ven'/dor

ven'/due'
ve/ne'/re/al dis/ease'
ve'/ni·al
ve/ni'/re
     _____ de no'/vo
     _____ fa'/ci/as
ve/ni'/re/man
ve'/nit et di'/cit
ven'/ter
ven'/ture
ven'/ue'
     _____ ju'/ris/dic'/tion
ve/ra'/cious
ve/rac'/i/ty
ve/ray'
ver'/ba
ver'/bal
     _____ as/sault'
     _____ pro'/cess
ver'/dict'
     _____ con'/trar'y to law
     _____ of not guilt'y
     _____ sub'/ject to
   o·pin'/ion of court
ve'/re/dic'/tum
ver'/i/fi/ca'/tion
ver'/i/fy'
   ver'/i/fied'
   ver'/i/fy'/ing
ver'/i/ty
ver'/sion
ver'/sus
ver'/ti/cal
ver'/ti/go'
ver'/sus
ver'y

ves'/sel
vest
    vest'/ed
    vest'/ing
vest'/ed
    vest'/ing
vest'/ed
    _____ de/vise'
    _____ es/tate'
    _____ in'/ter/est
    _____ leg'/a/cy
    _____ pen'/sion
    _____ re/main'/der
    _____ rights
ves/ti'/gial words
ves/tig'/i/um
ves'/try
ves'/tu/ra
ves'/ture
vet'/er/an
ve'/to
vex
    vexed
    vex'/ing
vex/a'/ri
vex/a'/ta quaes'/ti·o
vex/a'/tion
vex/a'/tious
    _____ ac'/tions
    _____ de/lay'
    _____ pro/ceed'/ing
    _____ re/fus'/al to pay
vi'a
    _____ ex/ec'/u/ti'/va
    _____ or'/di/na'/ri·a
    _____ pub'/li/ca

vi'/a/bil'/i/ty
vi'/a/ble
vic'/ar
vi/car'/i/ous li'/a·bil'/i/ty
vice
    _____ ad'/mi/ral
    _____ con'/sul
    _____ mar'/shal
    _____ pres'/i/dent
    _____ prin'/ci/pal
vice'/roy'
vice ver'/sa
vic'/i/nage
vi/cin'/i/ty
vi'/cious
vic'/tor
vict'/u·al
vic'/tus
vi'/de
    _____ an'/te
    _____ in'/fra
    _____ post
    _____ su'/pra
vi/de'/li/cet'
vi/du'/i·ty
vie
vi et ar'/mis
view
view'/er
vig'/il
vig'/i/lance
vig'/i/lant
vig'/or
vig'/or/ous
vil'/lage
vil'/lain

vil′/lein

   ____ re/gard′/ant

   ____ ser′/vices

vil′/len/age

vil′/len/ous judg′/ment

vin/a′/gi/um

vin′/di/ca′/re

vin′/di/cate′

   vin′/di/cat′/ed

   vin′/di/cat′/ing

vin′/di/ca′/tion

vint′/ner

vi′/o/late′

   vi′/o/lat′/ed

   vi′/o/lat′/ing

vi′/o/la′/tion

vi′/o/lence

vi′/o/lent

   ____ in′/ju/ry

   ____ pre/sump′/tion

vir

vi′/res

vir/ga′/ta

vir′/gate′

virge

vir′/tu/al

vir′/tu/ous

vir/tu′/te

   ____ of/fi′/ci·i

vis

   ____ ar/ma′/ta

   ____ clan′/des/ti′/na

   ____ com/pul′/si/va

   ____ di/vi′/na

   ____ ex/pul′/si/va

   ____ im/pres′/sa

vis (contd.)

   ____ in/er′/mis

   ____ in/ju′/ri/o′/sa

   ____ la′/i/ca

   ____ li/ci′/ta

   ____ ma′/jor

   ____ prox′/i/ma

   ____ sim′/plex′

vi′/sa

vis′/count′

vis′/i/bil′/i/ty

vis′/i/ble

vi′/sion

vis′/it

vis′/i/ta′/tion

vis′/i/tor

vi′/sus

vi′/tal

vi/tal′/i/ty

vi′/ti/ate′

   vi′/ti/at′/ed

   vi′/ti/at′/ing

vi/til′/i/gate′

   vi/til′/i/gat′/ed

   vi/til′/i/gat′/ing

vi/var′/i/um

vi′/va/ry

vi′/va vo′/ce

vi′/vum va′/di/um

vo/cab′/u/la ar′/tis

vo/cab′/u/lar′y

vo′/cal

vo/ca′/tion

vo/cif′/er/ous

vo′/co

voice

voice (contd.)
_____ ex/em′/plars′
_____ i·den′/ti/fi/ca′/
tion
void
_____ con′/tract′
_____ in to′/to
_____ judg′/ment
_____ leg′/a/cy
_____ mar′/riage
_____ pro′/cess
void′/a·ble
_____ con′/tract′
_____ pref′/er/ence
void′/ance
voir dire
vo′/lens′
vo/len′/ti non fit in/ju′/
ri·a
vo/li′/tion
vol′/un/tar′i/ly
vol′/un/tar′y
_____ dis/mis′/sal
_____ man′/slaugh′/ter
_____ waste
vol′/un/teer′
vote
vot′/ed
vot′/ing
vot′/er
vouch
vouched
vouch′/ing
vouch/ee′
vouch′/er

voy′/age
_____ char′/ter
_____ pol′/i/cy
voy/eur′/ism′
vul′/gar
vul′/gar′/i/ty

W

wa′/di·a
wage
_____ as/sign′/ment
_____ earn′/er
wa′/ger
wa′/ger/ing
_____ con′/tract′
wag′/on
wag′/on/age
waif
wait
wait′/ed
wait′/ing
waive
waived
waiv′/ing
waiv′/er
_____ by e·lec′/tion of
rem′/e/dies
_____ of ex/emp′/tion
_____ of im/mu′/ni/ty
_____ of tort

wall

wan′/der

    wan′/dered

    wan′/der/ing

want

    _____ of con/sid′/er/a′′/tion

    _____ of ju′/ris/dic′′/tion

want′/age

wan′/ton

    _____ act

    _____ con′/duct′

    _____ in′′/ju/ry

    _____ mis/con′/duct′

    _____ neg′/li/gence

wan′/ton/ness

ward

    _____ in chan′/cer·y

    _____ mote

    _____ pa′′/tient

    _____ of ad′/mi/ral/ty

war′/da

ward′/age

war′/den

ward′/ship′

ware′/house′

    _____ re/ceipt′

warn

    warned

    warn′/ing

warp

war′/rant

    _____ cred′/i/tor

    _____ of ar/rest′

war′/rant (contd.)

    _____ of at/tor′′/ney

    _____ of com/mit′′/ment

    _____ of′′/fi/cer

war′/ran/tee′

war′/ran/tor′

war′/ran/ty

    _____ deed

    _____ of fit′/ness

    _____ of hab′/it/a·bil′′/i/ty

    _____ of mer′/chant/a·bil′/i/ty

    _____ of ti′/tle

war′/ren

waste

wast′′/ing trust

watch

watch′/man

wa′/ter

    _____ course

    _____ dis′/trict′

    _____ pow′′/er

wa′/ter/course′

wa′/tered stock

wa′/ter/front′

wa′/ter/mark′

wa′/ter/way′

way

    _____ of ne/ces′′/si/ty

way′/bill′

way′/leave′

wealth

weap′/on

wear and tear
wear′/ing ap/par′/el
weath′/er
wed
    wed′/ded *or* wed
    wed′/ding
wed′/lock′
week
weigh′/age
weight
    _____ of ev′/i/dence
weir
wel′/fare′
welsh′/er
welsh′/ing
west
west′/ern
whale
whal′/er
wharf
wharf′/age
wharf′/in/ger
wheel′/age
when/ev′/er
where′/a·bouts′
where/as′
where′/fore′
where/in′
where′/of′
where′/to
where′/up/on′
wher/ev′/er
where′/with/al′
which
while
whim

whip
    whipped
    whip′/ping
whip′/lash′
whis′/key
white a′/cre
white′-/col′lar crime
who/ev′/er
whole
whole′/sale
    _____ deal′/er
    _____ price
whole′/sal′/er
whole′/some
whol′/ly
    _____ de/pen′/dent
    _____ dis/a′bled
whore
whore′/mas′/ter
wid′/ow
wid′/ow/er
wid′/ow/hood′
wife
wild′/cat′ strike
will
    _____ con′/test′
    _____ sub′/sti/tutes′
will′/ful
    _____ and ma/li′/cious
in′/ju/ry
    _____ and wan′/ton
in′/ju/ry
    _____ in/dif′/fer/ence
    _____ mis/con′/duct′
    _____ mur′/der
    _____ neg′/li/gence

will′/ful/ly
will′/ing/ly
wine
win′/ter
wire′/tap′
    wire′/tapped′
    wire′/tap′/ped
wire′/tap′/per
wish
wit
wit′/am
witch′/craft′
with con/sent′
with/draw′
    with/drew′
    with/drawn′
    with/draw′/ing
with/draw′/al
with/hold′
with/in′
with/out′
    _____ day
    _____ de/lay′
    _____ no′/tice
    _____ prej′/u/dice
    _____ re′/course′
    _____ re/serve′
wit′/ness
    wit′/nessed
    wit′/ness/ing
wit′/ting/ly
wom′/an
words
    _____ ac′/tion/a·ble in
    them/selves′
    _____ of lim′/i/ta′/tion

words (contd.)
    _____ of pro′/cre/a′tion
    _____ of pur′/chase
work
    _____ of ne/ces′/si/ty
    _____ prod′/uct
    _____ re/lief′
work′/a·way′
work′/ing
    _____ cap′/i/tal
work′/man
work′/men's com′/pen/
sa′/tion
work′/shop′
world′/ly
    _____ em/ploy′/ment
wor′/ry
    wor′/ried
    wor′/ry/ing
wor′/ship
worth
worth′/less
wor′/thy
would
wound
    wound′/ed
    wound′/ing
wrath
wreck
wreck′/er
wrench
writ
    _____ of as/sis′/tance
    _____ of as/so′/ci/a′/
tion
    _____ of at/tach′/ment

writ (contd.)

_____ of cer′/ti·o/ra′/ri

_____ of con/spir′′/a/cy

_____ of det′/i/nue′

_____ of e·ject′/ment

_____ of en′/try

_____ of er′/ror

_____ of ex′/e/cu′/tion

_____ of ex/tent′

_____ of grand dis/tress′

_____ of man′/da/mus

_____ of mesne

_____ of pos/ses′′/sion

_____ of priv′/i/lege

_____ of pro′/hi/bi′/tion

_____ of pro/tec′/tion

_____ of re/cap′/tion

_____ of re/plev′/in

_____ of res/ti/tu′/tion

_____ of sum′/mons

_____ pro re/tor′/no ha/ben′/do

write

   wrote

   writ′′/ten

   writ′′/ing

writ′′/ten

_____ con′′/tract′

_____ in′′/stru/ment

wrong′′/do′/er

wrong′′/ful

_____ birth ac′/tion

_____ con′/duct′

_____ death stat′/utes

wrong′/ful (contd.)

_____ lev′y

wrong′/ful/ly

wrong′/head′/ed

Y

yard

yea and nay

year

_____ and a day

_____ of mourn′/ing

year′/ly

yel′′low-/dog′ con′′/tract′

yel′/low jour′/nal/ism′

yeo′/man

yeo′/man/ry

yes′/ter/day

yield

   yield′/ed

   yield′/ing

young′′/er chil′′/dren

youth

Z

zeal

zeal′/ot

zeal′/ous

_____ wit′′/ness

Z′-/mark′

zone

zon′/ing

Section Two

LEGAL REFERENCE DATA

Abbreviations

A

A. *Atlantic Reporter*
A.2d *Atlantic Reporter, Second Series*
AAA American Arbitration Association; American Accounting Association
ABA American Bar Association; American Bankers Association
abbr. abbreviation
abr. abridgment
abs. absent
A.C. anno Christi (year of Christ)
a/c account; account current
acct. account
ACLU American Civil Liberties Union
A.D. anno Domini (in the year of our Lord)
A.D.2d Appellate Division, Second Series, New York
add. addenda
ad int. ad interim (in the meantime)
adj. sess. adjourned session
adjt. adjutant

Ad. L.   administrative law
ALR   *American Law Reports Annotated*
Am.   American
adm'r   administrator
adm'x   administratrix
ads   ad sectam (at the suit of)
AEC   Atomic Energy Commission
AFB   Air Force Base
AFDC   Aid to Families with Dependent Children
aff'd   affirmed
AFL–CIO   American Federation of Labor and Congress of
Industrial Organizations
AFTR   *American Federal Tax Reports*
AG   Attorney General
agcy.   agency
agt.   agent
AHA   American Hospital Association
AICPA   American Institute of Certified Public Accountants
AID   Agency for International Development
aka   also known as
Ala.   *Alabama Reports*
Ala. Acts   *Acts of Alabama*
Ala. App.   Alabama Appellate Court
Ala. Code   *Code of Alabama*
Alaska   *Alaska Reporter*
Alaska Sess. Laws   *Alaska Session Laws*
Alaska Stat.   *Alaska Statutes*
ALI   American Law Institute
ALR   *American Law Reports Annotated*
ALTA   American Land Title Association
A.M.   or a.m. ante meridiem (before noon)
AMA   American Medical Association
amal. or amalg.   amalgamated
Am. Bankr. Rep.   *American Bankruptcy Reports*
amend.   amendment

amt.   amount
ann. or annot.   annotated
anon.   anonymous
a/o   account of
APA   Administrative Procedure Act
app.   appendix; appointed; approximate; apprentice
App. Ct.   Appellate Court
appd.   approved
append.   appendix
approx.   approximate or approximately
APR   annual percentage rate
apt.   apartment
A.R.   anno regni (in the year of the reign)
arg.   arguendo
Ariz.   *Arizona Reports*
Ariz. App.   *Arizona Appeals*
Ariz. Rev. Stat. Ann.   *Arizona Revised Statutes Annotated*
Ark.   *Arkansas Reports*
Ark. Acts   *General Acts of Arkansas*
Ark. Stats. Ann.   *Arkansas Statutes Annotated*
art.   article
a/s   after sight; alongside (shipping)
ASE   American Stock Exchange
assem.   assembly
ass'n   association
assoc.   associate
Atl.   Atlantic
ATLA   American Trial Lawyers Association
ATS   at suit of
Att'y Gen.   Attorney General
AUC   ab urbe condita (from the founding of the city)
aug.   augmented
auth.   authority
auto.   automobile
aux.   auxiliary

ave.   avenue
avg.   average
AWOL   absent without leave
AWW   average weekly wage

B

b.   born; brother
Bank. Cas.   *Banking Cases*
Bank. L.J.   *Banking Law Journal*
bb   bail bond
B.C.   before Christ; bail court; bankruptcy cases
bd.   board
bd   bills discontinued; bank draft
b/d   brought down
BE   bill of exchange
bf   bonum factum (good deed—"approved")
bhd.   brotherhood
BIA   Bureau of Indian Affairs
bibliog.   bibliography
bkcy.   bankruptcy
bkg.   banking
bkpr.   bookkeeper
B/L   bill of lading
bldg.   building
BLS   Bureau of Labor Statistics
bros.   brothers
b/s   bill of sale
BTA   *Board of Tax Appeals Reports*
bur.   bureau
Burns' Ann. St.   *Burns Annotated Indiana Statutes*

C

C   Celsius; centigrade; Conservative
CAA   Civil Aeronautics Administration
CAB   Civil Aeronautics Board
Cal.   *California Reports*
Cal.2d   *California Reports, Second Series*
Cal. App.   *California Appellate Reports*
Cal. App.2d   *California Appellate Reports, Second Series*
Cal. Rptr.   *California Reporter*
canc.   cancel or canceled
CAP   Civil Air Patrol
cas.   casualty
ca. sa.   capias ad satisfaciendum (a writ of execution that deprives a party of liberty until damages are satisfied)
cat.   catalog
cav   curia advisare vult (the court will be advised)
CB   *Cumulative Bulletin of the Internal Revenue Service*
CBO   Congressional Budget Office
CBOE   Chicago Board of Options Exchange
CCA   Circuit Court of Appeals; County Court of Appeals
CCP   *Deering's California Codes (Code of Civil Procedure)*
CCPA   Court of Customs and Patent Appeals
cd   certificate of deposit
CD   Civil Defense; *Current Digest, American Digest System*
CEA   Council of Economic Advisers
cent.   central
cert.   certiorari; certificate; certified
cf.   confer (compare)
c/f   carried forward
c&f   cost and freight
CFR   *Code of Federal Regulations*
CFTC   Commodity Futures Trading Commission

CG   Coast Guard; Consul General
ch.   chapter; chancellor; courthouse
chem.   chemical
chm. or chmn.   chairman
CIA   Central Intelligence Agency
CIEP   Council on International Economic Policy
cir.   circuit
civ. code   civil code
CJ   corpus juris; chief justice; circuit judge
cl   civil law
c/l   cash letter
cl.   claim; class; clause
class.   classified; classification
clk.   clerk
CLU   Civil Liberties Union
CMA   Court of Military Appeals
co.   company
c/o   care of
Code Civ. Proc.   *Code of Civil Procedure*
Code Gen. Laws   *Code of General Laws*
Code Pub. Gen. Laws   *Code of Public General Laws*
coll.   collection or collector
collab.   collaboration or collaborator
Colo.   *Colorado Reports*
Colo. App.   *Colorado Court of Appeals Reports*
Colo. Rev. Stat.   *Colorado Revised Statutes*
Colo. Sess. Laws   *Colorado Session Laws*
comm.   committee
comm'n   commission
comm'r   commissioner
comp. st.   compiled statutes
Cong.   Congress
Cong. Rec.   *Congressional Record*
Conn.   *Connecticut Reports*
Conn. Gen. Stat.   *Connecticut General Statutes*

consol. consolidated
Const. Constitution
Const. Amend. Constitutional Amendment
constr. construction
coop. cooperative
corp. corporation
cp. compare
cp common pleas
CPA Certified Public Accountant
cr. credit
Cr. Code *Criminal Code*
Crim. L. Rep. *Criminal Law Reporter*
cs. case
CSC Civil Service Commission
ct. cent; county; court
Ct. Cl. United States Court of Claims
Cust. A. United States Customs Appeals
cwo cash with order

D

d. daughter; died; data
da deposit account
D/A documents for acceptance
dba doing business as
DC District Court; District of Columbia
DCA Defense Communications Agency
D.C. Code *District of Columbia Code*
dd de dato (today's date)
ddb double-declining-balance depreciation
DEA Drug Enforcement Administration
deb. debenture

dec.   deceased
def.   defendant; deferred
del.   delegate
Del.   *Delaware Reports*
Del. Ch.   *Delaware Chancery Reports*
Del. Code Ann.   *Delaware Code Annotated*
dem.   demise
Dem.   Democrat or Democratic
dep.   departure
dept.   department
desc.   descendant
dev.   development
dft.   draft
DI   Department of the Interior
DIA   Defense Intelligence Agency
dict.   dictionary; dictation
dig.   digest
dist.   district
distrib.   distribute, distributing, or distributor
div.   division; dividend
D.J.   district judge; doctor juris (doctor of law)
dl   demand loan
do.   delivery order
DOA   dead on arrival
DOD   Department of Defense
DOE   Department of Energy
DOT   Department of Transportation
D/P   documents against payment
dpl.   diplomat
dr.   drive; debtor
Dr.   doctor
dstn.   destination
D/W   dock warrant
dwi   died without issue

E

E east; eastern; English; equity; exchequer
e. eldest
ea. each
ecol. ecology or ecological
econ. economy or economic
ed. or edit. edition, editor, or edited
ED election district
educ. education or educational
EEOC Equal Employment Opportunity Commission
e.g. exempli gratia (for example)
elec. electric or electricity; electronics
ency. encyclopedia
eng'r engineer or engineering
EO executive order
EPA Environmental Protection Agency
eq. equity; equal
equip. equipment
esp. especially
est. estate; estimated; established or establishment
estab. established
eta estimated time of arrival
et al. et alii (and others)
etc. et cetera (and others)
etd estimated time of departure
et ux. et uxor (and wife)
evce. evidence
exch. exchange; exchequer
ex int. without interest
exp. expired; express; expenses; export
ex'r executor
ex'x executrix

F

F. *Federal Reporter*
F.2d *Federal Reporter, Second Series*
FAA Federal Aviation Agency
fam. family
FBI Federal Bureau of Investigation
FCA Farm Credit Administration
FCC Federal Communications Commission
FDA Food and Drug Administration
FDIC Federal Deposit Insurance Corporation
fed. federal
Fed. Cas. *United States Federal Cases*
Fed. L. Rev. *Federal Law Review*
Fed. R. App. P. *Federal Rules of Appellate Procedure*
Fed. R. Civ. P. *Federal Rules of Civil Procedure*
Fed. R. Crim. P. *Federal Rules of Criminal Procedure*
Fed. Sec. L. Rep. *Federal Securities Law Reporter*
fem. female or feminine
FHA Federal Housing Administration
FICA Federal Insurance Contributions Act
fid. fiduciary
fin. finance or financial
Fla. *Florida Reports*
Fla. Stat. *Florida Statutes*
fn. footnote
fob free on board
FOIA Freedom of Information Act
FPC Federal Power Commission
fr. fragmentum (fragment)
FRB Federal Reserve Board; Federal Reserve Bank
FRS Federal Reserve System
frt. freight
FSLIC Federal Savings and Loan Insurance Corporation

F. Supp. *Federal Supplement*
FTC Federal Trade Commission
fut. future
FWS Fish and Wildlife Service

G

GA General Assembly; General Agent
Ga. *Georgia Reports*
GAAP generally accepted accounting principles
Ga. App. *Georgia Appeals*
GAAS generally accepted auditing standards
Ga. Code Ann. *Code of Georgia, Annotated*
Ga. Dec. *Georgia Decisions*
GAO General Accounting Office
gdn. guardian
gen. general; gender
gloss. glossary
GNP gross national product
gov't government
gtc good till canceled
gtd. or guar. guaranteed

H

h. husband
H.A. hoc anno (in this year)
Haw. *Hawaii Reports*
Haw. Rev. Stat. *Hawaii Revised Statutes*
Haw. Sess. Laws *Session Laws of Hawaii*

HB   House Bill
HC   House of Commons
HEW   Department of Health, Education, and Welfare
HHS   Department of Health and Human Services (new
name of HEW)
hist.   history or historical
HL   House of Lords
hon.   honorable
hosp.   hospital
hous.   housing
HR   House of Representatives
hs   hoc sensu (in this sense)
HUD   Department of Housing and Urban Development

I

I   Independent
ibid.   ibidem (in the same place)
I.C.A.   *Iowa Code Annotated*
ICC   Interstate Commerce Commission; Indian Claims
Commission
Idaho   *Idaho Reports*
Idaho Code   *Idaho Code*
Idaho Sess. Laws   *Idaho Session Laws*
i.e.   id est (that is)
Ill.   *Illinois Reports*
Ill. Ann. Stat.   *Illinois Annotated Statutes*
Ill. App.   *Illinois Appellate Court Reports*
Ill. Laws   *Laws of Illinois*
Ill. Rev. Stat.   *Illinois Revised Statutes*
ILO   International Labor Organization
IMF   International Monetary Fund

inc.   incorporated; income; increase; included or inclusive
Ind.   *Indiana Reports*
Ind. Acts   *Indiana Acts*
Ind. App.   *Indiana Appellate Court Reports*
Ind. Code   *Indiana Code*
indem.   indemnity
indus.   industry, industries, or industrial
ins.   insurance
inst.   institute or institution
INTERPOL   International Criminal Police Organization
int'l   international
Int. Rev. Code   *Internal Revenue Code*
inv.   investment
Iowa   *Iowa Reports*
Iowa Code   *Iowa Code*
Iowa Code Ann.   *Iowa Code Annotated*
IRA   Individual Retirement Account
IRS   Internal Revenue Service
iv   increased value; invoice value

J

J   judge; justice; journal
JA   joint agent; judge advocate
JAG   judge advocate general
J.D.   juris doctor (doctor of jurisprudence or law)
JJ   judges or justices
Jones Ill. Stat. Ann.   *Jones Illinois Statutes Annotated*
JP   justice of the peace
jur.   juridical or jurist
juv.   juvenile

K

Kan.   *Kansas Reports*
Kan. App.   *Kansas Appeals*
Kan. Stat.   *Kansas Statutes*
K.B.   King's Bench
K.C.   King's Counsel
Ky.   *Kentucky Reports*
Ky. Dec.   *Kentucky Decisions*
Ky. Rev. Stat.   *Kentucky Revised Statutes*
Ky. Rev. Stat. Ann.   *Baldwin's Kentucky Revised Statutes Annotated*

L

L   Latin; law
La.   *Louisiana Reports*
La. Ann.   *Louisiana Annual Reports*
La. App.   Louisiana Court of Appeals
Lat.   Latin
law.   lawyer
lc   letter of credit
LC   Library of Congress
L. Ct.   Law Court
L. Div.   law division
L.Ed.   *Lawyers' Edition Supreme Court Reports*
leg.   legal; legislative or legislature
Leg.   *Acts of the Legislature*
legis.   legislation, legislative, or legislature
liab.   liability
Lib.   Liberal
L.J.   *Law Journal*; Law Judge
LL.B.   bachelor of laws

LL.D.   doctor of laws
LL.M.   master of laws
loc.   cit. loco citato (in the place cited)
L.R.   *Law Reports*
lsc   loco supra citato (in the place mentioned above)
ltd.   limited

M

m.   male; married
mach.   machine or machinery
mag.   magazine
mar.   maritime
mas.   masculine
Mass.   *Massachusetts Reports*
Mass. Ann. Laws   *Annotated Laws of Massachusetts*
Mass. App. Ct.   *Massachusetts Appeals Court Reports*
Mass. Elec. Ca.   *Massachusetts Election Cases*
mat.   maturity (bonds)
MC   Member of Congress
M.C.L.A.   *Michigan Compiled Laws Annotated*
Md.   *Maryland Reports*
Md. App.   *Maryland Appellate Reports*
Md. Code Ann.   *Annotated Code of Maryland*
Me.   *Maine Reports*
med.   mediator; medical
Me. Legis. Serv.   Maine Legislative Service
mem.   member; memorandum
Me. Rev. Stat. Ann.   *Maine Revised Statutes Annotated*
mfd.   manufactured
mfg.   manufacturing
mfr.   manufacturer
mgr.   manager

mgt.   management
MHR   Member of the House of Representatives
Mich.   *Michigan Reports*
Mich. App.   *Michigan Court of Appeals*
Mich. Comp. Laws   *Michigan Compiled Laws*
Mich. Comp. Laws Ann.   *Michigan Compiled Laws Annotated*
Mich. Pub. Acts   *Public and Local Acts of the State of Michigan*
mil.   military
Mil. L. Rev.   *Military Law Review*
min.   minor; minute
Minn.   *Minnesota Reports*
Minn. Ct. Rep.   *Minnesota Court Reporter*
Minn. Stat.   *Minnesota Statutes*
Minn. Stat. Ann.   *Minnesota Statutes Annotated*
misc.   miscellaneous or miscellany
Miss.   *Mississippi Reports*
Miss. Code   *Mississippi Code*
Miss. Code Ann.   *Mississippi Code Annotated*
Miss. Dec.   *Mississippi Decisions*
Miss. Laws   *General Laws of Mississippi*
Miss. St. Ca.   *Mississippi State Cases*
mkt.   market
mo.   month
Mo.   *Missouri Reports*
mo   money order
Mo. App.   *Missouri Appeal Reports*
Mont.   *Montana Reports*
Mont. Rev. Codes Ann.   *Revised Codes of Montana Annotated*
Mo. Rev. Stat.   *Missouri Revised Statutes*
MP   military police; member of Parliament
M.R.S.A.   *Maine Revised Statutes Annotated*
M.S.A.   *Minnesota Statutes Annotated*

mtg.　mortgage; meeting
mun.　municipal
mut.　mutual

N

N　north or northern
n.　natus (born); note; noon; number
n/a　no account
NAACP　National Association for the Advancement of Colored People
NAB　National Alliance of Businessmen
NAM　National Association of Manufacturers
NAS　National Academy of Science
NASA　National Aeronautics and Space Administration
nat.　native; national; natural
Nat. Bankr. R.　*National Bankruptcy Register*
nat'l　national
NATO　North Atlantic Treaty Organization
nb　nota bene (note well)
NBS　National Bureau of Standards
N.C　*North Carolina Reports*
N.C. App.　*North Carolina Appeals*
N.C. Gen. Stat.　*General Statutes of North Carolina*
NCUA　National Credit Union Administration
N.D.　*North Dakota Reports*
N.D. Cent. Code Ann.　*North Dakota Century Code, Annotated*
N.D. Sess. Laws　*Laws of North Dakota*
N.E.　*North Eastern Reporter*
N.E.2d　*North Eastern Reporter, Second Series*
Neb.　*Nebraska Reports*
Neb. Rev. Stat.　*Revised Statutes of Nebraska*
Nev.　*Nevada Reports*

Nev. Rev. Stat.   *Nevada Revised Statutes*
Nev. Stats.   *Statutes of Nevada*
N/F   no funds
NG   National Guard
NG   no good
N.H.   *New Hampshire Reports*
N.H. Judicial Council   New Hampshire Judicial Council
N.H. Rev. Stat.   *New Hampshire Revised Statutes*
N.H. Rev. Stat. Ann.   *New Hampshire Revised Statutes Annotated*
NHTSA   National Highway Transportation Safety Administration
N.J.   *New Jersey Supreme Court Reports*
N.J. Eq.   New Jersey Equity
N.J. Laws   *Laws of New Jersey*
N.J. Rev. Stat.   *Revised Statutes of New Jersey*
N.J. S.A. or N.J. Stat. Ann.   *New Jersey Statutes Annotated*
N.J. Super.   *New Jersey Superior Court Reports*
nka   now known as
NLRB   National Labor Relations Board
N.M.   *New Mexico Reports*
N.M. Laws   *Laws of New Mexico*
N.M. Stat. Ann.   *New Mexico Statutes Annotated*
no.   north or northern; number
NOAA   National Oceanic and Atmospheric Administration
nov   non obstante veredicto (notwithstanding verdict)
NP   notary public
NRC   Nuclear Regulatory Commission
NRS   *Nevada Revised Statutes*
NS   not sufficient (funds); new series
NSA   National Shipping Authority; National Standards Association
NSC   National Security Council
NTSB   National Transportation Safety Board
N.W.   *Northwestern Reporter*

N.W.2d   *Northwestern Reporter, Second Series*
N.Y.   *New York Court of Appeals Reports*
N.Y. Ann. Ca.   *New York Annotated Cases*
N.Y. Civ. Proc.   *New York Civil Procedure*
N.Y. Cr.R.   *New York Criminal Reports*
N.Y.L.C. Ann.   *New York Leading Cases Annotated*
N.Y. Misc.   *New York Miscellaneous Reports*
N.Y.S. or N.Y. Supp.   *New York Supplement*
N.Y.S.2d   *New York Supplement Reporter, Second Series*
NYSE   New York Stock Exchange

O

OAS   Organization of American States
O.C.D.   *Ohio Circuit Decisions*
od   overdrawn; on demand; overdose
o/d   overdraft
OEO   Office of Economic Opportunity
OEP   Office of Emergency Planning
off.   office
Ohio   *Ohio Reports*
Ohio App.   *Ohio Appellate Reports*
Ohio Cir. Ct. R.   *Ohio Circuit Court Reports*
Ohio Cir. Dec.   *Ohio Circuit Decisions*
Ohio Dec.   *Ohio Decisions*
Ohio Rev. Code Ann.   *Ohio Revised Code Annotated*
Ohio St.   *Ohio State Reports*
Okl.   *Oklahoma Reports*
Okl. Stat. Ann.   *Oklahoma Statutes Annotated*
OMB   Office of Management and Budget
Op. Attys. Gen.   *Opinions of the United States Attorneys General*
Or.   *Oregon Reports*

Or. App.   *Oregon Appeals*
Or. Rev. Stat.   *Oregon Revised Statutes*
ord.   ordinance; order
org.   organization
orig.   original
O.S.   *Ohio State Reports*
o/s   out of stock; outstanding (banking)
OTC   over-the-counter

P

P.   *Pacific Reporter*
P.2d   *Pacific Reporter, Second Series*
pa   power of attorney
Pa.   *Pennsylvania State Reports*
Pac.   Pacific
Pa. Commw.   *Pennsylvania Commonwealth Court Reports*
Pa. Cons. Stat. Ann.   *Pennsylvania Consolidated Statutes Annotated*
par.   paragraph
Pa. Stat. Ann.   *Purdon's Pennsylvania Statutes Annotated*
Pa. Super.   *Pennsylvania Superior Court Reports*
pat.   patent or patented
PAU   Pan American Union
P.C.   Penal Code; patent cases
pc   petty cash
P/C   prices current
pct.   percent
pd.   paid
pd   per diem
PD   police department
per.   period; person
pf., pfd.   preferred (stock)

pg.   page
PHA   Public Housing Administration
pm.   premium
pm   post mortem
PM   postmaster; prime minister
p.m. or P.M.   post meridiem (after noon)
pn   promissory note
PO   post office
pod.   port of debarkation
poe   port of embarkation or entry
Pol. Code   Political Code
pp   parcel post; postpaid; prepaid
ppd.   postpaid; prepaid
P.R. Laws Ann.   *Puerto Rico Laws Annotated*
pres.   president; present
prob.   probable or probably; problem; probate
proc.   procedure; proceedings; proclamation
prod.   product or production
prop.   property; proposition
propr.   proprietor
prov.   province or provincial; provisional; provost
P.R.R.   *Puerto Rico Supreme Court Reports*
P.S.   *Purdon's Pennsylvania Statutes Annotated*
PTO   Patent and Trademark Office
pub.   public; publication; published, publishing, or publisher
Pub. Gen. Laws   public general laws

Q

Q   queen
q.   question; query
qd   quasi dicat (as if he should say)
qe   quod est (which is)

qed   quod erat demonstrandum (which was to be demonstrated)
qef   quod erat faciendum (which was to be done)
qen   quare executionem non (execution should not be issued)
qq   questions
qqv   quae vide (which see, referring to something plural)
qtr.   quarter or quarterly
qv   quod vide (which see)

R

r   right
R   Republican; rabbi
rcd.   received
R&D   research and development
rd.   road; rendered
recd. or rec'd   received
ref.   reference; referee; refining
reg.   regiment; register or registered; regulation
rel.   religion; relative
rep.   republic; report
Rep.   Republican
rept.   report
res.   residence; resolution
rev.   revenue; revised or revision; review or reviewed
Rev. Civ. Code   Revised Civil Code
R.I.   *Rhode Island Reports*
R.I. Gen. Laws   *General Laws of Rhode Island*
rpt.   report
rr   railroad
R.S.   Revised Statutes
rt.   right
ry.   railway

S

s signature
S south or southern
sav. savings
SBA Small Business Administration
S.C. Supreme Court; *South Carolina Reports*; Superior Court
S.C.Eq. *South Carolina Equity Reports*
S.C.L. *South Carolina Law*
S. Ct. *Supreme Court Reporter*
S.D. *South Dakota Reports*
S.D. Comp. Laws *South Dakota Compiled Laws*
S.E. *South Eastern Reporter*
S.E.2d *South Eastern Reporter, Second Series*
SEC Securities and Exchange Commission
sec. securities; second; secondary; secretary
secy or sec'y secretary
sel. selection; selective
Sen. Senate; Senator
ser. series
serv. service
sgd. signed
sh. share
S.H.A. *Smith-Hurd Illinois Annotated Statutes*
shpt. shipment
sig. signal; signature
S.J. Res. Senate Joint Resolution
S&L savings and loan
so. south or southern
So. *Southern Reporter*
So.2d *Southern Reporter, Second Series*
soc'y society (case name)
sp sine prole (without issue)
sps sine prole superstite (without surviving issue)
SS steamship

SSA   Social Security Administration
SSS   Selective Service System
st.   statute; state; street
Stat.   *United States Statutes at Large*
subst.   substantive
sup., supp., or suppl.   supplement or supplementary
supt.   superintendent
sur.   surety
svgs.   savings
S.W.   *Southwestern Reporter*
S.W.2d   *Southwestern Reporter, Second Series*
sys. or syst.   system

T

t   tempore (in the time of)
tax.   taxation
tb   trial balance
T.C.   United States Tax Court
TD   Treasury Department
tech.   technical, technically, or technician; technique
tel.   telegraph; telephone
temp.   temporary
Tenn.   *Tennessee Reports*
Tenn. App.   *Tennessee Appeals*
Tenn. Ch. App.   *Tennessee Chancery Appeals*
Tenn. Code Ann.   *Tennessee Code Annotated*
ter. or terr.   territory or territorial
Tex.   *Texas Reports*
Tex. App.   *Texas Appeals Reports*
Tex. Civ. App.   *Texas Civil Appeals Reports*
tit.   title

tkt.   ticket
tl   total loss
TM   trademark
tnpk.   turnpike
transp.   transport or transportation
Treas. Dec.   *Treasury Decisions*
TT   Trust Territories
TU   trade union
TVA   Tennessee Valley Authority

U

u   united
U   university; union
UCC   *Uniform Commercial Code*
U.L.A.   *Uniform Laws Annotated*
UN   United Nations
UNICEF   United Nations International Children's Emergency Fund
univ.   university
unof.   unofficial
U.S.   *United States Supreme Court Reports*
U.S. Ap.   *United States Appeals*
USC   *United States Code*
U.S. Const.   United States Constitution
USDA   United States Department of Agriculture
USIA   United States Information Agency
USPS   United States Postal Service
Utah   *Utah Reports*
Utah 2d   *Utah Reports, Second Series*
Utah Code Ann.   *Utah Code Annotated*
util.   utility

V

VA　Veterans Administration
Va.　*Virginia Reports*
Va. Cas.　*Virginia Cases*
Va. Dec.　*Virginia Decisions*
val.　value or valued
var.　variable; variation; various
vat.　value-added tax
VC　vice-chancellor
VD　various dates; venereal disease
VFW　Veterans of Foreign Wars
V.I.　*Virgin Islands Reports*
viz.　videlicet (that is to say)
VP　vice president
Vt.　*Vermont Reports*
Vt. Stat. Ann.　*Vermont Statutes Annotated*

W

w　warehouse; withdrawn or withdrew
W　west or western
w/　with
war.　warrant
Wash.　*Washington Reports*
Wash. 2d　*Washington Reports, Second Series*
Wash. App.　*Washington Appellate Reports*
Wash. Rev. Code　*Revised Code of Washington*
West.　*Western Reporter*
WHO　World Health Organization
whsle.　wholesale
wi　when issued

Wis.   *Wisconsin Reports*
Wis. 2d   *Wisconsin Reports, Second Series*
Wis. Stat.   *Wisconsin Statutes*
W. Va.   *West Virginia Reports*
W. Va. Code   *West Virginia Code*
Wyo.   *Wyoming Reports*
Wyo. Sess. Laws   *Session Laws of Wyoming*
Wyo. Stat.   *Wyoming Statutes*

X

xcp   ex coupon
x div.   ex dividend
x war.   ex warrants

Y

y   year
yb.   yearbook

Z

z   zone

FORMS of ADDRESS:
HONORARY and Official Positions

The chart in this section gives the correct forms of written address, salutation, and complimentary close for letters to persons holding honorary or official titles, whether of high or low rank. It also gives the correct form of referring to those persons in a letter and the correct form to use in speaking to, or informally introducing, them. (The form of informal introduction and the form of reference to a person are usually similar. Where they differ, the form of reference is shown in parentheses.)

To facilitate usage, the forms of addresses are presented in nine groups:

United States Government Officials
State and Local Government Officials
Court Officials
United States Diplomatic Representatives
Foreign Officials and Representatives
The Armed Forces
Church Dignitaries
College and University Officials
United Nations Officials

You should make every effort to learn the name of the person addressed, as well as his or her title. Use the name in writing, except in those few instances where the name is omitted in the chart. If you know the person's title only, address him by the title prefaced by *The.* For example, *The Lieutenant Governor of Iowa.* The formal salutation would be *Sir* or *Madam.*

When a person is acting as an official, the word *acting* precedes the title in the address, but not in the salutation or spoken address. For example, *Acting Mayor of Memphis, Dear Mayor Blank.*

A person who has held a position entitling him to be addressed as *The Honorable* is addressed as *The Honorable* after retirement. The title itself, such as Senator or Governor, is not used in the address or salutation. Even a former president is called *Mr.* An exception to this practice is the title of *Judge.* A person who has once been a judge customarily retains his title even when addressed formally. Retired officers of the armed forces retain their titles, but their retirement is indicated, thus, *Lieutenant General John D. Blank, U.S.A., Retired.*

In many cases the name in the address is followed by the abbreviation of a scholastic degree. If you do not know whether the addressee has the degree, you should not use the initials. Nor should a person be addressed by a scholastic title unless he or she actually possesses the degree that the title indicates.

The wife of an American official does not share her husband's title. She is always addressed as *Mrs. Blank.* When they are addressed jointly, the address is, for example, *Ambassador and Mrs. Blank.* Nor does a husband share his wife's title. When they are addressed jointly, if he does not have a title, the traditional address is *Mr. and Mrs. J.W. Blank,* regardless of any high-ranking title she may hold. Alternatives to the traditional address that include her title if her husband is untitled are: *Ambassador* Ruth Blank and *Mr. J.W.* Blank (the titled person preceding the untitled person), *Ambassador* Ruth and *Mr. J.W.* Blank, *Ambassador* and *Mr.* Blank.

Women in official or honorary positions are addressed just as men in similar positions, except that Madam replaces Sir, and Mrs., Miss, or Ms. replaces Mr. Ms. may be substituted for *Miss* or *Mrs.* in cases where the marital status of the woman is unknown or where the woman has stipulated that she prefers the title *Ms.*

Note: In the following chart, Correct Forms of Address, the form of address for a man is used throughout, except where not applicable. To use the form of address for a woman in any of these positions, use the substitution *Madam* for *Sir,* and *Mrs., Miss,* or *Ms.* for *Mr.* Thus, Dear *Madam; Mrs.* Blank, Representative from New York; The Lieutenant Governor of Iowa, *Miss* Blank; The American Minister, *Ms.* Blank. The *Mr.* preceding a title becomes *Madam;* thus, *Madam* Secretary, *Madam* Ambassador. Use *Esquire* or *Esq.* in addressing a man, where appropriate; some organizations are beginning to use *Esquire* in addressing a woman.

Forms of Address:
Honorary And Official Positions

UNITED STATES GOVERNMENT OFFICIALS

Personage	Envelope and Inside Address (Add City, State, Zip)	Formal Salutation	Informal Salutation	Formal Close	Informal Close	1. Spoken Address 2. Informal Introduction or Reference
The President	The President The White House	Mr. President:	Dear Mr. President:	Respectfully yours,	Very respectfully yours, Very truly yours, or Sincerely yours,	1. Mr. President 2. Not introduced (The President)
Former President of the United States[1]	The Honorable William R. Blank (local address)	Sir:	Dear Mr. Blank:	Respectfully yours,	Sincerely yours,	1. Mr. Blank 2. Former President Blank or Mr. Blank
The Vice-President of the United States	The Vice-President of the United States United States Senate	Mr. Vice-President:	Dear Mr. Vice-President:	Very truly yours,	Sincerely yours,	1. Mr. Vice-President or Mr. Blank The Vice-President ___
The Chief Justice of the United States Supreme Court	The Chief Justice of the United States The Supreme Court of the United States	Sir:	Dear Mr. Chief Justice:	Very truly yours,	Sincerely yours,	1. Mr. Chief Justice 2. The Chief Justice
Associate Justice of the United States Supreme Court	Mr. Justice Blank The Supreme Court of the United States	Sir:	Dear Mr. Justice:	Very truly yours,	Sincerely yours,	1. Mr. Justice Blank or Justice Blank 2. Mr. Justice Blank
Retired Justice of the United States Supreme Court	The Honorable William R. Blank (local address)	Sir:	Dear Justice Blank:	Very truly yours,	Sincerely yours,	1. Mr. Justice Blank or Justice Blank 2. Mr. Justice Blank

[1] If a former president has a title, such as General of the Army, address him by it.

Source: From the book, Complete Secretary's Handbook, 4th Edition, Mary A. De Vries, Revisor. © 1977 Prentice-Hall, Inc. Published by Prentice-Hall, Inc., Englewood Cliffs, New Jersey 07632

290

UNITED STATES GOVERNMENT OFFICIALS continued

Personage	Envelope and Inside Address (Add City, State, Zip)	Formal Salutation	Informal Salutation	Formal Close	Informal Close	1. Spoken Address 2. Informal Introduction or Reference
The Speaker of the House of Representatives	The Honorable William R. Blank Speaker of the House of Representatives	Sir:	Dear Mr. Speaker: or Dear Mr. Blank:	Very truly yours,	Sincerely yours,	1. Mr. Speaker or Mr. Blank 2. The Speaker, Mr. Blank (The Speaker or Mr. Blank)
Former Speaker of the House of Representatives	The Honorable William R. Blank (local address)	Sir:	Dear Mr. Blank:	Very truly yours,	Sincerely yours,	1. Mr. Blank 2. Mr. Blank
Cabinet Officers addressed as "Secretary"[a]	The Honorable William R. Blank Secretary of State The Honorable William R. Blank Secretary of State of the United States of America (if written from abroad)	Sir:	Dear Mr. Secretary:	Very truly yours,	Sincerely yours,	1. Mr. Secretary or Secretary Blank or Mr. Blank 2. The Secretary of State, Mr. Blank (Mr. Blank or The Secretary)
Former Cabinet Officer	The Honorable William R. Blank (local address)	Dear Sir:	Dear Mr. Blank:	Very truly yours,	Sincerely yours,	1. Mr. Blank 2. Mr. Blank
Postmaster General	The Honorable William R. Blank The Postmaster General	Sir:	Dear Mr. Postmaster General:	Very truly yours,	Sincerely yours,	1. Mr. Postmaster General or Postmaster General Blank or Mr. Blank 2. The Postmaster General, Mr. Blank (Mr. Blank or The Postmaster General)

[a]Titles for cabinet secretaries are Secretary of State; Secretary of the Treasury; Secretary of Defense; Secretary of the Interior; Secretary of Agriculture; Secretary of Commerce; Secretary of Labor; Secretary of Health, Education, and Welfare; Secretary of Housing and Urban Development; Secretary of Transportation.

UNITED STATES GOVERNMENT OFFICIALS *continued*

Personage	Envelope and Inside Address (Add City, State, Zip)	Formal Salutation	Informal Salutation	Formal Close	Informal Close	1. Spoken Address 2. Informal Introduction or Reference
The Attorney General	The Honorable William R. Blank The Attorney General	Sir:	Dear Mr. Attorney General:	Very truly yours,	Sincerely yours,	1. Mr. Attorney General or Attorney General Blank 2. The Attorney General, Mr. Blank (Mr. Blank or The Attorney General)
Under Secretary of a Department	The Honorable William R. Blank Under Secretary of Labor	Dear Mr. Blank:	Dear Mr. Blank:	Very truly yours,	Sincerely yours,	1. Mr. Blank 2. Mr. Blank
United States Senator	The Honorable William R. Blank United States Senate	Sir:	Dear Senator Blank:	Very truly yours,	Sincerely yours,	1. Senator Blank or Senator 2. Senator Blank
Former Senator	The Honorable William R. Blank (local address)	Dear Sir:	Dear Senator Blank:	Very truly yours,	Sincerely yours,	1. Senator Blank or Senator 2. Senator Blank
Senator-elect	Honorable William R. Blank Senator-elect United States Senate	Dear Sir:	Dear Mr. Blank:	Very truly yours,	Sincerely yours,	1. Mr. Blank 2. Senator-elect Blank or Mr. Blank
Committee Chairman— United States Senate	The Honorable William R. Blank, Chairman Committee on Foreign Affairs United States Senate	Dear Mr. Chairman:	Dear Mr. Chairman: or Dear Senator Blank:	Very truly yours,	Sincerely yours,	1. Mr. Chairman or Senator Blank or Senator 2. The Chairman or Senator Blank
Subcommittee Chairman— United States Senate	The Honorable William R. Blank, Chairman, Subcommittee on Foreign Affairs United States Senate	Dear Senator Blank:	Dear Senator Blank:	Very truly yours,	Sincerely yours,	1. Senator Blank or Senator 2. Senator Blank

UNITED STATES GOVERNMENT OFFICIALS *continued*

Personage	Envelope and Inside Address (Add City, State, Zip)	Formal Salutation	Informal Salutation	Formal Close	Informal Close	1. Spoken Address 2. Informal Introduction or Reference
United States Representative or Congressman [3]	The Honorable William R. Blank House of Representatives The Honorable William R. Blank Representative in Congress (local address)(when away from Washington, DC)	Sir:	Dear Mr. Blank:	Very truly yours,	Sincerely yours,	1. Mr. Blank 2. Mr. Blank, Representative (Congressman) from New York or Mr. Blank
Former Representative	The Honorable William R. Blank (local address)	Sear Sir: or Dear Mr. Blank:	Dear Mr. Blank:	Very truly yours.	Sincerely yours,	1. Mr. Blank 2. Mr. Blank
Territorial Delegate	The Honorable William R. Blank Delegate of Puerto Rico House of Representatives	Dear Sir: or Dear Mr. Blank:	Dear Mr. Blank:	Very truly yours,	Sincerely yours,	1. Mr. Blank 2. Mr. Blank
Resident Commissioner	The Honorable William R. Blank Resident Commissioner of (Territory) House of Representatives	Dear Sir: or Dear Mr. Blank:	Dear Mr. Blank:	Very truly yours,	Sincerely yours,	1. Mr. Blank 2. Mr. Blank
Directors or Heads of Independent Federal Offices, Agencies, Commissions, Organizations, etc.	The Honorable William R. Blank Director, Mutual Security Agency	Dear Mr. Director (Commissioner, etc.):	Dear Mr. Blank:	Very truly yours,	Sincerely yours,	1. Mr. Blank 2. Mr. Blank
Other High Officials of the United States, in general: Public Printer, Comptroller General	The Honorable William R. Blank Public Printer The Honorable William R. Blank Comptroller General of the United States	Dear Sir: or Dear Mr. Blank:	Dear Mr. Blank:	Very truly yours,	Sincerely yours,	1. Mr. Blank 2. Mr. Blank

[3] The official title of a "congressman" is *Representative*. Strictly speaking, senators are also congressmen.

UNITED STATES GOVERNMENT OFFICIALS *continued*

Personage	Envelope and Inside Address (Add City, State, Zip)	Formal Salutation	Informal Salutation	Formal Close	Informal Close	1. Spoken Address 2. Informal Introduction or Reference
Secretary to the President	The Honorable William R. Blank Secretary to the President The White House	Dear Sir: or Dear Mr. Blank	Dear Mr. Blank:	Very truly yours,	Sincerely yours,	1. Mr. Blank 2. Mr. Blank
Assistant Secretary to the President	The Honorable William R. Blank Assistant Secretary to the President The White House	Dear Sir: or Dear Mr. Blank:	Dear Mr. Blank:	Very truly yours,	Sincerely yours,	1. Mr. Blank 2. Mr. Blank
Press Secretary to the President	Mr. William R. Blank Press Secretary to the President The White House	Dear Sir: or Dear Mr. Blank:	Dear Mr. Blank:	Very truly yours,	Sincerely yours,	1. Mr. Blank 2. Mr. Blank

STATE AND LOCAL GOVERNMENT OFFICIALS

Personage	Envelope and Inside Address (Add City, State, Zip)	Formal Salutation	Informal Salutation	Formal Close	Informal Close	1. Spoken Address 2. Informal Introduction or Reference
Governor of a State[1] or Territory [1]	The Honorable William R. Blank Governor of New York	Sir:	Dear Governor Blank:	Respectfully yours,	Very sincerely yours,	1. Governor Blank or Governor 2. a) Governor Blank b) The Governor c) The Governor of New York (used only outside his or her own state)
Acting Governor of a State or Territory	The Honorable William R. Blank Acting Governor of Connecticut	Sir:	Dear Mr. Blank:	Respectfully yours,	Very sincerely yours,	1. Mr. Blank 2. Mr. Blank

[1]The form of addressing governors varies in the different states. The form given here is the one used in most states. In Massachusetts by law and in some other states by courtesy, the form is *His (Her) Excellency, the Governor of Massachusetts.*

294

STATE AND LOCAL GOVERNMENT OFFICIALS *continued*

Personage	Envelope and Inside Address (Add City, State, Zip)	Formal Salutation	Informal Salutation	Formal Close	Informal Close	1. Spoken Address 2. Informal Introduction or Reference
Lieutenant Governor	The Honorable William R. Blank Lieutenant Governor of Iowa	Sir:	Dear Mr. Blank:	Respectfully yours, or Very truly yours,	Sincerely yours,	1. Mr. Blank 2. The Lieutenant Governor of Iowa, Mr. Blank or The Lieutenant Governor
Secretary of State	The Honorable William R. Blank Secretary of State of New York	Sir:	Dear Mr. Secretary:	Very truly yours,	Sincerely yours,	1. Mr. Blank 2. Mr. Blank
Attorney General	The Honorable William R. Blank Attorney General of Massachusetts	Sir:	Dear Mr. Attorney General:	Very truly yours,	Sincerely yours,	1. Mr. Blank 2. Mr. Blank
President of the Senate of a State	The Honorable William R. Blank President of the Senate of the State of Virginia	Sir:	Dear Mr. Blank:	Very truly yours,	Sincerely yours,	1. Mr. Blank 2. Mr. Blank
Speaker of the Assembly or The House of Representatives [2]	The Honorable William R. Blank Speaker of the Assembly of the State of New York	Sir:	Dear Mr. Blank:	Very truly yours,	Sincerely yours,	1. Mr. Blank 2. Mr. Blank
Treasurer, Auditor, or Comptroller of a State	The Honorable William R. Blank Treasurer of the State of Tennessee	Dear Sir:	Dear Mr. Blank:	Very truly yours,	Sincerely yours,	1. Mr. Blank 2. Mr. Blank
State Senator	The Honorable William R. Blank The State Senate	Dear Sir:	Dear Senator Blank:	Very truly yours,	Sincerely yours,	1. Senator Blank or Senator 2. Senator Blank

[2] In most states the lower branch of the legislature is the House of Representatives. The exceptions to this are: New York, California, Wisconsin, and Nevada, where it is known as the Assembly; Maryland, Virginia, and West Virginia—the House of Delegates; New Jersey—the House of General Assembly.

STATE AND LOCAL GOVERNMENT OFFICIALS continued

Personage	Envelope and Inside Address (Add City, State, Zip)	Formal Salutation	Informal Salutation	Formal Close	Informal Close	1. Spoken Address 2. Informal Introduction or Reference
State Representative, Assemblyman, or Delegate	The Honorable William R. Blank House of Delegates	Dear Sir:	Dear Mr. Blank:	Very truly yours,	Sincerely yours,	1. Mr. Blank 2. Mr. Blank or Delegate Blank
District Attorney	The Honorable William R. Blank District Attorney, Albany County County Courthouse	Dear Sir:	Dear Mr. Blank:	Very truly yours,	Sincerely yours,	1. Mr. Blank 2. Mr. Blank
Mayor of a city	The Honorable William R. Blank Mayor of Detroit	Dear Sir:	Dear Mayor Blank:	Very truly yours,	Sincerely yours,	1. Mayor Blank or Mr. Mayor 2. Mayor Blank
President of a Board of Commissioners	The Honorable William R. Blank, President Board of Commissioners of the City of Buffalo	Dear Sir:	Dear Mr. Blank:	Very truly yours,	Sincerely yours,	1. Mr. Blank 2. Mr. Blank
City Attorney, City Counsel, Corporation Counsel	The Honorable William R. Blank, City Attorney (City Counsel, Corporation Counsel)	Dear Sir:	Dear Mr. Blank:	Very truly yours,	Sincerely yours,	1. Mr. Blank 2. Mr. Blank
Alderman	Alderman William R. Blank City Hall	Dear Sir:	Dear Mr. Blank:	Very truly yours,	Sincerely yours,	1. Mr. Blank 2. Mr. Blank

COURT OFFICIALS

Personage	Envelope and Inside Address (Add City, State, Zip)	Formal Salutation	Informal Salutation	Formal Close	Informal Close	1. Spoken Address 2. Informal Introduction or Reference
Chief Justice [1] of a State Supreme Court	The Honorable William R. Blank Chief Justice of the Supreme Court of Minnesota [2]	Sir:	Dear Mr. Chief Justice:	Very truly yours,	Sincerely yours,	1. Mr. Chief Justice or Judge Blank 2. Mr. Chief Justice Blank or Judge Blank

[1] If his or her official title is *Chief Judge* substitute *Chief Judge* for *Chief Justice*, but never use *Mr., Mrs., Miss* or *Ms.* with *Chief Judge* or *Judge*. [2] Substitute here the appropriate name of the court. For example, the highest court in New York State is called the Court of Appeals.

COURT OFFICIALS *continued*

Personage	Envelope and Inside Address (Add City, State, Zip, or City, Country)	Formal Salutation	Informal Salutation	Formal Close	Informal Close	1. Spoken Address 2. Informal Introduction or Reference
Associate Justice of a Supreme Court of a State	The Honorable William R. Blank Associate Justice of the Supreme Court of Minnesota	Sir:	Dear Justice Blank:	Very truly yours,	Sincerely yours,	1. Mr. Justice Blank 2. Mr. Justice Blank
Presiding Justice	The Honorable William R. Blank Presiding Justice, Appellate Division Supreme Court of New York	Sir:	Dear Justice Blank:	Very truly yours	Sincerely yours,	1. Mr. Justice (or Judge) Blank 2. Mr. Justice (or Judge Blank)
Judge of a Court3	The Honorable William R. Blank Judge of the United States District Court for the Southern District of California	Sir:	Dear Judge Blank:	Very truly yours,	Sincerely yours,	1. Judge Blank 2. Judge Blank
Clerk of a Court	William R. Blank, Esquire Clerk of the Superior Court of Massachusetts	Dear Sir:	Dear Mr. Blank:	Very truly yours,	Sincerely yours,	1. Mr. Blank 2. Mr. Blank

UNITED STATES DIPLOMATIC REPRESENTATIVES

Personage	Envelope and Inside Address	Formal Salutation	Informal Salutation	Formal Close	Informal Close	1. Spoken Address 2. Informal Introduction or Reference
American Ambassador	The Honorable William R. Blank American Ambassador 1	Sir:	Dear Mr. Ambassador:	Very truly yours,	Sincerely yours,	1. Mr. Ambassador or Mr. Blank 2. The American Ambassador2(The Ambassador or Mr. Blank)

1When an ambassador or minister is not at his or her post, the name of the country to which he or she is accredited must be added to the address. For example: *The American Ambassador to Great Britain.* If he or she hold military rank, the diplomatic complimentary title *The Honorable* should be omitted, thus *General William R. Blank, American Ambassador (or Minister).*

2With reference to ambassadors and ministers to Central or South American countries, substitute *The Ambassador of the United States for American Ambassador or American Minister.*

3Not applicable to judges of the United States Supreme Court.

297

UNITED STATES DIPLOMATIC REPRESENTATIVES *continued*

Personage	Envelope and Inside Address (Add City, State, Zip, or City, Country)	Formal Salutation	Informal Salutation	Formal Close	Informal Close	1. Spoken Address 2. Informal Introduction or Reference
American Minister	The Honorable William R. Blank American Minister to Rumania	Sir:	Dear Mr. Minister:	Very truly yours,	Sincerely yours,	1. Mr. Minister or Mr. Blank 2. The American Minister, Mr. Blank (The Minister or Mr. Blank)
American Chargé d' Affaires, Consul General, Consul, or Vice Consul	William R. Blank, Esquire[3] American Chargé d'Affaires ad interim (or other title)	Sir:	Dear Mr. Blank:	Very truly yours,	Sincerely yours,	1. Mr. Blank 2. Mr. Blank
High Commissioner	The Honorable William R. Blank United States High Commissioner to Argentina	Sir:	Dear Mr. Blank	Very truly yours,	Sincerely yours,	1. Commissioner Blank or Mr. Blank 2. Commissioner Blank or Mr. Blank

[3]Do not use *Esquire* to refer to a woman in this position.

FOREIGN OFFICIALS AND REPRESENTATIVES

Personage	Envelope and Inside Address	Formal Salutation	Informal Salutation	Formal Close	Informal Close	1. Spoken Address 2. Informal Introduction or Reference
Foreign Ambassador[1] in the United States	His Excellency,[2] Erik Rolf Blankson Ambassador of Norway	Excellency:	Dear Mr. Ambassador:	Very truly yours,	Sincerely yours,	1. Mr. Ambassador or Mr. Blank 2. The Ambassador of Norway (The Ambassador or Mr. Blank)

[1]The correct title of all ambassadors and ministers of foreign countries is Ambassador (Minister) of _____ (name of country), with the exception of Great Britain. The adjective form is used with reference to representatives from Great Britain—British Ambassador, British Minister.

[2]When the representative is British or a member of the British Commonwealth, it is customary to use *The Right Honorable* and *The Honorable* in addition to *His (Her) Excellency* wherever appropriate.

FOREIGN OFFICIALS AND REPRESENTATIVES continued

Personage	Envelope and Inside Address (Add City, State, Zip, or City, Country)	Formal Salutation	Informal Salutation	Formal Close	Informal Close	1. Spoken Address 2. Informal Introduction or Reference
Foreign Minister [3] in the United States	The Honorable George Macovescu Minister of Rumania	Sir:	Dear Mr. Minister:	Very truly yours,	Sincerely yours,	1. Mr. Minister or Mr. Blank 2. The Minister of Rumania (The Minister or Mr. Blank)
Foreign Diplomatic Representative with a Personal Title [4]	His Excellency, [5] Count Allesandro de Bianco Ambassador of Italy	Excellency:	Dear Mr. Ambassador:	Very truly yours,	Sincerely yours,	1. Mr. Ambassador or Count Bianco 2. The Ambassador of Italy (The Ambassador or Count Bianco)
Prime Minister	His Excellency, Christian Jawaharal Blank Prime Minister of India	Excellency:	Dear Mr. Prime Minister:	Respectfully yours,	Sincerely yours,	1. Mr. Blank 2. Mr. Blank or The Prime Minister
British Prime Minister	The Right Honorable Godfrey Blank, K.G., M.C., M.P. Prime Minister	Sir:	Dear Mr. Prime Minister: or Dear Mr. Blank:	Respectfully yours,	Sincerely yours,	1. Mr. Blank 2. Mr. Blank or The Prime Minister
Canadian Prime Minister	The Right Honorable Claude Louis St. Blanc, C.M.G. Prime Minister of Canada	Sir:	Dear Mr. Prime Minister: or Dear Mr. Blanc:	Respectfully yours,	Sincerely yours,	1. Mr. Blanc 2. Mr. Blanc or The Prime Minister
President of a Republic	His Excellency, Juan Cuidad Blanco President of the Dominican Republic	Excellency:	Dear Mr. President:	I remain with respect, Very truly yours, (formal general usage) Sincerely yours, (less formal)	Sincerely yours,	1. Your Excellency 2. Not introduced (President Blanco or the President)

[3] The correct title of all ambassadors and ministers of foreign countries is Ambassador (Minister) of _____ (name of country), with the exception of Great Britain. The adjective form is used with reference to representatives from Great Britain—British Ambassador, British Minister.

[4] If the personal title is a royal title, such as His (Her) Highness, Prince, etc., the diplomatic title His (Her) Excellency or The Honorable is omitted.

[5] Dr., Señor Don, and other titles of special courtesy in Spanish-speaking countries may be used with the diplomatic title His (Her) Excellency or The Honorable.

FOREIGN OFFICIALS AND REPRESENTATIVES *continued*

Personage	Envelope and Inside Address (Add City, State, Zip, or City, Country)	Formal Salutation	Informal Salutation	Formal Close	Informal Close	1. Spoken Address / 2. Informal Introduction or Reference
Premier	His Excellency, Charles Yves de Blanc Premier of the French Republic	Excellency:	Dear Mr. Premier:	Respectfully yours,	Sincerely yours,	1. Mr. Blanc / 2. Mr. Blanc or The Premier
Foreign Chargé d'Affaires (de missi)[6] in the United States	Mr. Jan Gustaf Blanc Chargé d'Affaires of Sweden	Sir:	Dear Mr. Blanc:	Respectfully yours,	Sincerely yours,	1. Mr. Blanc / 2. Mr. Blanc
Foreign Chargé d'Affaires ad interim in the United States	Mr. Edmund Blanc Chargé d'Affaires ad interim[7] of Ireland	Sir:	Dear Mr. Blanc:	Respectfully yours,	Sincerely yours,	1. Mr. Blank / 2. Mr. Blank

[6]The full title is usually shortened to *Chargé d'Affaires.*
[7]The words "ad interim" should not be omitted in the address.

THE ARMED FORCES/THE ARMY

Personage	Envelope and Inside Address (Add City, State, Zip, or City, Country)	Formal Salutation	Informal Salutation	Formal Close	Informal Close	1. Spoken Address / 2. Informal Introduction or Reference
General of the Army	General of the Army William R. Blank, U.S.A. Department of the Army	Sir:	Dear General Blank:	Very truly yours,	Sincerely yours,	1. General Blank / 2. General Blank
General, Lieutenant General, Major General, or Brigadier General	General (Lieutenant General, Major General, or Brigadier General) William R. Blank, U.S.A.[1]	Sir:	Dear General Blank:	Very truly yours,	Sincerely yours,	1. General Blank / 2. General Blank
Colonel, Lieutenant Colonel	Colonel (Lieutenant Colonel) William R. Blank, U.S.A.	Dear Colonel Blank:	Dear Colonel Blank:	Very truly yours,	Sincerely yours,	1. Colonel Blank / 2. Colonel Blank
Major	Major William R. Blank, U.S.A.	Dear Major Blank:	Dear Major Blank:	Very truly yours,	Sincerely yours,	1. Major Blank / 2. Major Blank

[1]U.S.A. indicates regular services. A.U.S. (Army of the United States) signifies the Reserve.

THE ARMED FORCES/THE NAVY

Personage	Envelope and Inside Address (Add City, State, Zip, or City, Country)	Formal Salutation	Informal Salutation	Formal Close	Informal Close	1. Spoken Address 2. Informal Introduction or Reference
Captain	Captain William R. Blank, U.S.A.	Dear Captain Blank:	Dear Captain Blank:	Very truly yours,	Sincerely yours,	1. Captain Blank 2. Captain Blank
First Lieutenant, Second Lieutenant [2]	Lieutenant William R. Blank, U.S.A.	Dear Lieutenant Blank:	Dear Lieutenant Blank:	Very truly yours,	Sincerely yours,	1. Lieutenant Blank 2. Lieutenant Blank
Chief Warrant Officer, Warrant Officer	Mr. William R. Blank, U.S.A.	Dear Mr. Blank:	Dear Mr. Blank	Very truly yours,	Sincerely yours,	1. Mr. Blank 2. Mr. Blank
Chaplain in the U.S. Army [3]	Chaplain William R. Blank Captain, U.S.A.	Dear Chaplain Blank:	Dear Chaplain Blank:	Very truly yours,	Sincerely yours,	1. Chaplain Blank 2. Captain Blank (Chaplain Blank)
Fleet Admiral	Fleet Admiral William R. Blank, U.S.N. Chief of Naval Operations, Department of the Navy	Sir:	Dear Admiral Blank:	Very truly yours,	Sincerely yours,	1. Admiral Blank 2. Admiral Blank
Admiral, Vice Admiral, Rear Admiral	Admiral (Vice Admiral or Rear Admiral) William R. Blank, U.S.N. United States Naval Academy [1]	Sir:	Dear Admiral Blank:	Very truly yours,	Sincerely yours,	1. Admiral Blank 2. Admiral Blank
Commodore, Captain, Commander, Lieutenant Commander	Commodore (Captain, Commander, Lieutenant Commander) William R. Blank, U.S.N. U.S.S. Mississippi	Dear Commodore (Captain, Commander) Blank:	Dear Commodore (Captain, Commander) Blank:	Very truly yours,	Sincerely yours,	1. Commodore (Captain, Commander) Blank 2. Commodore (Captain, Commander) Blank

[1] U.S.N. signifies regular service; U.S.N.R. indicates the Reserve.

[2] In all official correspondence, the full rank should be included in both the envelope address and the inside address, but not in the salutation.

[3] Roman Catholic chaplains and certain Anglican priests are introduced as Chaplain Blank but are spoken to and referred to as Father Blank.

Personage	Envelope and Inside Address (Add City, State, Zip, or City, Country)	Formal Salutation	Informal Salutation	Formal Close	Informal Close	1. Spoken Address 2. Informal Introduction or Reference
Junior Officers: Lieutenant, Lieutenant Junior Grade, Ensign	(Lieutenant, etc.) William R. Blank, U.S.N. U.S.S. Wyoming	Dear Mr. Blank:	Dear Mr. Blank:	Very truly yours,	Sincerely yours,	1. Mr. Blank [2] 2. Lieutenant, etc., Blank (Mr. Blank)
Chief Warrant Officer, Warrant Officer	Mr. William R. Blank, U.S.N. U.S.S. Texas	Dear Mr. Blank:	Dear Mr. Blank:	Very truly yours,	Sincerely yours,	1. Mr. Blank 2. Mr. Blank
Chaplain	Chaplain William R. Blank Captain, U.S.N. Department of the Navy	Dear Chaplain Blank:	Dear Chaplain Blank:	Very truly yours,	Sincerely yours,	1. Chaplain Blank 2. Captain Blank (Chaplain Blank)

[2] Junior officers in the medical or dental corps are spoken to and referred to as *Dr.* but are introduced by their rank.

THE ARMED FORCES—AIR FORCE

Air Force titles are the same as those in the Army. *U.S.A.F.* is used instead of *U.S.A.*, and *A.F.U.S.* is used to indicate the Reserve.

THE ARMED FORCES—MARINE CORPS

Marine Corps titles are the same as those in the Army, except that the top rank is *Commandant of the Marine Corps. U.S.M.C.* indicates regular service, *U.S.M.R.* indicates the Reserve.

THE ARMED FORCES—COAST GUARD

Coast Guard titles are the same as those in the Navy, except that the top rank is *Admiral. U.S.C.G.* indicates regular service, *U.S.C.G.R.* indicates the Reserve.

CHURCH DIGNITARIES/CATHOLIC FAITH

Personage	Envelope and Inside Address (Add City, State, Zip, or City, Country)	Formal Salutation	Informal Salutation	Formal Close	Informal Close	1. Spoken Address 2. Informal Introduction or Reference
The Pope	His Holiness, The Pope or His Holiness Pope _____ Vatican City	Your Holiness: Most Holy Father:	Always Formal	Respectfully,	Always Formal	1. Your Holiness 2. Not introduced (His Holiness or The Pope)
Apostolic Delegate	His Excellency, The Most Reverend William R. Blank Archbishop of _____ The Apostolic Delegate	Your Excellency:	Dear Archbishop Blank:	Respectfully yours,	Respectfully,	1. Your Excellency 2. Not introduced (The Apostolic Delegate)
Cardinal in the United States	His Eminence, William Cardinal Blank Archbishop of New York	Your Eminence:	Dear Cardinal Blank:	Respectfully yours,	Respectfully, or Sincerely yours,	1. Your Eminence or less formally Cardinal Blank 2. Not introduced (His Eminence or Cardinal Blank)
Bishop and Archbishop in the United States	The Most Reverend William R. Blank, D.D. Bishop (Archbishop) of Baltimore	Your Excellency:	Dear Bishop (Archbishop) Blank:	Respectfully yours,	Respectfully, or Sincerely yours,	1. Bishop (Archbishop) Blank 2. Bishop (Archbishop) Blank
Bishop in England	The Right Reverend William R. Blank Bishop of Sussex (local address)	Right Reverend Sir:	Dear Bishop:	Respectfully yours,	Respectfully,	1. Bishop Blank 2. Bishop Blank
Abbot	The Right Reverend William R. Blank Abbot of Westmoreland Abbey	Dear Father Abbot:	Dear Father Blank:	Respectfully yours,	Sincerely yours,	1. Father Abbot 2. Father Blank

303

CHURCH DIGNITARIES/CATHOLIC FAITH continued

Personage	Envelope and Inside Address (Add City, State, Zip, or City, Country)	Formal Salutation	Informal Salutation	Formal Close	Informal Close	1. Spoken Address 2. Informal Introduction or Reference
Canon	The Reverend William R. Blank, D.D. Canon of St. Patrick's Cathedral	Reverend Sir:	Dear Canon Blank:	Respectfully yours,	Sincerely yours,	1. Canon Blank 2. Canon Blank
Monsignor	The Right (or Very) [1] Reverend Msgr. William R. Blank	Right Reverend and Dear Monsignor Blank: or Very Reverend and Dear Monsignor Blank:	Dear Monsignor Blank:	Respectfully yours,	Sincerely yours,	1. Monsignor Blank 2. Monsignor Blank
Brother	Brother John Blank 932 Maple Avenue	Dear Brother:	Dear Brother Brother Blank:	Respectfully yours,	Sincerely yours,	1. Brother Blank 2. Brother Blank
Superior of a Brotherhood and Priest[2]	The Very Reverend William R. Blank, M.M. Director	Dear Father Superior	Dear Father Superior:	Respectfully yours,	Sincerely yours,	1. Father Blank 2. Father Blank
Priest	With scholastic degree: The Reverend William R. Blank, Ph.D. Georgetown University	Dear Dr. Blank:	Dear Dr. Blank:	Respectfully,	Sincerely yours,	1. Doctor (Father) Blank 2. Doctor (Father) Blank
	Without scholastic degree: The Reverend William R. Blank St. Vincent's Church	Dear Father Blank:	Dear Father Blank:	Respectfully,	Sincerely yours,	1. Father Blank 2. Father Blank

[1] Dependent upon rank. See the *Official* (Roman) *Catholic Directory*.

[2] The address for the superior of a Brotherhood depends upon whether or not he is a priest or has a title other than superior. Consult the *Official Catholic Directory*.

CHURCH DIGNITARIES/CATHOLIC FAITH *continued*

Personage	Envelope and Inside Address (Add City, State, Zip, or City, Country)	Formal Salutation	Informal Salutation	Formal Close	Informal Close	1. Spoken Address 2. Informal Introduction or Reference
Sister Superior	The Reverend Sister Superior (order, if used) [3] Convent of the Sacred Heart	Dear Sister Superior:	Dear Sister Superior:	Respectfully,	Respectfully, or Sincerely yours,	1. Sister Blank or Sister St. Teresa 2. The Sister Superior or Sister Blank (Sister St. Teresa)
Sister	Sister Mary Blank St. John's High School	Dear Sister:	Dear Sister Blank:	Respectfully,	Sincerely yours,	1. Sister Blank 2. Sister Blank
Mother Superior of a Sisterhood (Catholic or Protestant)	The Reverend Mother Superior, O.C.A. Convent of the Sacred Heart	Dear Reverend Mother: or Dear Mother Superior:	Dear Reverend Mother: or Dear Mother Superior:	Respectfully,	Sincerely yours,	1. Reverend Mother 2. Reverend Mother
Member of Community	Mother Mary Walker, R.S.M. Convent of Mercy	Dear Mother Walker:	Dear Mother Walker:	Respectfully,	Sincerely yours,	1. Mother Walker 2. Mother Walker

CHURCH DIGNITARIES/JEWISH FAITH

Personage	Envelope and Inside Address (Add City, State, Zip, or City, Country)	Formal Salutation	Informal Salutation	Formal Close	Informal Close	1. Spoken Address 2. Informal Introduction or Reference

[3] The address of the superior of a Sisterhood depends upon the order to which she belongs. The abbreviation of the order is not always used. Consult *Official Catholic Directory.*

305

CHURCH DIGNITARIES/JEWISH FAITH *continued*

Rabbi	With scholastic degree: Rabbi William R. Blank, Ph.D.	Sir:	Dear Rabbi Blank: or Dear Dr. Blank:	Respectfully yours, or Very truly yours,	Sincerely yours,	1. Rabbi Blank or Dr. Blank 2. Rabbi Blank or Dr. Blank
	Without scholastic degree: Rabbi William R. Blank	Sir:	Dear Rabbi Blank:	Respectfully yours, or Very truly yours,	Sincerely yours,	1. Rabbi Blank 2. Rabbi Blank

CHURCH DIGNITARIES/PROTESTANT FAITH

Archbishop (Anglican)	The Most Reverend Archbishop of Canterbury or The Most Reverend John Blank, Archbishop of Canterbury	Your Grace:	Dear Archbishop Blank:	Respectfully yours,	Sincerely yours,	1. Your Grace 2. Not introduced (His Grace or The Archbishop)
Presiding Bishop of the Protestant Episcopal Church in America	The Most Reverend William R. Blank, D.D., LL.D. Presiding Bishop of the Protestant Episcopal Church in America Northwick House	Most Reverend Sir:	Dear Bishop Blank:	Respectfully yours,	Sincerely yours,	1. Bishop Blank 2. Bishop Blank
Anglican Bishop	The Right Reverend The Lord Bishop of London	Right Reverend Sir:	My dear Bishop:	Respectfully yours,	Sincerely yours,	1. Bishop Blank 2. Bishop Blank
Methodist Bishop	The Very Reverend William R. Blank Methodist Bishop	Reverend Sir:	Mr dear Bishop:	Respectfully yours,	Sincerely yours,	1. Bishop Blank 2. Bishop Blank
Protestant Episcopal Bishop	The Right Reverend William R. Blank, D.D., LL.D. Bishop of Denver	Right Reverend Sir:	Dear Bishop Blank:	Respectfully yours,	Sincerely yours,	1. Bishop Blank 2. Bishop Blank

CHURCH DIGNITARIES/PROTESTANT FAITH *continued*

Personage	Envelope and Inside Address (Add City, State, Zip, or City, Country)	Formal Salutation	Informal Salutation	Formal Close	Informal Close	1. Spoken Address 2. Informal Introduction or Reference
Archdeacon	The Venerable William R. Blank Archdeacon of Baltimore	Venerable Sir:	My dear Archdeacon:	Respectfully yours,	Sincerely yours,	1. Archdeacon Blank 2. Archdeacon Blank
Dean[1]	The Very Reverend William R. Blank, D.D. Dean of St. John's Cathedral	Very Reverend Sir:	Dear Dean Blank:	Respectfully yours,	Sincerely yours,	1. Dean Blank or Dr. Blank 2. Dean Blank or Dr. Blank
Protestant Minister	With scholastic degree: The Reverend William R. Blank, D.D., Litt.D. or The Reverend Dr. William R. Blank	Dear Dr. Blank:	Dear Dr. Blank:	Very truly yours,	Sincerely yours,	1. Dr. Blank 2. Dr. Blank
	Without scholastic degree: The Reverend William R. Blank	Dear Mr. Blank:	Dear Mr. Blank:	Very truly yours,	Sincerely yours,	1. Mr. Blank 2. Mr. Blank
Episcopal Priest (High Church)	With scholastic degree: The Reverend William R. Blank, D.D., Litt.D. All Saint's Cathedral or The Reverend Dr. William R. Blank	Dear Dr. Blank:	Dear Dr. Blank:	Very truly yours,	Sincerely yours,	1. Dr. Blank 2. Dr. Blank
	Without scholastic degree: The Reverend William R. Blank St. Paul's Church	Dear Mr. Blank: or Dear Father Blank:	Dear Mr. Blank: or Dear Father Blank:	Very truly yours,	Sincerely yours,	1. Father Blank or Mr. Blank 2. Father Blank or Mr. Blank

[1]Applies only to the head of a Cathedral or of a Theological Seminary.

COLLEGE AND UNIVERSITY OFFICIALS

President of a College or University	With a doctor's degree: Dr. William R. Blank or William R. Blank, LL.D., Ph.D. President, Amherst College	Sir:	Dear Dr. Blank:	Very truly yours,	Sincerely yours,	1. Dr. Blank 2. Dr. Blank
	Without a doctor's degree Mr. William R. Blank President, Columbia University	Sir:	Dear President Blank:	Very truly yours,	Sincerely yours,	1. Mr. Blank 2. Mr. Blank or Mr. Blank, President of the College
	Catholic priest: The Very Reverend William R. Blank, S.J., D.D., Ph.D. President, Fordham University	Sir:	Dear Father Blank:	Very truly yours,	Sincerely yours,	1. Father Blank 2. Father Blank
University Chancellor	Dr. William R. Blank Chancellor, University of Alabama	Sir:	Dear Dr. Blank:	Very truly yours,	Sincerely yours,	1. Dr. Blank 2. Dr. Blank.
Dean or Assistant Dean of a College or Graduate School	Dean William R. Blank School of Law or (If he holds a doctor's degree) Dr. William R. Blank, Dean (Assistant Dean) School of Law University of Virginia	Dear Sir: or Dear Dean Blank:	Dear Dean Blank:	Very truly yours,	Sincerely yours,	1. Dean Blank 2. Dean Blank or Dr. Bank, the Dean (Assistant Dean) of the School of Law
Professor	Professor William R. Blank or (If he holds a doctor's degree) Dr. William R. Blank or William R. Blank, Ph.D. Yale University	Dear Sir: or Dear Professor (Dr.) Blank:	Dear Professor (Dr.) Blank:	Very truly yours,	Sincerely yours,	1. Professor (Dr.) Blank 2. Professor (Dr.) Blank

308

COLLEGE AND UNIVERSITY OFFICIALS *continued*

Personage	Envelope and Inside Address (Add City, State, Zip, or City, Country)	Formal Salutation	Informal Salutation	Formal Close	Informal Close	1. Spoken Address 2. Informal Introduction or Reference
Associate or Assistant Professor	Mr. William R. Blank or (If he holds a doctor's degree) Dr. William R. Blank or William R. Blank, Ph.D. Associate (Assistant) Professor Department of Romance Languages Williams College	Dear Sir: or Dear Professor (Dr.) Blank:	Dear Professor (Dr.) Blank:	Very truly yours,	Sincerely yours,	1. Professor (Dr.) Blank or 2. Professor (Dr.) Blank
Instructor	Mr. William R. Blank or (If he holds a doctor's degree) Dr. William R. Blank or William R. Blank, Ph.D. Department of Economics University of California	Dear Sir: or Dear Mr. (Dr.) Blank:	Dear Mr. (Dr.) Blank:	Very truly yours,	Sincerely yours,	1. Mr. (Dr.) Blank 2. Mr. (Dr.) Blank
Chaplain of a College or University	The Reverend William R. Blank, D.D. Chaplain, Trinity College or Chaplain William R. Blank Trinity College	Dear Chaplain Blank: or (If he holds a doctor's degree) Dear Dr. Blank:	Dear Chaplain (Dr.) Blank:	Very truly yours,	Sincerely yours,	1. Chaplain Blank 2. Chaplain Blank or Dr. Blank

UNITED NATIONS OFFICIALS[1]

Personage	Envelope and Inside Address (Add City, State, Zip, or City, Country)	Formal Salutation[2]	Informal Salutation	Formal Close	Informal Close	1. Spoken Address 2. Informal Introduction or Reference
Secretary General	His Excellency, William R. Blank Secretary General of the United Nations	Excellency:[2]	Dear Mr. Secretary General:	Very truly yours,	Sincerely yours,	1. Mr. Blank or Sir 2. The Secretary General of the United Nations or Mr. Blank
Under Secretary	The Honorable William R. Blank Under Secretary of the United Nations The Secretariat United Nations	Sir:	Dear Mr. Blank:	Very truly yours,	Sincerely yours,	1. Mr. Blank 2. Mr. Blank
Foreign Representative (with ambassadorial rank)	His Excellency, William R. Blank Representative of Spain to the United Nations	Excellency:	Dear Mr. Ambassador:	Very truly yours,	Sincerely yours,	1. Mr. Ambassador or Mr. Blank 2. Mr. Ambassador or The Representative of Spain to the United Nations (The Ambassador or Mr. Blank)
United States Representative (with ambassadorial rank)	The Honorable William R. Blank United States Representative to the United Nations	Sir: or Dear Mr. Ambassador	Dear Mr. Ambassador:	Very truly yours,	Sincerely yours,	1. Mr. Ambassador or Mr. Blank 2. Mr. Ambassador or The United States Representative to the United Nations (The Ambassador or Mr. Blank)

[1]The six principal branches through which the United Nations functions are The General Assembly, The Security Council, The Economic and Social Council, The Trusteeship Council, The International Court of Justice, and The Secretariat.

[2]An American citizen should never be addressed as "Excellency."

Latin Words and Phrases

Legal dictation in every field contains many Latin words and phrases. Those that you are most likely to hear are listed below. The list also contains a few French terms. The list will enable you to write the words and phrases correctly; the almost literal translations will enable you to understand the meaning of the dictation. Foreign words and phrases are frequently italicized in printing and underlined in typing. However, many of them have become completely Anglicized and are not generally printed in italic type or underlined. The words and phrases that are italicized in the list should be underlined when typed. Those in roman type should not be underlined. You will notice that some words are not underlined unless used in a phrase or expression. For example, "animus" is not italicized when written alone, but is italicized in the phrase *animus furandi.*

a fortiori. With stronger reason; much more.
a mensa et thoro. From bed and board.
a priori. From what goes before; from the cause to the effect.
a vinculo matrimonii. From the bonds of marriage.
ab initio. From the beginning.
actiones in personam. Personal actions.
ad faciendum. To do.
ad hoc. For this (for this special purpose).
ad infinitum. Indefinitely; forever.
ad litem. For the suit; for the litigation (A guardian *ad litem* is a person appointed to prosecute or defend a suit for a person incapacitated by infancy or incompetency.)
ad quod damnum. To what damage; what injury. (A phrase used to describe the plaintiff's money loss or the damages he claims.)

311

ad respondendum. To answer.

ad satisfaciendum. To satisfy.

ad valorem. According to value.

aggregatio menium. Meeting of minds.

alias dictus. Otherwise called.

alibi. In another place; elsewhere.

alii. Others.

aliunde. From another place; from without (as evidence outside the document).

alius. Another.

alter ego. The other self.

alumnus. A foster child.

amicus curiae. Friend of the court.

animo. With intention, disposition, design, will.

animus. Mind; intention.

animus furandi. The intention to steal.

animus revertendi. An intention of returning

animus revocandi. An intention to revoke.

animus testandi. An intention to make a testament or will.

anno Domini (A.D.). In the year of the Lord.

ante. Before.

ante litem motam. Before suit brought.

arguendo. In the course of the argument.

assumpsit. He undertook; he promised.

bona fide. In good faith.

*bona vacantia.*Vacant goods. (Personal property that no one claims, which escheats to the state.)

capias. Take; arrest. (A form of writ directing an arrest.)

capias ad satisfaciendum (ca. sa.). Arrest to satisfy. (A form of writ.)

causa mortis. By reason of death.

caveat. Let him beware; a warning.

caveat emptor. Let the buyer beware.

cepit et asportavit. He took and carried away.

certiorari. To be informed of; to be made certain in regard to. (See glossary of legal terms.)

cestui (pl. cesuis). Beneficiaries. (Pronounced "setty.")

cestui que trust. He who benefits by the trust.

cestui que use. He who benefits by the use.

cestui que vie. He whose life measures the duration of the estate.

civiliter mortuus. Civilly dead.

Consensus, non concubitus, facit nuptias vel matrimonium. Consent, not cohabitation, constitutes nuptials or marriage.

consortium (*pl.* consortia). A union of lots or chances (a lawful marriage).

contra. Against.

contra bonos mores. Against good morals.

contra pacem. Against the peace.

coram non judice. In presence of a person not a judge. (A suit brought and determined in a court having no jurisdiction over the matter is said to be *coram non judice,* and the judgment is void.)

corpus. Body.

corpus delicti. The body of the offense; the essence of the crime.

corpus juris. A body of law.

corpus juris civilis. The body of the civil law.

Cujus est solum, ejus est usque ad coelum. Whose the soil is, his it is up to the sky.

cum testamento annexo (c.t.a.). With the will annexed. (Describes an administrator who operates under a will rather than in intestacy.)

damnum absque injuria. Damage without injury. (Damage without legal wrong.)

datum (*pl.* data). A thing given; a date.

de bonis non administratis. Of the goods not administered. Frequently abbreviated to *de bonis non.*

de bono et malo. For good and ill.

de facto. In fact; in deed; actually.

de jure. Of right; lawful.

De minimis non curat lex. The law does not concern itself with trifles.

de novo. Anew; afresh.

de son tort. Of his own wrong.

dies non. Not a day (on which the business of the courts can be carried on).

donatio mortis causa. A gift by reason of death. (A gift made by a person in sickness, under apprehension of death.)

duces tecum. You bring with you. (A term applied to a writ commanding the person upon whom it is served to bring certain evidence with him to court. Thus, we speak of a *subpoena duces tecum.*)

dum bene se gesserit. While he shall conduct himself well; during good behavior.

durante minore aetate. During minority.

durante viduitate. During widowhood.

e converso. Conversely; on the other hand.

eo instanti. Upon the instant.

erratum (*pl.* errata). Error.

et alii (et al.). And others.

et alius (et al.). And another.

et cetera (etc.). And other things.

ex cathedra. From the chair.

ex contractu. (Arising) from the contract.

ex delicto. (Arising) from a tort.

ex gratia. As a matter of favor.

ex necessitate legis. From legal necessity.

ex officio. From office; by virtue of his office.

ex parte. On one side only; by or for one party.

ex post facto. After the act.

ex rel (short for *ex relatione*). On information of; on behalf of a party or parties.

et uxor (et ux.). And wife.

et vir. And husband.

felonice. Feloniously.

feme covert. A married woman.

feme sole. A single woman (including one who has been married but whose marriage has been dissolved by death or divorce).

ferae naturae. Of a wild nature.

fiat. Let it be done. (A short order or warrant of a judge, commanding that something shall be done.)

fieri. To be made up; to become.

fieri facias. Cause to be made. (A writ directed to the sheriff to reduce the judgment debtor's property to money in the amount of the judgment.)

filius nullius. The son of nobody; a bastard.

filius populi. A son of the people.

flagrante delicto. In the very act of committing the crime.

habeas corpus. You have the body. (See glossary of legal terms.)

habendum clause. Clause in deed that defines extent of ownership by grantee.

habere facias possessionem. That you cause to have possession. (A writ of ejectment.)

habere facias seisinam. That you cause to have seisin. (A writ to give possession.)

honorarium (*pl.* honoraria). An honorary fee or gift; compensation from gratitude.

idem sonans. Having the same sound (as names sounding alike but spelled differently).

Ignorantia legis neminen excusat. Ignorance of the law excuses no one.

illicitum collegium. An unlawful association.

Impotentia excusat legem. Impossibility is an excuse in law.

in bonis. In goods; among possessions.

in esse. In being; existence.

in extremis. In extremity (in the last illness).

in fraudem legis. In circumvention of law.

in futuro. In the future.

in loco parentis. In the place of a parent.

in pari delicto. In equal fault.

in personam. A remedy where the proceedings are *against the person,* as contradistinguished from those against a specific thing.

in praesenti. At present; at once; now.

in re. In the matter.

in rem. A remedy where the proceedings are *against the thing,* as distinguished from those against the person.

in rerum natura. In nature; in life; in existence.

in specie. In the same, or like, form. (To decree performance *in specie* is to decree specific performance.)

in statu quo. In the condition in which it was. (See *status quo.*)

in terrorem. In terror.

in toto. In the whole; completely.

in transitu. In transit; in course of transfer.

indebitatus assumpsit. Being indebted, be promised, or undertook. (An action in which plaintiff alleges defendant is indebted to him.)

indicia. Marks; signs.

infra. Below.

innuendo. Meaning.

inter. Among; between.

inter vivos. Between the living.

interim. In the meantime.

intra. Within; inside.

ipse dixit. He himself said (it). (An assertion made but not proved.)

ipso facto. By the fact itself.

ita est. So it is.

jura personarum. Rights of persons.

jura rerum. Rights of things.

jurat. Portion of affidavit in which officer administering the oath certifies that it was sworn to before him. (See p. 230.)

jure divino. By divine right.

jure uxoris. In his wife's right.

jus (pl. jura). Law; laws collectively.

jus accrescendi. The right of survivorship.

jus ad rem. A right to a thing.

jus civile. Civil law.

jus commune. The common law; the common right.

jus gentium. The law of nations; international law.

jus habendi. The right to have a thing.

jus proprietatis. Right of property.

levari facias. Cause to be levied; a writ of execution.

lex loci. Law of the place (where the cause of action arose).

lex loci rei sitae. The law of the place where a thing is situated.

lex mercatoria. The law merchant.

lis pendens. Litigation pending; a pending suit.

locus delicti. The place of the crime or tort.

locus in quo. The place in which.

locus sigilii (L.S.). The place for the seal.

mala fides. Bad faith.

mala in se. Wrongs in themselves (acts morally wrong).

mala praxis. Malpractice.

mala prohibita. Prohibited wrongs or offenses.

malo animo. With evil intent.

malum in se. Evil in itself.

mandamus. We command. (See glossary of legal terms.)

manu forti. With a strong hand (forcible entry).

mens rea. Guilty mind.

nihil dicit. He says nothing. (Judgment against defendant who does not put in a defense to the complaint.)

nil debet. He owes nothing.

nisi prius. Unless before. (The phrase is used to denote the forum where the trial was held as distinguished from the appellate court.)

nolle prosequi. To be unwilling to follow up, or to prosecute. (A formal entry on the record by the plaintiff or the prosecutor that he will not further prosecute the case.)

nolo contendere. I will not contest it.

non compos mentis. Not of sound mind.

non est factum. It is not his deed.

non obstante. Notwithstanding.

non prosequitur (non pros.). He does not follow up, or pursue, or prosecute. (If the plaintiff fails to take some step that he should, the defendant may enter a judgment of *non pros.* against him.)

nudum pactum. A nude pact. (A contract without consideration.)

nul tiel record. No such record.

nul tort. No wrong done.

nulla bona. No goods. (Wording of return to a writ of *fieri facias.*)

nunc pro tunc. Now for then.

obiter dictum. Remark by the way. (See *dictum* in glossary of legal terms.)

onus probandi. The burden of proof.

opus (*pl. opera*). Work; labor.

ore tenus. By word of mouth; orally.

pari delicto. In equal guilt.

particeps criminis. An accomplice in the crime.

pater familias. The father (head) of a family.

peculium. Private property.

pendente lite. Pending the suit; during the litigation.

per annum. By the year.

per autre vie. For another's lifetime. (See also *pur autre vie.*)

per capita. By the head; as individuals. (In a distribution of an estate, if the descendants take per capita, they take share and share alike regardless of family lines of descent.)

per centum (per cent). By the hundred.

per contra. In opposition.

per curiam. By the court.

per diem. By the day.

per se. By itself; taken alone.

per stirpes. By stems or root; by representation. (In a distribution of an estate, if distribution is *per stirpes*, descendants take by virtue of their representation of an ancestor, not as individuals.)

postmortem. After death.

postobit. To take effect after death.

praecipe or *precipe.* Command. (A written order to the clerk of the court to issue a writ.)

prima facie. At first sight; on the face of it.

pro. For.

pro confesso. As confessed.

pro forma. As a matter of form.

pro hac vice. For this occasion.

pro rata. According to the rate or proportion.

pro tanto. For so much; to that extent.

pro tempore (pro tem.). For the time being; temporarily.

prochein ami. Next friend.

publici juris. Of public right.

pur autre vie. For, or during, the life of another. (See also *per autre vie.*)

quaere. Query; question; doubt. (This word indicates that a particular rule, decision, or statement that follows it is open to question.)

quantum meruit. As much as he deserved.

quantum valebant. As much as they were (reasonably) worth (in absence of agreement as to value).

quare. Wherefore.

quare clausum fregit. Wherefore he broke the close. (A form of trespass on another's land.)

quasi. As if; as it were. (Indicates that one subject resembles another, but that there are also intrinsic differences between them. Thus, we speak of quasi contracts, quasi torts, etc.)

quid pro quo. What for what; something for something. (A term denoting the consideration for a contract.)

quo warranto. By what right or authority. (See glossary of legal terms.)

quoad hoc. As to this.

quod computet. That he account.

reductio ad absurdum. Reduced to the absurd.

res. A thing; an object; the subject matter.

res gestae. Things done; transactions.

res ipsa loquitur. The thing speaks for itself.

res judicata. A matter adjudicated.

scienter. Knowingly.

scilicet (SS. or ss.) To wit. (sc. is not used in legal papers)

scintilla. A spark; the least particle.

scire facias. Cause to know; give notice. (A writ used to revive a judgment that has expired.)

se defendendo. In self-defense; in defending oneself.

semper. Always.

semper paratus. Always ready. (A plea by which the defendant alleges that he has always been ready to perform what is demanded of him.)

seriatim. Severally; separately.

sigillum. A seal.

simplex obligato. A simple obligation.

sine die. Without day. (Without a specified day being assigned for a future meeting or hearing.)

situs. Situation; location.

stare decisis. To abide by decided cases.

status quo. State in which (the existing state of things at any given date.) See *in statu quo.*

sub judice. Under consideration.

sub modo. Under a qualification; in a qualified way.

sub nom. Under the name.

sui juris. Of his own right (having legal capacity to act for himself).

supersedeas. That you supersede. (A writ commanding a stay of the proceedings.)

supra. Above.

terminus a quo. The starting point.

ultra vires. Without power; beyond the powers of. (See glossary of legal terms.)

venire facias. That you cause to come (a kind of summons).

Verba fortius accipiuntur contra proferentem. Words are to be taken most strongly against the one using them.

versus (vs., v.). Against.

vi et armis. By force and arms.

via. A road; a right of way; by way of.

vice versa. On the contrary; on opposite sides.

videlicet (viz.) (contraction of *videre* and *licet*). It is easy to see (that is, namely).

virtute officii. By virtue of his office.

viva voce. By the living voice; by word of mouth.

voir dire. To speak the truth. (Denotes a preliminary examination to determine the competency of a witness.)

Note: Some states' statutes permit wills to be self-proved when certain formalities are followed. States that permit self-proved wills include Alaska, Arizona, Colorado, Delaware, Florida, Idaho, Indiana, Kansas, Kentucky, Minnesota, Montana, Nebraska, New Mexico, North Dakota, Oklahoma, Texas, and Utah.

COURTS OF RECORD AND JUDICIAL CIRCUITS
(TABLES I, II, III AND IV)

I. FEDERAL COURTS OF RECORD IN THE UNITED STATES
AND THEIR MEMBERS

Court	Members
Supreme Court of the United States	Chief Justice
	Associate Justices
United States Court of Appeals for the District of Columbia	Circuit Justice
	Chief Judge
	Circuit Judges
United States Court of Appeals for the (First) Circuit	Circuit Justice
	Chief Judge
	Circuit Judges
United States District Court for the (Southern) District of (New York)	Chief Judge
Or where the state is all in one district	District Judges
United States District Court for the District of (Maryland)	
United States Court of Claims	Chief Judge
	Associate Judges
United States Court of Customs and Patent Appeals	Chief Judge
	Associate Judges
United States Customs Court	Chief Judge
	Judges
United States Court of Military Appeals	Chief Judge
	Associate Judges
The Tax Court of the United States	Chief Judge
	Judges
Temporary Emergency Court of Appeals of the United States	Chief Judge
	Associate Judges

II. STATE COURTS OF RECORD IN THE UNITED STATES
AND THEIR MEMBERS
(Asterisks indicate intermediate appellate courts.
Municipal courts are not included.)

State	Court	Members of Court
Alabama	Supreme Court	Chief Justice
		Associate Justices
	*Court of Appeals	Presiding Judge
		Associate Judges
	Circuit Courts	Judges
	Probate Courts	Judge

continued

State	Court	Members of Court
Alaska	Supreme Court	Chief Justice
		Associate Justices
	Superior Court	Judges
Arizona	Supreme Court	Chief Justice, Justices
	Court of Appeals	Judges
	Superior Courts	Judges
Arkansas	Supreme Court	Chief Justice
		Associate Justices
	Circuit Courts	Judges
	Chancery Courts	Chancellors
	Probate Courts	Judges
California	Supreme Court	Chief Justice
		Associate Justices
	*Courts of Appeal	Presiding Justice
		Justices
	Superior Courts	Judges
Colorado	Supreme Court	Chief Justice, Justices
	Court of Appeals	Judges
	District Court	Judges
	Superior Courts	Judges
	County Courts	Judges
	Probate Courts (Denver only)	Judges
Connecticut	Supreme Court	Chief Justice
		Associate Justices
	Superior Court	Judges
	Courts of Common Pleas	Judges
	Probate Courts	Judges
Delaware	Supreme Court	Chief Justice
		Associate Justices
	Court of Chancery	Chancellor
		Vice Chancellor
	Superior Court	President Judge
		Associate Judges
	Registers' Courts	Register of Wills
District of Columbia	U.S. District Court	Chief Judge
		Judges
	District of Columbia Superior Court	Chief Judge
		Associate Judges
Florida	Supreme Court	Chief Justice, Justices
	*District Courts of Appeal	Chief Judge, Judges
	Circuit Courts	Judges
	County Courts	Judges
	Probate Courts	Judges

continued

State	Court	Members of Court
Georgia	Supreme Court	Chief Justice Presiding Justice Associate Justices
	*Court of Appeals	Chief Judge Presiding Judge Judges
	Superior Courts	Judges
	Probate Courts	Probate Judges
Hawaii	Supreme Court	Chief Justice Justices
	*Circuit Courts	Judges
	District Courts	District Judges
Idaho	Supreme Court	Chief Justice Justices
	District Courts	Judges
Illinois	Supreme Court	Chief Justice Justices
	*Appellate Courts	Judges
	Circuit Courts	Judges
	Court of Claims	Chief Judge Judges
Indiana	Supreme Court	Chief Justice Associate Judges
	*Court of Appeals	Chief Judge Presiding Judge Associate Judges
	Superior Courts	Judges
	Circuit Court	Judges
	Probate Courts	Judges
Iowa	Supreme Court	Chief Justice Justices
	*Court of Appeals	Judges
	District Courts	Judges
Kansas	Supreme Court	Chief Justice Justices
	*Court of Appeals	Judges
	District Court	Judges
Kentucky	Supreme Court	Chief Justice Associate Justices
	*Court of Appeals	Commissioners of Appeals Special Commissioners
	Circuit Courts	Judges
	District Courts	Judges

continued

321

State	Court	Members of Court
Louisiana	Supreme Court	Chief Justice
		Associate Justices
	*Court of Appeal	Judges
	(New Orleans only)	
	District Courts	Judges
Maine	Supreme Judicial Court	Chief Justice
		Associate Justices
	Superior Court	Justices
	State District Courts	Chief Judge, Judges
	Probate Courts	Judges
Maryland	Court of Appeals	Chief Judge
		Associate Judges
	Court of Special Appeals	Judges
	Circuit Courts	Chief Judges, Judges
	Orphans' Courts	Judges
Massachusetts	Supreme Judicial Court	Chief Justice
		Associate Justices
	*Appeals Court	Justices
	Superior Court	Chief Justice
		Associate Justices
	Probate Courts	Judges
	Land Court	Judge, Associate Judges
Michigan	Supreme Court	Chief Justice
		Associate Justices
	Court of Appeals	Justices
	Circuit Courts	Circuit Judge
		Judges
	Court of Claims	Judge
	Probate Courts	Judges
Minnesota	Supreme Court	Chief Justice
		Associate Justices
	District Court	Judges
	County Courts	Judges
	Probate Courts	Judges
Mississippi	Supreme Court	Chief Justice
		Associate Justices
	Circuit Courts	Judges
	Chancery Courts	Chancellors
	County Courts	Judges
Missouri	Supreme Court	Chief Justice
		Presiding Judge
		Associate Judges
	*Courts of Appeals	Presiding Judge
		Associate Judges

continued

322

State	Court	Members of Court
Missouri (con't.)	Court of Common Pleas	Judges
	Circuit Courts	Judges
	Probate Courts	Judges
Montana	Supreme Court	Chief Justice
		Associate Justices
	District Court	Judges
Nebraska	Supreme Court	Chief Justice
		Associate Justices
	District Court	Judges
	County Courts	Judges
Nevada	Supreme Court	Chief Justice
		Associate Justices
	District Court	Judges
New Hampshire	Supreme Court	Chief Justice
		Associate Justices
	Superior Court	Chief Justice
		Justices
	Probate Courts	Presiding Judges
New Jersey	Supreme Court	Chief Justice
		Justices
	*Superior Court,	Senior Judge
	Appellate Division	Judges
	Superior Court,	Judges
	Chancery Division	
	Superior Court,	Judges
	Law Division	
	County Courts	Judges
	Surrogate's Courts	Surrogates
New Mexico	Supreme Court	Chief Justice
		Justices
	*Court of Appeals	Chief Judge
		Judges
	District Court	Presiding Judge
		Judges
	Probate Courts	Judges
New York	Court of Appeals	Chief Judge
		Associate Judges
	*Supreme Court,	Presiding Justice
	Appellate Division	Justices
	Supreme Court	Justices
	County Courts	Judges
	Surrogates' Courts	Surrogates
	Court of Claims	Judges
	City and District Courts	Judges
	(in larger cities and	
	counties)	

continued

State	Court	Members of Court
North Carolina	Supreme Court	Chief Justice
		Associate Justices
	*Court of Appeals	Judges
	Superior Courts	Judges
North Dakota	Supreme Court	Chief Justice
		Judges
	District Court	Judges
	County Courts	Judges
Ohio	Supreme Court	Chief Justice
		Justices
	*Courts of Appeals	Judges
	Court of Claims	Judges
	Courts of Common Pleas	Judges
Oklahoma	Supreme Court	Chief Justice
		Vice Chief Justice
		Justices
	*Criminal Court of	Presiding Judge
	Appeals	Judges
	*Court of Appeals	Judges
	District Courts	Judges
Oregon	Supreme Court	Chief Justice
		Associate Justices
	*Court of Appeals	Judges
	Tax Court	Judges
	Circuit Courts	Judges
	County Courts	County Judges
Pennsylvania	Supreme Court	Chief Justice
		Justices
	Superior Court	Presiding Judge
		Judges
	Commonwealth Court	Judges
	Courts of Common Pleas	Judges
Rhode Island	Supreme Court	Chief Justice
		Associate Justices
	Superior Court	Presiding Justice
		Justices
	Family Court	Judges
	District Court	Judges
	Probate Courts	Judges
South Carolina	Supreme Court	Chief Justice
		Associate Justice
	Circuit Courts	Judges
	County Courts	Judges
	Probate Courts	Judges

continued

324

State	Court	Members of Court
South Dakota	Supreme Court	Presiding Judge
		Judges
	Circuit Courts	Judges
Tennessee	Supreme Court	Chief Justice
		Associate Justices
	*Court of Appeals	Presiding Judge
		Associate Judges
	*Court of Criminal Appeals	Judges
Tennessee (Continued)	Chancery Courts	Chancellors
	Circuit Courts	Judges
	County Courts	Judges
	Probate Courts, Shelby and Davidson Counties	Judge
Texas	Supreme Court	Chief Justice
		Associate Justices
	*Court of Civil Appeals	Chief Justice
		Associate Justices
	Court of Criminal Appeal	Presiding Judge, Judges
		Commissioners
	District Courts	Judges
	County Courts	Judges
Utah	Supreme Court	Chief Justice
		Justices
	District Court	Judges
	Circuit Courts	Judges
Vermont	Supreme Court	Chief Justice
		Associate Justices
	Superior Courts	Judges
	Probate Courts	Judges
Virginia	Supreme Court	Chief Justice
		Justices
	Circuit Courts	Judges
Virgin Islands	District Court	Judge
	Territorial Courts	Judges
Washington	Supreme Court	Chief Justice
		Associate Judges
	Court of Appeals	Judges
	Superior Courts	Judges

continued

II. State Courts of Record—*continued*

State	Court	Members of Court
West Virginia	Supreme Court of Appeals	President
		Judges
	Circuit Courts	Judges
	County Commissions	Commissioners
Wisconsin	Supreme Court	Chief Justice
		Associate Justices
	*Court of Appeals	Judges
	Circuit Courts	Judges
	County Courts	Judges
Wyoming	Supreme Court	Chief Justice
		Associate Justice
	District Courts	Judges

III. JUDICIAL CIRCUITS AND THE STATES AND TERRITORIES IN EACH CIRCUIT

District of Columbia Circuit	District of Columbia
First Circuit	Maine, Massachusetts, New Hampshire, Puerto Rico, Rhode Island
Second Circuit	Connecticut, New York, Vermont, Virgin Islands,
Third Circuit	Delaware, New Jersey, Pennsylvania, Virgin Islands
Fourth Circuit	Maryland, North Carolina, South Carolina, Virginia, West Virginia
Fifth Circuit	Alabama, Canal Zone, Florida, Georgia, Louisiana, Mississippi, Texas
Sixth Circuit	Kentucky, Michigan, Ohio, Tennessee
Seventh Circuit	Illinois, Indiana, Wisconsin
Eighth Circuit	Arkansas, Iowa, Minnesota, Missouri, Nebraska, North Dakota, South Dakota, Territory of Guam
Ninth Circuit	Alaska, Arizona, California, Hawaii, Idaho, Montana, Nevada, Oregon, Washington
Tenth Circuit	Colorado, Kansas, New Mexico, Oklahoma, Utah, Wyoming

continued

State	Circuit	State	Circuit
Alabama	Fifth Circuit	Montana*	Ninth Circuit
Alaska*	Ninth Circuit	Nebraska*	Eighth Circuit
Arizona*	Ninth Circuit	Nevada*	Ninth Circuit
Arkansas	Eighth Circuit	New Hampshire*	First Circuit
California	Ninth Circuit	New Jersey*	Third Circuit
Canal Zone*	Fifth Circuit	New Mexico*	Tenth Circuit
Colorado*	Tenth Circuit	New York	Second Circuit
Connecticut*	Second Circuit	North Carolina	Fourth Circuit
Delaware*	Third Circuit	North Dakota*	Eighth Circuit
Florida	Fifth Circuit	Ohio	Sixth Circuit
Georgia	Fifth Circuit	Oklahoma	Tenth Circuit
Guam	Eighth Circuit	Oregon*	Ninth Circuit
Hawaii*	Ninth Circuit	Pennsylvania	Third Circuit
Idaho*	Ninth Circuit	Puerto Rico	First Circuit
Illinois	Seventh Circuit	Rhode Island*	First Circuit
Indiana	Seventh Circuit	South Carolina	Fourth Circuit
Iowa	Eighth Circuit	South Dakota*	Eighth Circuit
Kansas*	Tenth Circuit	Tennessee	Sixth Circuit
Kentucky	Sixth Circuit	Texas	Fifth Circuit
Louisiana	Fifth Circuit	Utah*	Tenth Circuit
Maine*	First Circuit	Vermont*	Second Circuit
Maryland*	Fourth Circuit	Virginia	Fourth Circuit
Massachusetts*	First Circuit	Virgin Islands	Second Circuit
Michigan	Sixth Circuit	Washington	Ninth Circuit
Minnesota*	Eighth Circuit	West Virginia	Fourth Circuit
Mississippi	Fifth Circuit	Wisconsin	Seventh Circuit
Missouri	Eighth Circuit	Wyoming*	Tenth Circuit

*Only one district court.

327

State	When an instrument is notarized outside the state for recording within the state, must it be authenticated if notary affixes his seal?	Who authenticates acknowledgments taken by notary public in state for use in another state?
Alabama	No	Clerk of Circuit Court
Alaska	No	Lieutenant Governor
Arizona	No	Clerk of Superior Court
Arkansas	Yes[1]	Superior Court Clerk
California	Yes	Clerk of Court of Record
Colorado	No[1]	Secretary of State
Connecticut	Customary[1]	Clerk of Superior Court, Waterbury District Clerk
Delaware	No	Prothonotary
District of Columbia	No	Secretary of District Council
Florida	No	Secretary of State
Georgia	No	Clerk of Superior Court
Hawaii	No	Clerk of Circuit Court
Idaho	No	Clerk of District Court
Illinois	No	County Clerk or Secretary of State may grant certificates of magistracy to notaries
Indiana	No	Clerk of Circuit Court
Iowa	Yes	Secretary of State
Kansas	No[1]	Clerk of Court of Record
Kentucky	No[1]	Clerk of County (District) Court
Louisiana	No	Clerk of District Court
Maine	No[1]	Clerk of Court
Maryland	No	Clerk of Circuit Court (Clerk of Superior Court of Baltimore City)
Massachusetts	No	State Secretary; Clerk of Superior Court
Michigan	No	Clerk of County
Minnesota	No[1]	Clerk of District Court, Secretary of State
Mississippi	No	Chancery Clerk, Secretary of State
Missouri	No	Clerk of County Court (Clerk of Circuit Court for City of St. Louis)
Montana	No	Secretary of State or County Clerk
Nebraska	No[1]	County Clerk
Nevada	No[1]	County Clerk
New Hampshire	No[1]	Secretary of State or Clerk of Court of Record
New Jersey	Yes	County Clerk
New Mexico	Not required but customary	County Clerk
New York	Yes	County Clerk
North Carolina	No	Secretary of State or Register of Deeds
North Dakota	No[1]	Clerk of District Court
Ohio	No[1]	Clerk of Common Pleas Court

continued

State	When an instrument is notarized outside the state for recording within the state, must it be authenticated if notary affixes his seal?	Who authenticates acknowledgments taken by notary public in state for use in another state?
Oklahoma	No[1]	Secretary of State
Oregon	No	County Clerk or Secretary of State
Pennsylvania	No[1]	Prothonotary of Common Pleas Court
Rhode Island	No	Superior, Supreme, and District Court Clerks
South Carolina	No'	Clerk of Court
South Dakota	No	Clerk of Circuit Court
Tennessee	No	Clerk of County, Secretary of State fo. Notaries at Large
Texas	No	County Clerk
Utah	No	Secretary of State
Vermont	No (banks usually request authentication)	County Clerk
Virginia	No[1]	Clerk of Court
Virgin Islands	No	Clerk of District Court
Washington	No	Secretary of State or County Clerk
West Virginia	No[1]	Clerk of County Court
Wisconsin	No[1]	Clerk of Circuit Court
Wyoming	No	County Clerk

1. Uniform Recognition of Acknowledgements Act adopted.

NOTARIES PUBLIC

State	Appointments made by	Length of term	Notary must affix		Record of acts required	Bond required
			Seal	Date commission expires		
Alabama	Judges of Probate	4	Yes	No	Yes	Yes
Alaska . ..	Secretary of State	4	Yes	Yes	Yes	Yes
Arizona	Secretary of State	4	Yes	Yes	Yes	Yes
Arkansas	Governor	4	Yes	Yes	Yes	Yes
California	Secretary of State	4	Yes	No	Yes	Yes
Colorado	Secretary of State	4	Yes	Yes	Yes	Yes

continued

329

State	Appointments made by	Length of term	Notary must affix		Record of acts required	Bond required
			Seal	Date commission expires		
Connecticut	Secretary of State	5	Yes	No	No	No
Delaware	Governor	2	Yes	No	No	No
District of Columbia	D.C. Commissioners	5	Yes	No	Yes	Yes
Florida	Governor	4	Yes	Yes	No	Yes
Georgia	Clerks of Superior Court	4	Yes	No	No	No
Hawaii	Atty. Gen.	4	Yes	Yes	Yes	Yes
Idaho	Governor	4	Yes	No	Yes	Yes
Illinois	Secretary of State	4	Yes	No	No[2]	Yes
Indiana	Governor	4	Yes	Yes	No	Yes
Iowa	Secretary of State	3	Yes	No	Yes	Yes
Kansas	Secretary of State	4	Yes	Yes	No	Yes
Kentucky	Secretary of State	4	No	Yes	No[1]	Yes
Louisiana	Governor	Indefinite	No	No	Yes	Yes
Maine	Governor	7	Yes	No	No[3]	No
Maryland	Governor	4	Yes	Yes	Yes	No
Massachusetts .	Governor	7	No	Yes	No	No
Michigan	Governor	4	No	Yes	No	Yes
Minnesota	Governor	7	Yes	Yes	No[1]	Yes
Mississippi	Governor	4	Yes	Yes	Yes	Yes
Missouri	Secretary of State	4	Yes	Yes	Yes	Yes
Montana	Governor	3	Yes	Yes	No[1]	Yes
Nebraska	Governor	4	Yes	Yes	No	Yes
Nevada	Secretary of State	4	Yes[6]	Yes	No	Yes
New Hampshire	Governor	5	Yes[4]	Yes	No	No
New Jersey	Secretary of State	5	No	No	Yes	No
New Mexico	Governor	4	Yes	Yes	Yes	Yes
New York	Secretary of State	2	Yes	Yes	No	No
North Carolina	Secretary of State	5	Yes	Yes	No	No
North Dakota ..	Secretary of State	6	Yes	Yes	No[1]	Yes
Ohio	Governor	5	Yes[4]	No	No[1]	Yes
Oklahoma	Secretary of State	4	Yes	Yes	Yes	Yes

continued

State	Appointments made by	Length of term	Notary must affix		Record of acts required	Bond required
			Seal	Date commission expires		
Oregon	Governor	4	Yes	Yes	No[1]	Yes
Pennsylvania ..	Secretary of the Commonwealth	4	Yes	Yes	Yes	Yes
Rhode Island ..	Governor	5	No	No	No	No
South Carolina .	Governor	10	Yes	Yes	No	No
South Dakota ..	Governor	8	Yes	Yes[4]	No[1]	Yes
Tennessee	Governor	4	Yes	Yes	Yes	Yes
Texas	Secretary State	2	Yes	Yes	Yes	Yes
Utah	Governor	4	Yes	Yes	No[1]	Yes
Vermont	Judges of the County Court	2	Yes	No	No	No
Virginia	Governor	4	No	Yes	No	Yes
Washington	Governor	4	Yes	No	No	Yes
West Virginia ..	Governor	10	No	Yes	No	Yes
Wisconsin	Governor	4	Yes	Yes	No	Yes
Wyoming	Governor	4	Yes	Yes	Yes[5]	Yes

[1] Except with reference to commercial papers.
[2] Except with reference to negotiable instruments.
[3] Except with reference to mercantile and marine protests.
[4] In practice, but not by statute.
[5] For official acts required by law to be recorded.
[6] Stamp, rather than seal.

STATUTES OF LIMITATIONS IN NUMBER OF YEARS

State	Open Accounts	Notes	Written Contracts	Contracts Under Seal
Alabama	3	6[7]	6[7]	10
Alaska	6[7]	6[7]	6[7]	10
Arizona	3	6[1]	6[7]	6[1]
Arkansas	3	5	5[7]	5
California	4	4[2]	4	4
Colorado	6	6	6[3, 7]	6[3, 7]
Connecticut	6	6	6[7]	17
Delaware	3	6	3[7]	--
District of Columbia	3[7]	3[7]	3[7]	12
Florida	3	5	5[7]	20
Georgia	4	6	6[7]	20

continued

State	Open Accounts	Notes	Written Contracts	Contracts Under Seal
Hawaii	6[7]	6[7]	6[7]	6
Idaho	4	5	5	5
Illinois	5	10	10[7]	10[4]
Indiana	6	10	10-20	20
Iowa	5	10	10[7]	10
Kansas	3	5	5[7]	5
Kentucky	5	15[5]	15[7]	15
Louisiana	3	5	10	10
Maine	6	6[6]	6[7]	20
Maryland	3[7]	3[7]	3[7]	12
Massachusetts	6	6[6]	6[7]	20
Michigan	6[7]	6[7]	6[7]	6[7]
Minnesota	6	6[7]	6[7]	6
Mississippi	3	6	6	6
Missouri	5	10[7]	10[7]	10[7]
Montana	5	8	8[7]	8
Nebraska	4	5	5[7]	5
Nevada	4	6[7]	6[7]	6[7]
New Hampshire	6[7]	6[7]	6[7]	20
New Jersey	6[7]	6[7]	6[7]	16
New Mexico	4	6	6[7]	6
New York	6[7]	6[7]	6[7]	6[7]
North Carolina	3	3	3	10
North Dakota	6[7]	6[7]	6[1, 7]	6[3]
Ohio	15	15	15	15
Oklahoma	3	5	5	5
Oregon	6[7]	6[7]	6[7]	--
Pennsylvania	6	6	6[7]	20
Rhode Island	6[7]	6[7]	6	20
South Carolina	6	6	6	20
South Dakota	6[7]	6[7]	6[7]	20
Tennessee	6[7]	6[7]	6[7]	6[7]
Texas	2	4	4	4
Utah	4	6	6[7]	6
Vermont	6	6[8]	6[7]	8
Virginia	3	5	5[7]	10
Washington	3	6	6[7]	6
West Virginia	5	10	10[7]	10
Wisconsin	6[7]	6[7]	6[7]	10-20
Wyoming	8	10	10[7]	10

[1] Executed without the state, 4 years.
[2] Corporate notes, 6 years.
[3] Contracts affecting real property, 10 years.
[4] Vendor's lien, mortgage, 20 years.
[5] 5-year period applies if note is placed on the footing of a bill of exchange.
[6] Witnessed notes, 20 years.
[7] Sales contracts, 4 years (Uniform Commercial Code).
[8] Witnessed notes, 14 years.

Official report	Cite as
Alabama Reports	Ala.
Alabama Appellate Reports	Ala. App.
Alaska Reports	P. 2d
Arizona Reports	Ariz.
Arkansas Reports	Ark.
California Appellate Reports	Cal. App.
California Appellate Reports, Second Series	Cal. App. 2d
California Reports	Cal.
California Reports, Second Series	Cal. 2d
Colorado Reports	Colo.
Connecticut	Conn.
Delaware Reports	By name of Rep.
Delaware Chancery Reports	Del. Ch.
Florida Reports[1]	Fla.
Georgia Reports	Ga.
Hawaii Reports	H.
Idaho Reports	Idaho
Illinois Reports	Ill.
Illinois Appellate Court Reports	Ill. App.
Indiana Reports	Ind.
Indiana Appellate Reports	Ind. App.
Iowa Reports	Iowa
Kansas Reports	Kan.
Kentucky Reports[2]	Ky.
Louisiana Reports	La.
Maine Reports	Me.
Maryland Reports	Md.
Massachusetts Reports	Mass.
Michigan Reports	Mich.
Minnesota Reports	Minn.
Mississippi Reports	Miss.
Missouri Reports	Mo.
Missouri Appeal Reports	Mo. App.
Montana Reports	Mont.
Nebraska Reports	Neb.
Nevada Reports	Nev.
New Hampshire Reports	N.H.
New Jersey Equity Reports	N.J. Eq.
New Jersey Reports	N.J.
New Jersey Superior Court Reports	N.J. Super.
New Mexico Reports	N.M.
New York Appellate Division Reports	N.Y. App. Div.
New York Miscellaneous Reports	N.Y. Misc.
New York Reports	N.Y.
North Carolina Reports	N.C.

continued

Official report	Cite as
North Dakota Reports	N.D.
Ohio Appellate Reports	Ohio App.
Ohio State Reports	Ohio St.
Oklahoma Reports	Okl.
Oklahoma Criminal Reports	Okl. Cr.
Oregon Reports	Or.
Pennsylvania Reports	Pa.
Pennsylvania Superior Court Reports	Pa. Sup.
Rhode Island Reports	R.I.
South Carolina Reports	S.C.
South Dakota Reports	S.D.
Tennessee Reports	Tenn.
Tennessee Appeals Reports	Tenn. App.
Texas Reports	Tex.
United States Reports	U.S.
United States Court of Appeals, District of Columbia	U.S. App. D.C.
Utah Reports	Utah
Vermont Reports	Vt.
Virginia Reports	Va.
Washington Reports	Wash.
Washington Reports, Second Series	Wash. 2d
West Virginia Reports	W. Va.
Wisconsin Reports	Wis.
Wyoming Reports	Wyo.

[1] Up to Vol. 160 only. Now the Southern Reporter is official.
[2] Up to Vol. 314 only. Now the Southwestern Reporter is official.

Name of reporter	Cite as	Courts covered
Supreme Court Reporter	S. Ct.	United States Supreme Court
Federal Reporter	F	United States Circuit Courts of Appeals and the District Courts
Federal Reporter, Second Series	F. 2d	United States Courts of Appeals, United States Court of Customs and Patent Appeals, United States Emergency Court of Appeals
Federal Supplement	F. Supp.	United States District Courts, United States Court of Claims
Atlantic Reporter Atlantic Reporter, Second Series	A. A. 2d	Connecticut Delaware Maine Maryland New Hampshire New Jersey Pennsylvania Rhode Island Vermont District of Columbia
New York Supplement New York Supplement, Second Series	N.Y. Supp. N.Y.S. 2d	New York Court of Appeals Appellate Division of the Supreme Court Miscellaneous Courts
Northeastern Reporter Northeastern Reporter, Second Series	N.E. N.E. 2d	Illinois Indiana New York Massachusetts Ohio
Northwestern Reporter Northwestern Reporter, Second Series	N.W. N.W. 2d	Iowa Michigan Minnesota Nebraska North Dakota South Dakota Wisconsin

continued

Name of reporter	Cite as	Courts covered
Pacific Reporter Pacific Reporter, Second Series	P. P. 2d	} Alaska Arizona California Colorado Hawaii Idaho Kansas Montana Nevada New Mexico Oklahoma Oregon Utah Washington Wyoming
Southeastern Reporter Southeastern Reporter, Second Series	S.E. S.E. 2d	} Georgia North Carolina South Carolina Virginia West Virginia
Southern Reporter Southern Reporter, Second Series	So. So. 2d	} Alabama Florida Louisiana Mississippi
Southwestern Reporter Southwestern Reporter, Second Series	S.W. S.W. 2d	} Arkansas Kentucky Missouri Tennessee Texas

State	Title of compilation	How cited
Ala.	Code of Alabama, Recompiled 1958	Code of Ala. Tit. 10, § 101
Alaska	Alaska Statutes 1962	A.S. § 08.04.310
Ariz.	Arizona Revised Statutes Annotated	ARS § 10-101
Ark.	Arkansas Statutes Annotated 1947	Ark. Stats. (1947) Sec. 10-101
Calif.	Deering's California Codes (Code of Civil Procedure)	CCP § 101
Colo.	Colorado Revised Statutes, 1963	101-1-7, C.R.S. '63
Conn.	General Statutes, Revision of 1958	Conn. G.S. 1958 Sec. 101
Del.	Delaware Code Annotated, 1953	10 Del. C. § 110
D.C.	District of Columbia Code Annotated, 1961	D.C. Code 1961, Title 26, § 703
Fla.	Florida Statutes, 1967	Florida Statutes, 1967, § 101.011
Ga.	Code of Georgia, Annotated	Ga. Code Ann. § 10-1010
Hawaii	Revised Laws of Hawaii, 1955	R.L.H. 1955 § 172-1
Idaho	Idaho Code	Idaho Code, Sec. 26-1850
Ill.	Illinois Revised Statutes 1951	Ill. Rev. Stat. 1951 Ch. 10, §101
	Smith-Hurd Illinois Annotated Statutes	S.H.A. Ch. 10, § 101
	Jones Illinois Statutes Annotated	Jones Ill. Stat. Ann. Ch. 10, § 101
Ind.	Burns Annotated Indiana Statutes	Burns Ann. St. Sec. 25-101
Iowa	Code of Iowa, 1966	Code of Iowa, 1966, § 110.10
Kan.	Kansas Statutes Annotated, 1963	K.S.A. 48-101
Ky.	Kentucky Revised Statutes, 1962	KRS 101.010 (1)
La.	Louisiana Revised Statutes of 1950	R.S. 10:101
Maine	Revised Statutes of Maine, 1964	R.S. of Maine 1964, T. 10 § 51
Md.	Annotated Code of Maryland, 1957	Md. Code (1957), Art. 10, Sec. 101
Mass.	Annotated Laws of Massachusetts, 1966	A.L., C. 8 § 10
Mich.	1948 Compiled Laws of Michigan	C.L. 1948, § 10.101
	Michigan Statutes Annotated	Stat. Ann. § 10.101
Minn.	Minnesota Statutes 1967	Minn. Stat. 1967, Sec. 101.51
Miss.	Mississippi Code, 1942, Annotated	Miss. Code, 1942, Ann., § 101

continued

State	Title of compilation	How cited
Mo.	Missouri Revised Statutes, 1959	R.S. Mo. 1959, § 101.010
Mont.	Revised Codes of Montana, 1947, Annotated	RCM 1947, § 10-101
Nebr.	Nebraska Revised Statutes, 1943	Sec. 1-101, R.S. Nebr., 1943
	Reissue Revised Statutes of Nebraska, 1943	Sec. 1-101, R.R.S. Nebr., 1943
Nev.	Nevada Revised Statutes	NRS § 19.010
N.H.	1966 New Hampshire Revised Statutes Annotated	RSA 101:1
N.J.	Revised Statutes of New Jersey, 1937	N.J.R.S., 10:101-10
	New Jersey Statutes Annotated	N.J.S.A., 2A: 4-30.1
N.M.	New Mexico Statutes Annotated, 1953	NMSA Comp., 3-7-16
N.Y.	McKinney's Consolidated Laws of New York	Business Corporation Law, § 101
N.C.	General Statutes of North Carolina, 1965	G.S. § 10-101
N.D.	North Dakota Century Code, Annotated, 1961	N.D.C.C.A. § 9-08-05
Ohio	Baldwin's Ohio Revised Code, Annotated	R.C. § 1110.10
Okla.	Oklahoma Statutes, 1961	10 O.S. 1961 § 101
Ore.	Oregon Revised Statutes	ORS 11.010
Penn.	Purdon's Pennsylvania Statutes Annotated	10 P.S. § 101
R.I.	General Laws of Rhode Island of 1956	Gen. Laws 1956, 1-1-10
S.C.	Code of Laws of S.C. 1962	1962 Code, § 10-101
S.D.	South Dakota Code of 1939	SDC 10.1010 (10)
	South Dakota Code Supplement of 1960	SDC 1960 Supp. 11.0111
Tenn.	Tennessee Code Annotated	T.C.A., § 10-101
Tex.	Vernon's Texas Statutes, 1948	Vernon's Texas St. 1948, Art. 101
	Vernon's Texas Statutes, 1962 Supplement	Vernon's Texas C.C.P., 1962 Supp., Art. 5728
Utah	Utah Code Annotated, 1953	UCA 1953, 10-10-1
Vt.	Vermont Statutes Annotated	VSA, Title I, § 51
Va.	Code of Virginia, 1950	Code, § 10-101
Wash.	Revised Code of Washington, 1968 Supplement	RCW 10.11.101
W. Va.	West Virginia Code Annotated (1966)	Michie's § 17-3-6
Wis.	Wisconsin Statutes 1967	Stats. § 84.12
Wyo.	Wyoming Statutes 1957	WS, § 10-10